The History of the Origins of Christianity

Book II - The Apostles

By Joseph Ernest Renan

Edited by Anthony Uyl

Devoted Publishing

Woodstock, Ontario, 2017

The History of the Origins of Christianity Book II - The Apostles

By Joseph Ernest Renan

Member of the French Academy

Edited by Anthony Uyl

Originally Published by:

London: Mathieson & Company, 25, Paternoster Square E.C.

The text of The History of the Origins of Christianity - Book II: The Apostles is all in the Public Domain. This edition is published by Devoted Publishing a division of 2165467 Ontario Inc.

What kind of philosophies do you have? Let us know!

Contact us at: devotedpub@hotmail.com

Visit us on Facebook: @DevotedPublishing

Get more products via our website: www.devotedpublishing.com

Published in Woodstock, Ontario, Canada 2016

For bulk educational rates, please contact us at the email address above.

ISBN: 978-1-988297-70-5

Table of Contents

INTRODUCTION

CRITICISM OF ORIGINAL DOCUMENTS

The first book of our history of the Origins of Christianity has traced the story as far as the death and burial of Jesus. We must now resume the narrative at the point where we left it--to wit, Saturday, 4th April, 33. This will be for some time yet a continuation, in some sort, of the Life of Jesus. Next, after the months of joyous rapture, during which the great Founder laid the foundation of a new order for humanity, these last years were the most decisive in the history of the world. It is still Jesus, some sparks of whose sacred fire have been deposited in the hearts of a few friends who created institutions of the greatest originality, moves, transforms souls, imprints upon everything his divine seal. We have to show how, under this ever active and victorious influence over death, the faith of the resurrection, the influence of the holy Spirit, the gift of tongues, and the power of the Church, established themselves. We shall describe the organization of the Church at Jerusalem, its first trials, its first conquests, the earliest missions which it despatched. We shall follow Christianity in its rapid progress in Syria, as far as Antioch, where was formed a second capital, more important in a sense than that of Jerusalem, which it was destined to supplant. In this new centre, where the converted Pagans constituted the majority, we shall see Christianity separating itself definitely from Judaism, and receiving a name of its own; we shall see especially the birth of the grand idea of distant missions, destined to carry the name of Jesus into the world of the Gentiles. We shall pause at the important moment when Paul, Barnabas, and John Mark set out for the execution of this great design. There we shall interrupt our narrative, and cast a glance at the world which those daring missionaries undertook to convert. We shall endeavour to give an account of the intellectual, political, religious, and social condition of the Roman Empire about the year 45, the probable date of the departure of Saint Paul upon his first mission.

Such is the subject-matter of this second book, which we have entitled, The Apostles, for the reason that it expounds the period of common action during which the small family created by Jesus acted in concert, and was grouped morally around a single point--Jerusalem. Our next work, the third, will take us out of this company, and we shall be devoted almost exclusively to the man who, more than any other, represents conquering and travelling Christianity--Saint Paul. Although, from a certain epoch, he called himself an apostle, Paul had not the same right to the title as the Twelve; he is a workman of the second hour, and almost an intruder. The state in which historical documents have reached us are at this stage-misleading. As we know infinitely more of the history of St. Paul than that of the Twelve, as we possess his authentic writings and original memoirs detailing minutely certain periods of his life, we assign to him an importance of the first order, almost exceeding that of Jesus. This is an error. Paul was a great man: in the foundation of Christianity he played a most important part. Still, we must not compare him with Jesus, nor even with any of the immediate disciples of the latter. Paul never saw Jesus, nor did he ever taste the ambrosia of the Galilean preaching. Hence, the most commonplace man who had had his part of the celestial manna, was from that very circumstance superior to him who had only had an after-taste. Nothing can be more false than an opinion which has become fashionable in these days, that Paul was really the founder of Christianity. The real founder of Christianity was Jesus. The first places, next to him, ought to be reserved to those grand and obscure companions of Jesus, to those faithful and zealous women, who believed in him despite his death. Paul was, in the first century, a kind of isolated phenomenon. He did not leave an organized school. On the contrary he left bitter opponents, who strove, after his death, to banish him from the Church and to place him, in a sort of way, on the same footing as Simon Magus. They tried to take away from him that which we regard as the peculiar work--the conversion of the Gentiles. The church of Corinth, which he himself had founded, claimed to owe its origin to him and to St. Peter. In the second century Papias and St. Justin never mention his name. It was later, when oral tradition came to be regarded as nothing, and when the Scriptures took the place of everything, that Paul assumed a leading part in Christian theology. Paul, it was true, had a theology. Peter and Mary Magdalene had none. Paul left behind him considerable works: none of the writings of the other apostles are to be compared with his, either in regard to their importance or authenticity.

At first glance the documents for the period embraced in this volume are rare and altogether insufficient. The direct testimony is reduced to the first chapters of the Acts of the Apostles--chapters, the historical value of which is open to serious objections. Yet, the light which these last chapters of the Gospels cast upon that obscure interval, especially the Epistles of St. Paul, dispels, to some extent, the darkness. An old writing serves to make known, first, the exact date at which it was composed, and, secondly, the period which preceded its composition. Every writing suggests, in fact, retrospective inductions as to the state of society which produced it. Composed, for the most part, between the years 53 and 62, the Epistles of St. Paul are replete with information concerning the early years of Christianity. Moreover, seeing that we are here speaking of great events without precise dates, the essential point is to show the conditions under which they formed themselves. On this subject I ought to remark once for all that the current date inscribed at the head of each chapter is never more than approximate. The chronology of these first years has but a very small number of fixed land-marks. Yet, thanks to the care which the editor of the Acts has taken, not to interrupt the succession of events; thanks to the Epistle to the Galatians, where are to be found some numerical indications of the greatest value; and to Josephus, who gives the dates of events of profane history connected with some facts concerning the apostles, we are able to create for the history of these last a very probable canvas upon which the chances of error are confined within very narrow limits.

I shall again repeat at the beginning of this book what I have already said at the beginning of my Life of Jesus. In histories of that kind, where the general effect alone is certain, and where almost all the details lend themselves more or less to doubt, in consequence of the legendary character of the documents, hypothesis is essential. Upon periods of which we know nothing no hypothesis is possible. To endeavour to reproduce a group of ancient sculpture, which has certainly existed, but of which we possess only a few fragments, and concerning which we possess scarcely any written account, is an altogether arbitrary work. But to attempt to recompose the entire building of the Parthenon from what remains to us by the aid of the ancient text, availing ourselves of the drawing made in the seventeenth century of all the information possible; in one word, inspiring ourselves with the style of those inimitable fragments, trying to seize their soul and their life--what can be more legitimate? We need not boast of having found the ancient sculptor once more; but we have done what we could to approach him. Such a work is so much the more legitimate in history since language permits doubtful forms, which marble does not allow. There is oven nothing to prevent the reader from proposing a choice between diverse theories. The conscience of the writer may be easy since he has put forward as certain that which is certain, as probable that which is probable, as possible that which is possible. In those places where the footing between history and legend is uncertain, the general effect alone is all that need be sought after. Our third book, for which we shall have absolutely historical documents, where we shall have to paint characters of flesh and blood, and to speak of clearly defined facts, will offer a more definite story. It will be seen, however, that the character of that period is not known with greater certainty. Absolute facts speak more loudly than biographical details. We know very little of the incomparable artists who have created these masterpieces of Greek art. But these masterpieces tell us more about the personality of their authors and the public who appreciate them, than the most circumstantial narratives, and the most authentic texts could do.

For the knowledge of the decisive events which happened in the first days after the death of Jesus the authorities are the last chapters of the Gospels containing the narratives of the appearance of the resuscitated Christ. I need not repeat here what I have said in the Introduction to my Life of Jesus as to the value of these documents. On that side we have happily a control which was too often wanting in the life of Jesus; I intend to imply an important passage of St. Paul (1 Cor. xv 5-8), which establishes: 1st the reality of the appearances; 2nd, the long duration of the apparitions as opposed to the narrative of the synoptical Gospels; 3rd, the variety of places in which the apparitions took place in contradiction to Mark and Luke. The study of this fundamental text, together with other reasons, confirms us in the views which we have enunciated as to the reciprocal relation of the Synoptics with the fourth Gospel. In all that concerns the narrative of the resurrection and the apparitions, the fourth Gospel maintains that superiority which it has for all the rest of the Life of Jesus. If we wish to find a consecutive logical narrative, which allows that which is hidden behind the allusions to be conjectured, it is there that we must look for it. I am approaching the most difficult of the questions connected with the origin of Christianity. "What is the historic value of the fourth Gospel?" The use which I have made of it in my Life of Jesus is the point to which enlightened critics have taken the most objection. Almost all the scholars who apply the rational method to the history of theology reject the fourth Gospel as apocryphal in every aspect. I have anew reflected much upon this problem, and I am unable sensibly to modify my first opinion. Only as I differ on this point from the general opinion I have thought it necessary to explain in detail the reasons for my persistency. I intend to make it the subject of an appendix at the end of a revised and corrected edition of the Life of Jesus which will shortly appear.

The Acts of the Apostles are the most important document for the history which we are about to relate. I ought to explain myself hero as to the character of that work, its historical value, and the use which I have made of it.

The one thing beyond question is that the Acts had the same author as the third Gospel, of which

5

they are a continuation. It is not worth while to stop to prove this position, which, however, has never been disputed. The preface at the beginning of both writings, the dedication of both to Theophilus, the perfect similarity of style and of ideas furnish abundant demonstrations in this regard.

A second proposition, which is not quite so self-evident, but which may be regarded as very probable is, that the author of the Acts was a disciple of Paul, who accompanied him during a great part of his journeyings. At the first glance this proposition appeared indubitable. In many places beginning with the 10th verse of chapter xvi., the author in his story makes use of the pronoun "we," indicating that that thenceforward he made one of the company of Paul. That appears to be beyond question. One issue only presents itself to destroy the force of this argument: it is that of supposing that the passages where the pronoun "we" appears have been copied by the last editor of the Acts from an earlier manuscript by, for example, Timothy, and that the editor, out of inadvertence, had omitted to substitute for "we" the name of the narrator. This explanation is scarcely admissible. Such an inadvertence might easily occur in a vulgar compilation. But the third Gospel and the Acts are compositions most carefully edited, composed with reflection, and even with art, written by the same hand, and according to a deliberate plan. The two books together form a whole of absolutely the same style, offering the same favourite locutions, and the same manner of quoting the Scripture. A blunder of editing so really shocking as that would be inexplicable. We are then forced invincibly to conclude that he who wrote the end of the work wrote the beginning also, and that the narrator of all is he who wrote "we" in the passages mentioned.

This becomes still more striking, if we note in what circumstances the narrator thus puts himself in company with Paul. The use of "we" begins at the moment when Paul goes into Macedonia for the first time (xvi. 10). It ceases at the moment when Paul leaves Philippi, It is renewed when Paul, visiting Macedonia for the last time, again goes by way of Philippi (xx. 5-6.) Thenceforward the narrator never again separates himself from Paul until the end. If we further remark that the chapters in which the narrator accompanies the apostle have a specially precise character, it is impossible to believe that the narrator could have been a Macedonian, or rather a man of Philippi, who went before Paul to Troas during his second mission, who remained at Philippi after the departure of the apostle, and who at the last passage of the apostle through that city (third mission) joined him, not again to leave him. Can it be understood that an editor, writing at a distance, could thus have allowed himself to be ruled by the remembrance of another? Such memories would spoil the unity of the whole, The narrator who says "we" would have his own style; his special expressions; he would be more Paulinian than the editor himself. Now that is not so: the work is perfectly homogeneous.

There will, perhaps, be some surprise that a thesis so evident should have been contradicted. But criticism of the writings of the New Testament shows that many things which appear to be perfectly clear are, upon examination, full of uncertainty. In the matter of style, thoughts, and doctrines, the Acts are scarcely what might be expected from a disciple of Paul. They in no way resemble his epistles. There is not a trace of the lofty doctrines which constitute the originality of the Apostle of the Gentiles. The temperament of Paul is that of a stiff and self-contained Protestant; the author of the Acts gives us the impression of a good Catholic, docile, optimist, calling every priest a "holy father," every bishop "a great bishop," ready to swallow any fiction, rather than believe that these holy fathers and great bishops quarrel amongst themselves and often make rude war. Whilst professing a great admiration for Paul, the author of the Acts avoids giving him the title of apostle, and is anxious that the initiative of the conversion of the Gentiles should belong to Peter. We should say, in short, that he is a disciple of Peter, rather than of Paul. We shall soon show that, in two or three circumstances, his principles of conciliation have led him gravely to falsify the biography of Paul; he makes mistakes and omissions of things which are very strange in a disciple of this last. He does not mention a single one of his epistles; he keeps back, in the most surprising fashion, explanations of the first importance. Even in the part, where he must have been the companion of Paul, he is sometimes singularly dry, ill-informed and dull. In short, the softness and vagueness of some of his narratives, the conventionality which may be discerned in them, suggest to us a writer who had no personal communication with the apostles, and who wrote between the years 100 and 120.

Must we insist upon these objections? I think not, and I persist in believing that the last editor of the Acts is really the disciple of Paul who says "we" in the last chapters. All the difficulties, insoluble though they may appear, should be, if not set on one side, at least held in suspense by an argument as decisive as that which results from this word "we." We may add, that by attributing the Acts to a companion of Paul, two important peculiarities are explained: on the one hand, the disproportion of the work of which more than three-fifths are consecrated to Paul; on the other, the disproportion which may be remarked, even in the biography of Paul himself, whose first mission is dispatched with great brevity, whilst certain parts of the second and third missions, especially his last journey, are told with minute details. A man altogether a stranger to the apostolic history, would not have exhibited these inequalities. His work would have been better planned as a whole. That which distinguishes history composed from documents, from history written wholly or in part by an actor in it, is exactly this disproportion: The historian of the closet takes for his framework the events themselves; the author of memoirs takes his recollections for his framework, or, at least, his personal relations. An ecclesiastical historian, a sort of Eusebius, writing about the year 120, would have bequeathed to us a book very differently distributed after chapter xiii. The bizarre fashion in which the Acts at this time leaves the orbit in which they had revolved until then can, to my thinking, be explained only by the peculiar situation of the author and by his relations with Paul. This result will be naturally confirmed if we find amongst the known fellow labourers of Paul the name of the author to whom tradition attributes our writing.

This is in effect what took place. Manuscripts and tradition assign as the author of the third Gospel a certain Lucas or Lucanus. From what has been said it is evident that if Lucas be really the author of the third Gospel, he is also the author of the Acts. Now we find this Lucas mentioned precisely as the companion of Paul in the Epistle to the Colossians (iv. 14); in that to Philemon (24), and in the II Timothy (iv. 11.) This last Epistle is of more than doubtful authenticity. The Epistle to the Colossians and to Philemon on their side, although very probably authentic, are not, however, the most undoubted of Paul's Epistles. But those writings are, in any ease, of the first century, and suffice to prove that there was a Luke amongst the disciples of Paul. The fabricator of the Epistles to Timothy, in short, is certainly not the author of those to the Colossians and to Philemon (supposing, contrary to our opinion, that these last are apocryphal). To admit that a forger should have attributed an imaginary companion to Paul is to suppose something very improbable. But assuredly different forgers would not have pitched upon the same name. Two circumstances give to this reasoning a peculiar force. The first is that the name of Luke, or Lucanus, is an uncommon one amongst the early Christians; the second that the Luke of the Epistles had no other celebrity. To write a celebrated name at the top of a document, as is done in the second Epistle of Peter, and very probably in Paul's Epistles to Titus and Timothy, was in no way contrary to the habits of the time. But to write at the top of such a document a false name, otherwise obscure, is not to be believed. Was it the intention of the forger to throw over his book the authority of Paul? If it were, why did he not take the name of Paul himself? or at least the name of Timothy or Titus, disciples of the Apostle of the Gentiles, who were much bettor known? Luke scarcely had a place in tradition, legend, or history. The three passages of the Epistles above mentioned are not sufficient to make his name a generally accepted guarantee. The Epistles to Timothy were probably written after the Acts. The mention of Luke in the Epistles to the Colossians and to Philemon are equivalent to one only, the two documents being really but one. We think, therefore, that the author of the Acts was really Luke, the disciple of Paul.

The very name of Luke, or Lucanus, and the profession of physician, which the disciple of Paul thus named exercised, answer completely to the indications which the two books furnish as to their author. We have shown in effect that the author of the third Gospel and of the Acts was probably from Philippi, a Roman colony, where Latin was the prevailing language. Further, the author of the Gospel and of the Acts knew little of Judaism and the affairs of Palestine; he scarcely knew Hebrew. He is abreast of the ideas of the Pagan world, and he writes Greek with tolerable correctness. The work was composed far from Judea for the use of people who knew little of its geography, who cared nothing for either profound Rabbinical learning's or for Hebrew names. The dominant idea of the author is, that if the people had been free to follow their inclinations they would have embraced the faith of Jesus, and that it was the Jewish aristocracy who prevented them. The word Jew is always used by him in a bad sense, and as synonymous with enemy of Christians. On the other hand he shows himself very favourable to the Samaritan heretics.

What date may we give to the composition of this important document? Luke appears for the first time in company with Paul on the occasion of the first journey of the apostle to Macedonia, about the year 52. Suppose that lie was then 25 years of age; there is nothing unnatural in supposing him to have lived to the year 100. The narrative of the Acts stops at the year 63. But the edition of the Acts being evidently later than that of the third Gospel, and the date of that third Gospel being fixed with sufficient precision in the years which followed the destruction of Jerusalem (70), we cannot dream of placing the production of the Acts earlier than 71 or 72.

If it were certain that the Acts were composed immediately after the Gospel we might stop at this point. But doubt is permissible. Some facts lead to the belief that a considerable interval passed between the composition of the third Gospel and that of the Acts. Thus there is a singular contradiction between the last chapters of the Gospel and the first of the Acts. According to the former account the ascension took place on the very day of the resurrection; according to the Acts it took place only after forty days. It is clear that the second version presents the legend to us in a more advanced form--a form which was adopted when the need was felt for creating a place for the various apparitions, and for giving to the life beyond the tomb of Jesus a complete and logical frame-work. We are even tempted to suppose that the new fashion of conceiving things was not told to the author or did not come into his head except in the interval between the composition of the two works. In any case it is very remarkable that the author finds himself compelled to add new circumstances to his first account and to extend it. If his first book were still in his hands why did he not make the additions to his first account which, separated as they are, look so awkward? That, however, is not decisive, and a grave circumstance leads to the belief that Luke conceived at the same time the plan of both. That is the preface placed at the head of the Gospel, which appears common to the two books. The contradiction we have pointed out may perhaps be explained by the little rare which was taken to present an accurate account of the way in which the time was spent. This it is which makes all the accounts of the life of Jesus after his resurrection in complete disagreement as to the duration of that life. So little care was taken to be historical that the same narrator made no scruple about proposing two irreconcilable systems in succession. The three accounts of the conversion of Paul in the Acts present also little differences, which prove simply that the author did not trouble himself much about the exactness of the details.

It appears then that we shall be very near the truth in supposing that the Acts were written about the year 80. The spirit of the book, in fact, corresponds completely with the age of the first Flavians. The author carefully avoids all that can wound the Romans. He loves to show how favourable the Roman authorities were to the new sect; how they sometimes even embraced it; how they at least defended it against the Jews; how greatly superior is imperial justice to the passions of the local powers. He insists especially on the advantages which Paul owed to his rights as a Roman citizen. He abruptly cuts his narrative short at the moment of the arrival of Paul at Rome, perhaps in order to avoid the necessity of relating the cruelties of Nero towards the Christians. The contrast with the Apocalypse is striking. The Apocalypse, written in the year 68, is full of the memory of the iniquities of Nero; a horrible hatred of Rome overspreads it. Here we see a mild man, who lives in a period of calm. After about the year 70 until the last years of the first century, the situation was not altogether unpleasant for the Christians. Personages of the Flavian family attached themselves to Christianity. Who knows if Luke did not know Flavius Clemens, if he were not of his familia, if the Acts were not written for that powerful personage, whose official position required caution? Some indications have led to the belief that this book was composed at Rome. One might have said indeed that the principles of the Roman Church weighed upon the author. That Church, from the earliest ages, had the political and hierarchical character which has always distinguished it. The good Luke could enter into that spirit. His ideas of ecclesiastical authority are very advanced: we see the form of the episcopate sprouting. He writes history in that tone of an apologist at any cost which is that of the official historians of the court of Rome. He acts as an ultramontane historian of Clement XIV would act; praising at the same time the Pope and the Jesuits, and seeking to persuade by a narrative full of compunction that both sides in that debate observed the rules of charity. In two hundred years it will also be settled that Cardinal Antonelli and Mgr de Merode loved each other like two brothers. The author of the Acts was, but with a simplicity which will not again be equalled, the first of those complacent narrators, sanctimoniously satisfied, determined to believe that everything goes on in the Church in an evangelic fashion. Too loyal to condemn his master Paul, too orthodox not to share the official opinion which prevailed, he smoothed over differences of doctrine, to allow only the common end to be seen--that end which all these great founders pursued in effect by paths so opposed and through rivalries so energetic.

We can understand how a man who has placed himself intentionally in such a disposition of mind, is the least capable in the world of representing things as they really happened. Historical fidelity is a matter of indifference to him; edification is all he cares for. Luke scarcely conceals this; he writes in order that Theophilus may recognise the truth of what the catechists have taught him. There was then already a recognised system of ecclesiastical history, which was officially taught, and the framework of which, as well as that of the Gospel history itself, was probably already settled. The dominant character of the Acts, like that of the third Gospel, is a tender piety, a lively sympathy with the Gentiles, a conciliatory spirit, an extreme pro. occupation with the supernatural, love for the humble and lowly, a grand democratic sentiment, or rather the persuasion that the people are naturally Christian, that it is the great who prevent them from following their good instincts, an exalted idea of the power of the Church and of its heads, a remarkable taste for community of life. The system of composition is the same in both books, so that we are with respect to the history of the apostles on the same footing as we should be with regard to the Gospel history if we had one single text only, the Gospel of Luke.

The disadvantages of such a situation are manifest. The life of Jesus, as related by the third evangelist alone, would be extremely defective and incomplete. We know it, because so far as the life of Jesus is concerned, comparison is possible. Together with Luke we possess (without speaking of the fourth Gospel) Matthew and Mark, who, as compared with Luke, are in part, at least, original. We can lay a finger on the violent proceedings by means of which Luke dislocates or mixes up anecdotes, on the way in which he modifies the colour of certain facts according to his personal views, of the pious legends which he adds to the most authentic traditions. Is it not evident that if we could make such a comparison of the Acts, we should find faults of a precisely similar description? The first chapters of the Acts would even appear, without doubt, inferior to the third Gospel, for these chapters were probably composed with fewer and less universally accepted documents.

A fundamental distinction, in fact, is here necessary. From the point of view of historical value, the book of the Acts divides itself into two parts; one, including the first twelve chapters, and relating the principal facts of the history of the primitive Church; the other containing the remaining sixteen chapters, all devoted to the missions of St. Paul. That second part includes in itself two distinct kinds of narrative; those on the one hand, of which the narrator gives himself out as eye-witness; on the other, those in which he relates only what he has been told. It is clear that oven in the last case his authority is great. Often the conversations of Paul have furnished his information. Towards the end, moreover, the narrative assumes an astonishing character of precision. The last pages of the Acts are the only completely historical pages which we possess of the origins of Christianity. The first, on the contrary, are those which are most open to attack of all the New Testament. It is especially in the first years that the author obeyed impulses like those which preoccupied him in the composition of his gospel, and even more deceptive. His system of forty days; his account of the ascensions, closing by a species of final carrying off, theatrical solemnity; the strange life of Jesus; his manner of relating the descent of the Holy Ghost, and the miraculous preachings; his mode of understanding the gift of tongues, so different from that of St. Paul, unveil the preoccupation of a period relatively low when the legend is very ripe, rounded as it were in all parts. Everything is done with him with a strange setting and a great display of the marvellous. It must be remembered that the author wrote half a century after the events, far from the country where they happened, concerning incidents which neither he nor his master had seen, according to traditions in part fabulous or transmogrified. Not merely is Luke of another generation than the first founders of Christianity, but he is of another world; he is Hellenist with but very little of the Jew, almost a stranger to Jerusalem and the secrets of the Jewish life; he has not touched the primitive Christian society; he has scarcely known its last representatives. We see in the miracles, which he relates, rather inventions a priori than transformed facts; the miracles of Peter and Paul form two series, which answer each other. His persons resemble each other. Peter differs in nothing from Paul, nor Paul from Peter. The discourses, which he puts into the mouths of his heroes, though admirably appropriate to the circumstances, are all in the same style, and belong to the author rather than to those to whom he attributes them. We even find impossibilities. The Acts, in a word, are a dogmatic history, arranged to support the orthodox doctrine of the time, or to inculcate the ideas which seemed most agreeable to the piety of the author. Let us add that it could be no otherwise. The origin of every religion is known only by the narratives of the faithful. It is only scepticism which writes history ad narrandum.

These are not simple suspicions, conjectures of a criticism defiant to excess. They are solid inductions; every time that we are permitted to examine the narrative of the Acts, we find it incorrect and unsystematic. The examination of the Gospels, which can be done only by comparison with the Synoptics, we can make with the help of the Epistles of Paul, especially of the Epistle of Paul to the Galatians. It is clear that where the Acts and the Epistles clash, the preference ought always to be given to the Epistles--texts of an absolute authenticity, more ancient, of a complete sincerity, and free from legends. In history documents have the more authority the less they possess of historical form. The authority of all the chronicles must yield to that of an inscription, of a medal, of a map, of an authentic letter. From this point of view, the letters of certain authors, or of certain dates, are the basis of all the history of the origins of Christianity. Without them, it might be said that doubt would attach to them, and would ruin, from top to bottom, even the life of Jesus itself. Now, in two very important particulars, the Epistles put in a striking light the private tendencies of the author of the Acts, and his desire to efface all trace of the divisions which existed between Paul and the Apostles of Jerusalem.

And first, the author of the Acts says that Paul, after the incident at Damascus (ix, 19 et seq., xxii, 17 et seq.), having come to Jerusalem at a period when his conversion was hardly known; that he was presented to the Apostles; that he lived with the Apostles and the faithful on a footing of the greatest cordiality; that he disputed publicly with the Hellenist Jews; that a plot of theirs, and a celestial revelation, brought about his departure from Jerusalem. Now Paul tells us that things came about very differently. To prove that he owed nothing to the Twelve, and that he received his doctrine and his mission from Jesus, he asserts (Gal. i., 11 et seq.), that after his conversion he avoided taking counsel with anyone whatever, or going to Jerusalem to those who were apostles before him; that he went of his own accord, and without commission from anyone, to preach in Hauran; that three years later, it is true, he accomplished the journey to Jerusalem to make acquaintance with Peter; that he stayed there fifteen days with him; but that he saw no other apostle unless it were James, the Lord's brother, so that his face was unknown to the churches of Judea. The effort to soften down the asperities of the rude apostle by presenting him as a follow worker with the Twelve, labouring at Jerusalem in concert with them, evidently appears hero. Jerusalem is made his capital and point of departure; it is desired that his doctrine shall be so identified with that of the apostles, that he might in some sort replace them in the preaching; his first apostolate is reduced to the synagogues of Damascus; he is described as having been disciple and auditor, which he certainly never was; the time between his conversion and his first journey to Jerusalem is materially abridged; his stay in that city is prolonged; he is described as preaching there to the general satisfaction; as having lived intimately with all the apostles, although he himself says that he saw only two; the brethren of Jerusalem are described as watching over him, whilst Paul declares that his face was unknown to them.

The desire to make of Paul an assiduous visitor to Jerusalem, which has led our author to advance and to prolong his first stay in that city after his conversion, appears to have induced him to ascribe to the apostle one journey too many. According to him Paul came to Jerusalem with Barnabas, bearing the offering of the faithful during the famine of the year 44 (Acts xi. 30, xii. 25). Now Paul declares expressly that between the journey which took place three years after his conversion and the journey about the business of the circumcision, he did not go to Jerusalem (Gal. i. and ii.) In other words, Paul formally excludes the idea of any journey between Acts ix. 26 and Acts xv. 2. If we were to deny, against all reason, the identity of the journey related Acts xv. 2, et seq. we should not obtain the smallest contradiction. "After three years," says St. Paul, "I went up to Jerusalem to see Peter . . . Then fourteen years after I went up again to Jerusalem with Barnabas." It has been doubted whether these fourteen years date from the conversion, or the journey which followed three years after that event. Let us take the first hypothesis, which is the most favourable to those who would defend the account in the Acts. There would then be eleven years, at least, according to St. Paul, between his first and his second journey to Jerusalem; now. surely there were not eleven years between what is told Acts ix. 26 et seq. and what is told Acts xi, 30! And if against all probability that hypothesis is maintained, we find ourselves in the presence of another impossibility. In fact, what is told in Acts xi. 30 is contemporaneous with the death of James the son of Zebedee, which furnishes the only date fixed by the Acts of the Apostles, since it proceeded by very little the death of Herod Agrippa I. which happened in the year 44. The second journey of Paul having taken place at least fourteen years after his conversion, if Paul had really made that journey in the year 44, the conversion would have taken place in the year 30, which is absurd. It is, therefore, impossible to maintain for the journey related Acts xi. 30 and xii. 35 any reality.

These comings and goings appear to have been related by our author in a very inexact fashion. In comparing Acts xvii. 14-16; xviii. 5, with I. Thess. iii. 1-2, we find another disagreement. But seeing that does not concern matters of dogma, we need not speak of it here.

That which is most important about our present subject which furnishes thin critical ray of light for the difficult question of the historical value of the Acts is a comparision of the passages relative to the business of the circumcision in the Acts (chap. xv.) and in the Epistle to Galatians (chap. ii). According to the Acts the brethren in Judea being come to Antioch and having maintained the necessity of circumcision for the converted Pagans, a deputation, composed of Paul, Barnabas and many others was sent from Antioch to Jerusalem to consult the apostles and the elders in this question. They were received with much warmth by the whole community; a great assembly took place. Dissension scarcely showed itself, checked as it was under the effusions of a common charity and the happiness of finding themselves together. Peter announces the opinion which he had expected to find in the mouth of Paul, that converted Pagans do not become subject to the law of Moses. James appends to that only a very slight restriction. Paul does not speak, and, to say the truth, is under no necessity of speaking, since his doctrine is put into the mouth of Peter. The opinion of the brethren of Judea is supported by none. A solemn decree is formulated by the advice of James. This decree is signified to the churches by deputies specially appointed.

Let us now compare the account of Paul in the Epistle to the Galatians. Paul's version is that the journey to Jerusalem which he undertook on that occasion was the effect of a spontaneous movement, and even the result of a revolution. Arrived at Jerusalem, he communicates his gospel to those whom it concerned; he has, in particular, interviews with those who appear to be considerable personages. They do not offer him a single criticism; they communicate nothing to him; they only ask that he should remember the poor of Jerusalem. If Titus, who accompanied him, consented to allow himself to be circumcised it is "because of false brethren unawares brought in." Paul makes this passing concession to them, but he does not submit himself to them. As to men of importance (Paul speaks of them only with a shade of bitterness and irony), they have taught him nothing new. More, Peter, having come later to Antioch, Paul "withstood him to the face, because he was to be blamed." First, in effect, Peter ate with all indiscriminately. The emissaries of James having arrived, Peter hides himself and avoids the uncircumcised. "Seeing that they walked not uprightly according to the truth of the Gospel," Paul apostrophises Peter before them all, and reproaches him bitterly with his conduct.

The difference is palpable. On the one hand a solemn agreement, on the other anger ill-restrained, extreme susceptibilities. On the one side a sort of council; on the other nothing resembling it. On one side a formal decree issued by a recognized authority; on the other different opinions, which remain in existence without any reciprocal yielding, save for form's sake. It is useless to say which version merits the preference. The account in the Acts is scarcely probable, since according to this account the council was occasioned by a dispute of which no trace is to be found when the council has met. The two orators expressed themselves in a sense altogether different from that which we know to have been otherwise their usual part. The decree which the council is said to have decided upon is assuredly a fiction. If this decree of which James would have settled the terms had been really promulgated, why those terrors of the good and timid Peter? Why did he hide himself? He and the Christian community of Antioch were acting in the fullest conformity with the decree the terms of which had been settled by James himself. The business of the circumcision occurred about the year 51. Some years afterwards, about the year 56, the quarrel which the decree ought to have ended is more lively than ever. The Church of Galatia is troubled by new envoys from the Church of Jerusalem. Paul answered this new attack of his enemies by his thundering epistle. If the decree mentioned in Acts xv. had had any real existence, Paul had a very simple means of silencing debate--he had only to quote it. Now all that he says supposes the non-existence of this decree. In 57, Paul, writing to the Corinthians, ignores the same decree, and even violates its prescriptions. The decree orders abstinence from meats offered to idols. Paul, however, is of opinion that those meats may be eaten if no one is scandalized thereby, but they ought to be abstained from in cases where scandal would arise. In 58, then, about the time of the last journey of Paul to Jerusalem, James is more obstinate than ever. One of the characteristic features of the Acts--a feature which proves plainly that the author proposes to himself less to prevent historical truth and even to satisfy logic, than to edify pious readers--is the circumstance that the question of the admission of the uncircumcised is always settled, yet is always open. It is settled at first by the baptism of the eunuch of Queen Candace, then by the baptism of the centurion Cornelius, both miraculously ordained; then by the foundation of the church of Antioch (xi. 19, et. seq.) then by the pretended Council of Jerusalem, which does not prevent that; on the last pages of the book (xxi. 20-21.) the question is still in suspense. To tell the truth it has always remained in that state. The two fractions of the nascent Christianity never agreed upon it. One of them, however, that which clung to the practices of Judaism remained infertile, and faded into obscurity. Paul was so far from being accepted by all that after his death a part of Christendom anathematized him, and pursued him with calumnies.

In our third book we shall have to deal in detail with the question which lies at the root of all those curious incidents. Here we have desired to give only some examples of the manner in which the author of the Acts understands history, of his system of conciliation, of his preconceived ideas. Must we conclude from them that the first chapters of the Acts are devoid of authority, as some celebrated critics think, that fiction so far enters as to create both pieces and persons, such as the eunuch of Candace, the centurion Cornelius, and even the deacon Stephen and the pious Tabitha? I think by no means. It is probable that the author of the Acts has not invented the persons, but is a skilful advocate, who writes to prove his case, and who makes the most of the facts which have come to his knowledge to support his favourite theories, which are the legitimacy of the calling of the Gentiles, and the divine institution of the hierarchy. Such a document must be used with great caution, but to reject it absolutely is as uncritical as to follow it blindly. Some paragraphs, besides, even in the first part, have a universally recognised value, and represent authentic memoirs extracted by the last editor. Chapter xii., in particular, is excellent matter, and may have been the work of John-Mark.

It may be seen in what distress we should be if the only documentary authorities we have for this history were a legendary book like this. Happily, we have others which refer directly to the period which will be the subject of our third book, and which shed a great light upon this. These are the Epistles of St. Paul. The Epistles to the Galatians especially is a veritable treasury, the basis of the chronology of this age, the key which opens everything, the testimony which ought to re-assure the most sceptical as to the reality of matters concerning which they might doubt. I beg, serious readers who may be tempted to regard me as too bold or too credulous, to read again the two first chatters of that remarkable document. They are certainly the two most important chapters for the study of nascent Christianity. The Epistles of St. Paul have, in fact, an unequalled advantage in that history: their absolute authenticity. No doubt has ever been raised by serious criticism as to the authenticity of the Epistle to the Galatians. of the two Epistles to the Corinthians, of the Epistle to the Romans. The reasons for which the two Epistles to the Thessalonians and that to the Philippians, have been attacked are valueless. At the beginning of our third volume we shall have to discuss the more specious, although indecisive, objections which have been raised against the Epistle to the Colossians, and the note to Philemon; the special problem presented by the Epistle to the Ephesians; the strong reasons, finally, which point to the rejection of the two Epistles to Timothy, and that to Titus. The epistles of which we shall have to make use in this volume are those whose authenticity is indisputable; for, at least, the inductions which we shall draw from the others are independent of the question of whether they have or have not been dictated by St. Paul.

It is not necessary to refer in this place to the rules of criticism which have been followed in the composition of this work; that has already been done in the introduction to the Life of Jesus. The first twelve chapters of the Acts are in effect a document analogous to the synoptical Gospels, and require to be treated in the same fashion. Documents of this kind, half historical, half legendary, can never be regarded as wholly legend or wholly history. Almost everything in them is false in detail, nevertheless it may enclose some precious truths. To translate these narratives pure and simple is not to write history. These narratives are, in fact, often contradicted by other and more authentic texts. In consequence, even when there is only one text, one is always constrained to fear that if there had been others there would have been the same contradictions. For the Life of Jesus the narrative of Luke is continually controlled and corrected by the two other synoptical Gospels and by the fourth. Is it not probable, I repeat, that if we had for the Acts the analogue of the Synoptics and of the fourth Gospel, the Acts would be corrected on a host of points where we have now only their testimony? In our third book, where we shall be in clear and definite history, and where we shall have in our hands original and often biographical information, we shall be guided by other rules. When St. Paul himself tells us the story of some episode of his life which he had no interest in presenting in any particular light, it is clear that all that we need do is to insert his very words, word for word, in our narrative, according to the method of Tillemont. But when we are concerned with a narrator preoccupied with a system, writing as the advocate of certain ideas, editing after this infantine fashion, with vague and soft outlines, colours absolute, and strongly marked such as legend always offers, the duty of the critic is not to stick close to the text; his duty is to discover what truth the text may embody, without ever being too certain of having found it. To debar criticism from such interpretations would be as unreasonable as to command an astronomer to concern himself only with the apparent state of the heavens. Does not astronomy, on the contrary, consist in rectifying the parallax caused by the position of the observer, and to construct a real and veracious chart instead of a deceptive apparent one?

How besides can it be pretended that documents should be followed to the letter when they are full of impossibilities? The first twelve chapters of the Acts are a tissue of miracles. Now it is an absolute rule of criticism to give no place in historical documents to miraculous circumstances. This is not the result of a metaphysical system, but simply a matter of observation. Facts of that kind can never be verified. All the pretended miracles that we can study closely resolve themselves either into illusions or impostures. If a single miracle were proved, we could hardly reject all those of ancient history in a mass, for after all, admitting that a great number of these last were false, it is still possible to believe that certain of them were true. But it is not thus. All discussable miracles fade away. May we not reasonably conclude from that fact that the miracles which are removed from us by centuries, and concerning which there is no way of establishing an exhaustive discussion, are also without reality? In other words, there is no miracle except when one believes it; the substance of the supernatural is faith. Catholicism itself, which pretends that the miraculous power is not yet extinct within its bosom, undergoes the power of this law. The miracles which it pretends to work happen only in places of its choice. When there is so simple a method of proving its authenticity, why not do so in open daylight? A miracle in Paris, under the eyes of competent and learned men, would put an end to all doubts. But alas! that is what never happens. Never has a miracle been wrought before the public whom it is desirable to convert, I would say before the incredulous. The condition of the miracle is the credulity of the witness. No miracle is performed before those who might discuss and criticise it. To that rule there is not a single exception. Cicero said, with his usual good sense and acuteness, "Since when has that secret force disappeared? Is it not since men have become less credulous?"

"But," it is said, "if it is impossible to prove that there has ever been a supernatural fact, it is equally impossible to prove that there has not been one. The positive savant who denies the supernatural proceeds then as gratuitously as the believer who admits it." In no way. It is for him who affirms a proposition to prove it. He, before whom it is affirmed, has but one thing to do, to wait for the proof, and to yield if it is good. Supposing we had called upon Buffon to give a place in his Natural History to sirens and centaurs, Buffon would have answered, "Show me a specimen of these beings, and I will admit them; until you do, they do not exist for me"--"But prove that they do not exist?"--"It is for you to prove that they exist." The burden of proof in science rests upon those, who make the assertion. Why do we not believe in angels or devils, although innumerable historic texts assume their existence? Because the existence of an angel or a devil has never yet been proved.

To maintain the reality of the miracle appeal is made to the phenomena, which, it is said, could have been produced only by going beyond the laws of nature, the creation of man for example. "The creation of man," it is said, "could have come about only by the direct intervention of the Deity; why should not that intervention be repeated at other decisive moments of the development of the universe?" I shall not insist upon the strange philosophy, and the paltry idea of the Divinity which such a method of reasoning involves, for history has its method, independent of all philosophy. Without entering, in the smallest degree, upon the province of theodicy, it is easy to show how defective such an argument is. It is equivalent to saying that everything which does not happen in the existing state of the world, everything which we cannot explain by the existing condition of science, is miraculous. But then the sun is a miracle, for science is far from having explained the sun; the conception of every man is a miracle, for philosophy is still silent on that point; conscience is a miracle, for it is an absolute mystery; every animal is a miracle, for the origin of life is a problem concerning which we have almost no information. If we say that all life, that every soul is in effect of a superior order in nature, we are simply playing upon words. We are anxious that this should be understood; but then there must be an explanation of the word miracle. Can that be a miracle which happens every day and every hour? Miracle is not the unexplained; it is a formal derogation in the name of a particular will of known laws. What we deny is the exceptional; those are the private interventions, like that of a clockmaker, who has made a clock, very well, it is true, but to which he is from time to time obliged to put his hand to supply the deficiencies of the wheel-work. That God permeates everything, especially everything that lives, is distinctly our theory; we only say that no special intervention of a supernatural force has ever been proved. We deny the reality of private supernaturalism until a demonstrated fact of this kind has been presented to us. To seek this fact before the creation of man; to fly beyond history to periods, where all verification is impossible, in order to escape from verifying historical miracles, is to take refuge behind a cloud, to prove one obscure thing by another still morn obscure, to dispute a known law, because of a fact of which we are not certain. Miracles are appealed to which took place before any witness existed, simply because it is impossible to quote one of which there is any credible witness.

Without doubt, in distant ages, things happened in the universe, phenomena which offer themselves no more, at least upon the same scale in the actual state of things. But these phenomena may be explained by the date at which they have occurred. In the geological formation a great number of minerals and precious atones are found, which it would appear are no longer produced in nature. Nevertheless Messrs. Mitscherlich, Ebelman, de Sénarmont, Daubree have artificially recomposed the majority of these minerals and precious stones. If it is doubtful whether they will ever succeed in artificially producing life, it is because the artificial reproduction of the circumstances under which life commences (if it ever does commence) will be always out of the reach of humanity. How can we bring back a state of the planet which has disappeared for thousands of years? How are we to try an experiment which will occupy centuries? The diversity of the moans and the centuries of slow evolution--these are the things that are forgotten when we speak of the phenomena of old times, which do not happen to-day as miracles. In some celestial body at the present moment things are perhaps being done which have ceased upon this earth for an infinite period of time. Surely the formation of humanity is the most shocking and absurd thing in the world, if it is supposed to be sudden, instantaneous. It reverts to general analogies (without ceasing to be mysterious) if we see in it the result of a slow progress continued during incalculable periods. We must not apply the laws of maturity to embryonic life. The embryo develops all its organs one after another; the adult man, on the contrary, creates no more organs. He creates no more because he is no longer of an age to create; he does not even invent language because he is not called upon to invent it. But what is the use of meeting adversaries who continually evade the question? We ask for an authenticated historical miracle; we are told that there were such things before history existed. Assuredly, if a proof were required of the necessity for supernatural beliefs in certain states of the soul, it might be found in the fact that minds penetrating enough in every other respect have been able to rest the edifice of their faith on such a desperate argument.

Others, abandoning miracles of the physical order, entrench themselves behind moral miracles, without which they maintain that these events cannot be explained. Certainly the formation of Christianity is the greatest event in the religious history of the world. But it is not a miracle for all that. Buddhism, Babism have had martyrs as numerous, as exalted, as resigned as Christianity. The miracles of the foundation of Islam are of a wholly different character, and I confess that they affect me little. It must, however, be remarked that the Mussulman doctors base upon the establishment of Islam, upon its diffusion as by a train of fire, upon its rapid conquests, upon the force which gives it everywhere an absolute reign, the same reasonings which the Christian apologists base upon the establishment of Christianity, and assert that they clearly behold there the finger of God. Let us allow, if it is desired, that the foundation of Christianity is a unique fact. Hellenism is another absolutely unique fact, understanding by that word the ideal perfection in literature, in art, in philosophy, which Greece has achieved. Greek art surpasses all other art, as Christianity surpasses all other religions, and the Acropolis at Athens--a collection of masterpieces by the side of which everything else is no bettor than clumsy fumbling, or more or less successful imitation--is perhaps that which in its way most successfully defies comparison. Hellenism, in other words, is as much a miracle of beauty as Christianity is a miracle of sanctity. A unique thing is not a miraculous thing. God is in varying degrees in all that is beautiful, good, and true. But he is never in one of his manifestations in so exclusive a fashion that the presence of his breath in a religious or a philosophical movement ought to be deemed a privilege or exception.

I hope that the interval of two years and a half passed since the publication of the Life of Jesus will lead some of my readers to consider these problems with greater calmness. Religious controversy is always one of bad faith, without any intention or desire that it should be so. There is no independent discussion; no anxious seeking for the truth; it is the defence of a position already taken up to prove that the dissident is ignorant or dishonest. Calumnies, misinterpretations, falsifications of ideas and of texts, triumphant reasonings over things that an opponent has never said, cries of victory over mistakes which he has not made, nothing appears disloyal to the man who would hold in his hand the interests of absolute truth. I should have ignored history if I had not expected all that. I am cool enough to be almost insensible to it, and I have a sufficiently lively taste for matters of faith to be able to understand in a kindly spirit what there is that is often touching in the sentiment which inspired those who contradicted me. Often, in seeing so much simplicity, such a pious assurance, a wrath coming so frankly from good and pure souls, I have said, with John Huss, at the sight of an old woman who sweated under a faggot for his burning: Oh, sancta simplicitas! I have regretted certain emotions, which could only be profitless. According to the beautiful expression of the Scriptures, "God is not in the tempest." Ah! without doubt, if this trouble led to the discovery of the truth, we should be consoled for many agitations. But it is not thus: truth does not exist for the passionate man. It is reserved for the minds of those who seek for it without prejudice, without persistent love, without lasting hatred, with an absolute liberty, and without any after intention of acting in the business of humanity. These problems are only some of the innumerable questions of which the world is full, and which the curious examine. No one is offended by the enunciation of a theoretical opinion. Those who hold to their faith as to a treasure have a very simple method of defending it--that of taking no note of works written in a sense different from their own. The timid do better not to read them.

There are practical persons who, with regard to a work of science, ask what political party the author proposes to satisfy, and who are anxious that every poem should convey a moral lesson. Such persons do not admit that it is possible to write for something else besides a propaganda. The idea of art and of science aspiring only to find the true, and to realize the beautiful, outside of all politics, is to them incomprehensible. Between us and such persons misunderstandings are inevitable. "These people," as the Greek philosopher said, "take back with their left hand what they give with their right." A host of letters, dictated by a worthy sentiment, which I have received, may be summed up thus:-- "What do you want? What end do you propose?" Good God! the same that every one proposes in writing history. If I had many lives at my disposal I would devote one to writing the history of Alexander, another to writing the history of Athens, a third, it may be, to writing a history of the French Revolution, or a history of the Order of St. Francis. What end should I propose to myself in writing those works? One only, to find the truth and to make it live, to work so that the great things of the past may be known with the greatest possible exactitude, and expounded in a manner worthy of them. The notion of overthrowing the faith of anyone is far removed from me. These works ought to be executed with a supreme indifference, as if one were writing for a deserted planet. Every concession to scruples of an inferior order is a failure in the worship of art and of truth. Who does not admit that the absence of the proselytising spirit is at once the quality and the defect of a work composed in this spirit?

The first principle of the critical school in effect is that in matters of faith everyone admits what he wants to admit, and, as it were, makes the bed of his belief in proportion to his own stature. Why should we be so senseless as to mix ourselves up with what depends upon circumstances concerning which no one knows anything? If anyone accepts our principles, it is because he possesses the turn of mind and the necessary education for them; all our efforts would give neither, did one not already possess those qualities. Philosophy differs from faith, inasmuch as faith operates by itself, independently of the understanding that we have of the dogmas. We believe, on the contrary, that a truth has no value, save when it is reached by itself, when one sees the whole order of ideas to which it belongs. We do not force ourselves to silence such of our opinions as are not in harmony with the belief of a portion of our fellow-man; we make no sacrifice to the exigencies of divergent orthodoxies; but on the other hand we do not dream of attacking or provoking them; we act as though they did not exist. For myself, the day when I may be convicted of an effort to convert to my views a single adherent who did not come of himself would cause me the most acute pain. I should conclude from it, either that my mind had lost its freedom and calmness, or that something was oppressing me so that I could not content myself any longer with the free and joyous contemplation of the universe.

If, moreover, my aim had been to make war upon established religions, I should have worked in another way, undertaking only to point out the impossibilities and the contradictions of the texts and dogmas held as sacred. That minute task has been done a thousand times, and done well. In 1856, I wrote as follows:--"I protest once for all against the false interpretation which would be put upon my labours, if the various essays upon the history of religions which I have or may publish in the future, be treated as polemical works. Looked at as such, I should be the first to admit that these essays were very weak. Controversy requires tactics to which I am a stranger; it is necessary to know the weak side of one's adversary, to hold to it, never to touch doubtful questions, to avoid all concession, that is to say, to renounce the very essence of the scientific spirit. Such is not my method. The fundamental question upon which religious discussion must turn, that is to say, the question of revelation and of the supernatural, I never touch, not that that question may not be resolved for me with entire certainty, but because the discussion of such a question is not scientific, or rather because independent science supposes it to be resolved beforehand. Assuredly if I had any polemical or proselytising object in view, this would be a cardinal fault, it would be to transport into the region of delicate and obscure problems a question which is usually treated in the coarsest terms by controversialists and apologists. So far from regretting the advantages which I should thus give my opponent, I rejoice in them, if thereby I might convince the theologians that my writings are of another order than theirs, that in them they must look only for pure researches of study, open to attack as such, wherein an attempt is sometimes made to apply to the Jewish religion and to the Christian the principles of criticism which are followed in other branches of history and philology. I intend at no time to enter into the discussion of questions of pure theology any more than M.M. Burnouf, Creuzer, Guigniaut, and so many other critical historians of the religions of antiquity have thought themselves obliged to undertake the reputation of, or the apology for, the forms of worship with which they were occupied. The history of humanity is for me a vast whole, where everything is essentially unequal and diverse, but where everything of the same order arises from the same causes and obeys the same laws. These laws I inquire into with no other intention than that of discovering the exact tint of what really is. Nothing will make the change an obscure position, but one which is fruitful for science for the part of controversialist, an easy fact, inasmuch as it wins for the writer an assured favour amongst people who think it their duty to oppose war to war. In that polemic, the necessity for which I am far from disputing, but which is neither to my taste nor to my abilities, Voltaire is enough. One cannot be at the same time a good controversialist and a good historian. Voltaire, weak in scholarship; Voltaire, who appears so devoid of the sentiment of antiquity to us who are initiated into a better method; Voltaire is twenty times victorious over those who are even more innocent of criticism than he is himself. A new edition of the works of this great man would satisfy the want which appears to be felt at the present moment of answering the encroachments of theology; an answer bad in itself, but worthy of what it has to fight against; an old-fashioned answer to a science that is out of date. Let us do better, we who possess love of truth and a vast curiosity; let us leave these disputes to those whom they please; let us labour for the small number of those who march in the front rank of the human mind. Popularity, I know, belongs by preference to writers who, instead of pursuing the most elevated form of truth, apply themselves to struggling against the opinion of their times; but by a just revenge they have no value so soon as the opinion they have contested has ceased to exist. Those who refuted the magic and judicial astrology in the XVIth and XVIIth centuries, rendered an immense service to reason, yet their writings are unknown at the present day; their very victory has caused them to be forgotten.

I intend to hold invariably to this rule of conduct--the only one worthy of a scholar. I know that the researches of religious history touch upon living questions which appear to demand a solution. Persons familiar with free speculation do not understand the calm deliberation of thought; practical minds grow impatient with science, which does not answer to their eagerness. Let us avoid these vain excitements. Let us avoid finding anything. Let us rest in our respective Churches, profiting by their daily worship and their tradition of virtue, participating in their good work, and rejoicing in the poetry of their past. Nor should their intolerance repel us, We may even forgive that intolerance, for it is like egotism, one of the necessities of human nature. To suppose that it will henceforward form now religious families, or that the proportion amongst those which now exist will ever greatly change is to go against all appearances. There will soon be great schism in the Catholic Church; the days of Avignon, of the anti-popes, of the Clementists and the Urbanists will probably return. The Catholic Church may have its fourteenth Century again, but, notwithstanding her divisions, she will still remain the Catholic Church. It is probable that within a hundred years the relations between the number of Protestants, of Catholics, and of Jews will not have sensibly changed. But a great alteration will be made, or, rather, will have become apparent to the eyes of all. Each of these religious families will have two sorts of faithful ones; some believing absolutely as in the Middle Ages; others sacrificing the letter and holding only to the spirit. This second fraction will grow in every communion, and as the spirit agrees as much as the letter divides, the spiritualists of each communion will have reached such a point of agreement that they will altogether neglect to amalgamate. Fanaticism will be lost in a general tolerance. Dogma will become a mysterious ark which no one will ever want to open. If the ark is empty, then what matters it. One single religion will, I fear, resist this dogmatic softening; that is Islamism. There are amongst certain Mussulmans of the old school and amongst certain eminent men in Constantinople, there are in Persia, especially, forms of a large and conciliatory spirit. If these good forms are suffocated by the fanaticism of the ulemas, Islamism will perish, for two things are evident: the first, that modern civilization does not desire that the ancient religions should die out altogether; the second is, that it will not allow itself to be hampered in its work by old religious institutions. These last have the choice between submission and death.

As for pure religion, the pretension of which is not to be a sect or a Church apart, why should it submit to the inconveniences of a position of which it has none of the advantages? Why should it raise flag against flag when it knows that salvation is possible everywhere and to everybody; that it depends on the degree of nobility which each carries in himself? We can understand how Protestantism in the sixteenth century brought about an open rupture. Protestantism began with a very absolute faith. Far from corresponding to a weakening of dogmatism, the Reformation marked a renaissance of the most rigid Christian spirit. The movement of the nineteenth century, on the contrary, springs from a sentiment which is the very reverse of dogmatism; it arises not in sects or separate Churches, but in a general softening of all the Churches. The marked divisions increase the fanaticism of orthodoxy and provoke reactions. The Luthers and Calvins made the Caraffa, the Ghislieri, the Loyolas, the Philip II.'s. If our Church rejects them let us not recriminate; let us learn to appreciate the sweetness of modern manners, which has rendered those hatreds powerless; let us console ourselves by dreaming of that invisible Church which takes in the excommunicated saints, the best souls of every century. The banished of a Church are always its best men; they are in advance of their times; the heretic of to-day is the orthodox of to-morrow. What besides is the excommunication of men? Our Heavenly Father excommunicates only dry souls and narrow hearts. If the priest refuses to admit us to the cemetery, let us forbid our families to cry out. God is the Judge; the earth is a good mother who makes no differences; the corpse of a good man entering the unconsecrated corner carries consecration with it.

Undoubtedly there are circumstances in which the application of these principles is difficult. The spirit breathes where it will; the spirit is liberty. Now it is to persons who are as it were chained to absolute faith I would speak; of men in holy orders or clothed with some ministerial authority. Even then a fine soul knows how to find the ways of issue. A worthy country priest, by his solitary studies and by the purity of his his, comes to see the impossibility of literal dogmatism; must he sadden those whom he has hitherto consoled by explaining to them simple changes which they cannot understand? God forbid! There are not two men in the world who have exactly the same duties. The good Bishop Colenso accomplished an act of honesty such as the Church has not seen since its origin, in writing his doubts as soon as they came to him. But the humble Catholic priest, in a country of narrow and timid minds, ought to hold his tongue. How many discreet tombs around our village churches hide in this way poetic reserves--angelic silences! Will those whose duty it has been to speak equal the merit of those secrets known to God alone?

Theory is not practice. The ideal must remain the ideal; it must fear lest it soil itself by contact with reality. Thoughts which are good for those who are preserved by their nobility from all moral danger may not be, if they are, applied without their inconveniences for those who are surrounded with baseness. Great things are achieved only with ideas strictly defined; the man absolutely without prejudice would be powerless. Let us enjoy the liberty of the sons of God; but let us take care lest we become accomplices in the diminution of virtue which would menace society if Christianity were to grow weak. What should we be without it? What could replace the great schools of seriousness and respect, such as St. Sulpice, or the devoted ministry of the Sisters of Charity? How can we avoid being affrighted by the pettiness and the cold heartedness which have invaded the world? Our disagreement with persons who believe in positive religions is, after all, purely scientific; at heart we are with them! We have only one enemy who is theirs also--vulgar materialism, the baseness of the interested man.

Peace then, in God's name! Let the various orders of humanity live side by side, not falsifying their own intelligence in order to make reciprocal concessions which will lessen them, but in naturally supporting each other. Nothing ought to reign here below to the exclusion of its opposite. No one force ought to be able to suppress the others. The harmony of humanity results from the free emission of the most discordant notes. If orthodoxy should succeed in killing science we know what would happen. The Mussulman world of Spain died from having too conscientiously performed that task. If Rationalism wishes to govern the world without regard to the religious needs of the soul, the experience of the French Revolution is there to teach us the consequences of such a blunder. The instincts of art, carried to the highest point of refinement, but without honesty, made of the Italy of the Renaissance a den of thieves, an evil abode. Weariness, stupidity, mediocrity are the punishment of certain Protestant countries where, under the pretence of good sense and Christian spirit, art has been suppressed and science reduced to something paltry. Lucretius and St. Theresa, Aristophanes and Socrates, Voltaire and Francis of Assisi, Raphael and Vincent, St. Paul have an equal right to exist, and humanity would be the less if one of the elements which compose it were wanting.

CHAPTER I

FORMATION OF BELIEFS RELATIVE TO THE RESURRECTION OF JESUS--THE APPARITIONS AT JERUSALEM

Jesus, although speaking constantly of resurrection, of new life, never stated distinctly that he would rise again in the flesh. The disciples, in the hours immediately following his death, had not, in this respect, any settled expectations. The sentiments, in which they have so unaffectedly taken us into their confidence, implied even that they believed all was finished. They wept, and interred their friend, if not as they would at the death of a common person, at least as a person whose loss was irreparable. They were sad and cast down. The hope that they had cherished of seeing him realise the salvation of Israel is now proved to have been vanity. They were spoken of as men who had been robbed of a grand and dear illusion.

But enthusiasm and love do not recognise conditions barren of results. They dallied with the impossible, and, rather than abdicate hope, they did violence to all reality. Several phrases of the Master, which were recalled, especially those in which he predicted his future advent, might be interpreted in the sense that he would leave the tomb. Such a belief was, besides, so natural that the faith of the disciples would have sufficed to create it in every part. The great prophets, Enoch and Elijah, had not tasted death. They began even is believe that the patriarchs and the men of the first order in the old law, were not really dead, and that their bodies were in their sepulchres at Hebron, alive and animated. It was to happen to Jesus, what had happened to all men who have captivated the attention of their fellow-men. The world, accustomed to attribute to them superhuman virtues, cannot admit that they would have to undergo the unjust, revolting and iniquitous law, to wit, a common death. At the moment when Mahomet expired, Omar issued from the tent, sabre in hand, and declared that he would strike off the head of anyone who dared to say that the prophet was no more. Death is a thing so absurd--when it strikes down a man of genius, or the large-hearted man--that people will not believe in the possibility of such an error in nature. Heroes do not die. Is not true existence that which is implanted in the hearts of those whom we love? This adored Master had filled for some years the little world which pressed around him with joy and with hope; would people consent to leave him to rot in the tomb? No; he had lived too much in those who surrounded him for people not to declare after his death that he still lived.

The day which followed the burial of Jesus (Saturday, 15th April) was crowded with these thoughts. People were interdicted from all manner of manual labour, because of the Sabbath. But never was repose more fruitful. The Christian conscience had on that day but one object--the Master laid low in the tomb. The women, in particular, embalmed him in ointment with their most tender caresses. Not for a moment did their thoughts abandon that sweet friend, reposing in his myrrh, whom the wicked had killed! Ah! the angels are doubtless surrounding him, veiling their faces in his shroud! He, indeed, did say that he should die, that his death would be the salvation of the sinner, and that he should rise in the kingdom of his Father. Yes; he shall live again; God will not leave his Son to be a prey to hell; He will not suffer his chosen one to see corruption. What is this tombstone which weighs upon him? He will raise it up; he will reascend to the right hand of his Father, whence he descended. And we shall see him again; we shall hear his charming voice; we shall enjoy anew his conversations, and it is in vain that they have crucified him.

The belief in the immortality of the soul, which, through the influence of the Grecian philosophy, has become a dogma of Christianity, readily permits of one resigning oneself to death, inasmuch as the dissolution of the body in that hypothesis was only a deliverance of the soul, freed henceforth from vexatious bonds, without which it can exist. But that theory of man, considered as a being composed of two substances, did not appear very clear to the Jews. To them the reign of God and the reign of Spirit consisted in a complete transformation of the world and in the annihilation of death. To acknowledge that death could be victorious over Jesus, over him who came to extinguish its empire, was the height of absurdity. The very idea that he could suffer had previously disgusted his disciples. The latter, then, had no choice between despair or heroic affirmation. A man of penetration might have announced on that Saturday that Jesus would rise again; the little Christian Society on that day wrought the veritable miracle; it resurrected Jesus in its heart, because of the intense love that it bore for him. It decided that Jesus had not died. The love of these passionate souls was, in truth, stronger than death; and, as the property of passion is to be communicative, to light like a torch a sentiment which resembles itself, and, consequently, to be indefinitely propagated; Jesus, in a sense, at the moment of which we speak, is already risen from the dead. Let but one material fact, insignificant itself, permit the belief that his body is no longer here below, and the dogma of the resurrection will be established for eternity.

It was that which happened in the circumstances which, though part obscured, because of the incoherency of the traditions, and especially because of the contradictions which they presented, can, nevertheless, be grasped with a sufficient degree of probability.

Early on Sunday morning, the Galilean women who on Friday evening had hastily embalmed the body, visited the tomb in which he had been temporarily deposited. These were Mary Magdalene, Mary Cleophas, Salome, Joanna, wife of Kouza, and others. They came, probably, each on her own account, for it is difficult to call in question the tradition of the three synoptical gospels, according to which several women came to the tomb; on the other hand, it is certain that in the two most authentic narratives which we possess of the resurrection, Mary Magdalene alone played a part. In any case she had, at that solemn moment, taken a part altogether out of line. It is she whom we must follow step by step, for she bore on that day, for an hour, all the burden of a Christian conscience; her testimony decided the faith of the future.

Let us not forget that the vault in which the body of Jesus had been enclosed, was a vault which had been recently cut in the rock, and was situated in a garden near the place of execution. It had, for the latter reason been specially taken, seeing that it was late in the day and that they were desirous of not desecrating the Sabbath. The first gospel alone adds one circumstance, to wit, that the vault belonged to Joseph of Arimathæa. But, in general, the anecdotical circumstances annexed by the first gospel to the common fund of the tradition, are without any value, especially when the matter in hand is the last days of the life of Jesus. The same gospel mentions another detail which, in view of the silence of the others, has not any probability; we refer to the public seals and a guard being placed at the tomb. We must also remember that the mortuary vaults were low chambers, cut into an inclining rock, in which was contrived a vertical cutting. The door, ordinarily downwards, was closed by a very heavy stone, fitted into a groove. These chambers had not a lock and key, the weight of the stone was the sole safeguard that one had against thieves or profaners of tombs; it was likewise so arranged that, to remove it, either a machine or the combined efforts of several persons were required. All the traditions agree on that point, that the stone had been put at the mouth of the vault on the Friday evening.

But when Mary Magdalene arrived on the Sunday morning, the stone was not in its place. The vault was open. The body was no longer there. In her mind the idea of the resurrection was as yet little developed. That which filled her soul was a tender regret and the desire to render funeral honours to the body of her divine friend. Her first sentiments, moreover, were those of surprise and of sadness. The disappearance of the cherished body had stripped her of the last joy upon which she had calculated. She could not touch him again with her hands! And what had become of him? The idea of a desecration was present to her and she was shocked at it. Perhaps, at the same time, a glimmer of hope crossed her mind. Without losing a moment, she ran to a house in which Peter and John were together. "They have taken away the body of our Master," said she, "and I know not where they have laid him."

The two disciples got up hastily and ran with all their might to see. John, the younger, arrived first. He stooped down to look into the interior. Mary was right. The tomb was empty. The linen which had served to enshroud him was scattered about the sepulchre. They both entered, examined the linen, which was no doubt stained with blood, and remarked in particular the napkin, which had enveloped his head, rolled up in a corner apart. Peter and John returned home extremely perplexed. If they did not now pronounce the decisive words: "He is risen!" we may be sure that such a consequence was the irrevocable conclusion, and that the generating dogma of Christianity was already established.

Peter and John departed from the garden; Mary remained alone at the mouth of the sepulchre. She wept profusely. One single thought engaged her: Where have they put the body? Her woman's heart did not go beyond the desire of holding the well-beloved body again in her arms. Suddenly she heard a slight noise behind her. A man is standing near her. She thinks at first it is the gardener. "Sir," said she, "if thou have borne him hence, tell me where thou hast laid him, and I will take him away." In response, she heard herself called by her name, "Mary!" It was the voice which had so often before thrilled her. It was the voice of Jesus. "Oh, my master!" she exclaimed. She made as if to touch him. A sort of instinctive movement induced her to kneel down and kiss his feet. The vision gently receded, and said to her: "Touch me not!" Gradually the shadow disappeared. But the miracle of love was accomplished. What Cephas was not able to do, Mary had done. She knew how to extract life, sweet and penetrating words, from the empty tomb. It was no longer a question of deducing consequences or of framing conjectures. Mary had seen and heard. The resurrection had its first immediate witness.

Frantic with love, inebriated with joy, Mary returned to the city and said to the first disciples whom she met: "I have seen him; he has spoken to me." Her greatly troubled imagination, her broken and incoherent discourse, made her to be taken by some as mad. Peter and John, in their turn, related what they had seen. Other disciples went to the tomb and saw likewise. The conviction reached by the whole of this first group was that Jesus had risen. Many doubts still existed. But the assurances of Mary, of Peter and of John, imposed upon the others. Subsequently, this was called "the vision of Peter." Paul, in particular, does not speak of the vision of Mary, and awards all the honour of the first apparition to Peter. But that statement was very inexact. Peter only saw the empty sepulchre, the napkin and the winding sheet. Mary alone loved enough to dispense with nature and to have revived the phantom of the perfect master. In these sorts of marvellous crises, to see after others have seen--goes for nothing; all the merit consists in being the first to see; for others afterwards model their visions on the received type. It is the characteristic of good organisations to perceive the image promptly, accurately, and as if by a sort of innate sense of design. The glory, then, of the resurrection belongs to Mary Magdalene. Next to Jesus, it is Mary who has done the most for the establishment of Christianity. The image created by the delicate sensibility of Mary Magdalene hovers over the world still. Queen and patroness of idealists, Magdalene knew better than any other person how to verify her dream, how to impose upon all the holy vision of her passionate soul. Her great woman's affirmation, "He is risen!" has been the basis of the faith of humanity. Begone hence, powerless reason! Seek not to apply cold analysis to this masterpiece of idealism and of love. If wisdom renounces the part of consoling that poor human race, betrayed by fate, let folly attempt the enterprise. Where is the sage who has given to the world so much joy as Mary Magdalene, the possessed of devils?

The other women who had been to the tomb spread meanwhile the news abroad. They had not seen Jesus; but they spoke of a man in white, whom they had seen in the sepulchre, and who had said to them: "He is not here; return into Galilee; he will go before you there; there shall ye see him." Perhaps it was these white linen clothes which had originated this hallucination. Perhaps, again, they saw nothing, and only commenced to speak of their vision when Mary Magdalene had related hers. Indeed, according to one of the most authentic texts, they kept silence for some time--a silence which was afterwards attributed to terror. However this may be, these recitals increased every hour, and underwent some singular transformations. The man in white became the angel of God; it was told that his garments shone like the snow; that his face seemed like lightning. Others spoke of two angels; one of whom appeared at the head, the other at the foot of the sepulchre. By evening, many, perhaps, already believed that the women had seen this angel descend from heaven, move away the stone, and Jesus issue forth with a great noise. Doubtless they varied in their depositions; suffering from the effect of the imagination of others, as is always the case with common people; they borrowed every embellishment, and thus participated in the creation of the legend which grew up around them and suited their ideas.

The day was stormy and decisive. The little company was greatly dispersed. Some had already departed for Galilee; others hid themselves for fear. The deplorable scene of the Friday; the afflicting spectacle which they had had before their eyes, in seeing him of whom they had expected so much expire upon the gibbet, without his Father coming to deliver him, had, moreover, extinguished the faith of many. The news imparted by the women and Peter was received on every side with scarcely dissembled credulity. Of the diverse stories, some were believed; the women went hither and thither with singular and inconsistent stories, enriching them as they went. Statements, the most opposed, were put forth. Some still wept over the sad event of the day before; others were already triumphant; all were disposed to entertain the most extraordinary accounts. Nevertheless, the distrust which the excitement of Mary Magdalene inspired, the little authority which the women had, the incoherency of their narratives, produced grave doubts. People were living in the expectation of seeing new visions, and which could not fail but come. The state of the sect was altogether favourable to the propagation of strange rumours. If all the members of the little church had been assembled, the legendary creation would have been impossible; those who knew the secret of the disappearance of the body, would probably have reclaimed against the error. But in the confusion which prevailed, the door was opened for the most prolific misapprehensions.

It is the characteristic of those states of the soul, in which originate ecstasy and apparitions, to be contagious. The history of all the great religious crises, proves that these sort of visions are infectious. In an assembly of persons, entertaining the same beliefs, it is sufficient for one member of the body to affirm having seen or heard something supernatural for others to see and to hear also. Amongst the persecuted Protestants, a report was spread that people had heard the angels singing psalms upon a recently destroyed temple: They all went there and heard the same psalm. In cases of this kind, it is the most excited who give law, and who regulate the temperature of the common atmosphere. The exaltation of a few is transmitted to all; no one desires to be left behind, or likes to confess that he is less favoured than the others. Those who see nothing, are carried away, and finish by believing either that they are less clear-sighted, or that they do not take proper account of their sensations. In any case, they take care not to avow it; they would be disturbers of the common joy, would cause sadness to others, and would be playing a disagreeable part. When, therefore, one apparition is brought forward in such assemblies, it is customary for everyone to see it, or believe he has seen it. It is necessary to remember, however, what was the degree of intellectual culture possessed by the disciples of Jesus. What is called a weak head, very often, is associated with infinite goodness of heart. The disciples believed in phantoms; they imagined themselves to be compassed about with miracles; they participated in nothing which had relation to the positive science of the times. This science existed amongst some hundreds of men, scattered over those countries alone where Grecian culture had penetrated. But the commonality, in every country, participated very little in it. Palestine was, in this respect, one of the most backward countries. The Galileans were the most ignorant people of Palestine, and the disciples of Jesus might be counted amongst the persons the most simple of Galilee. It was to this very simplicity that they were indebted for their heavenly election. Among such people, belief in marvellous deeds found the most extraordinary facilities for propagating itself. Once the opinion on the resurrection of Jesus had been noised abroad, numerous visions were sure to follow. And so in fact they did follow.

On the same Sabbath day, at an advanced hour of the morning, when the tales of the women had already been circulated, two disciples, one of whom was named Cleopatros or Cleopas, set out on a short journey to a village named Emmaus, situated a short distance from Jerusalem. They talked together of recent events, and were filled with sadness On the way, an unknown companion joined them, and inquired as to the cause of their sorrow. "Art thou only a stranger in Jerusalem?" said they, "And hast not known the things which are come to pass in these days?" And he said unto them, "What things?" And they said unto him, "Concerning Jesus of Nazareth, which was a prophet mighty in deed and word before God and all the people: And how the chief priests and our rulers delivered him to be condemned to death and have crucified him. But we trusted that it had been he which should have redeemed Israel: and besides all this, to-day is the third day since these things were done. Yea, and certain women also of our company made us astonished, which were early at the sepulchre: and when they found not his body, they came, saying, that they had also seen a vision of angels, which said that he was alive. And certain of them which were with us went to the sepulchre, and found it even so as the women had said: but him they saw not." The unknown individual was a pious man, well versed in the Scriptures, citing Moses and the prophets. These three good people became friendly. Approaching Emmaus, the stranger was making as if he would continue his journey, the two disciples begged him to come and break bread with them. The day was far spent; the recollections of the two disciples became then more vivid. This hour of the evening for refreshments, was the one which they looked back to as being at once the most charming and most melancholy. How many times had they not seen, during that hour, their beloved Master forget the burden of the day, in the abandon of gay conversation, and enlivened by several sips of excellent wine, spoke to them of the fruit of the vine, which he would drink anew with them in the Kingdom of his Father. The gesture which he made in the breaking of bread, and in offering it to them, according to the custom of the heads of Jewish families, was deeply engraven on their memories. Filled with a tender sadness, they forgot the stranger: it was Jesus they saw holding the bread, then breaking and offering it to them. These recollections engrossed them to such an extent, that they scarcely perceived that their companion, anxious to continue his journey, had quitted them. And when they had awakened out of their reverie: "Did we not perceive," they said, "something strange? Do you not remember how our hearts burned while he talked with us by the way? And the prophecies which he cited, proved clearly that Messiah must suffer before entering into his glory." "Did you not recognize him at the breaking of bread?" "Yes: up to that time our eyes were closed; they were only opened when he vanished." The conviction of the two disciples was that they had seen Jesus. They returned with all haste to Jerusalem.

The main body of the disciples were, just at that moment, assembled at the house of Peter. Night had completely set in. Each was relating his impressions, and what he had seen and heard. The general belief already willed that Jesus had risen. At the entrance of the two disciples, the brethren hastened to speak to them of that which was called, "the vision of Peter." They, on their side, told what had befallen them on the way to Emmaus, and how that they had recognized him in the breaking of bread. The imaginations of everyone became quite excited. The doors were shut; for they feared the Jews. Oriental cities are silent after sunset. The silence, hence, for some moments in the interior was frequently profound. Every slight sound which was accidentally produced was interpreted in the sense of the common expectation. Expectation, as is usual, was the progenitor of its object. During a moment of silence, a slight breath of wind passed over the face of the assembly. At these decisive times, a current of air, a creaking window, a casual murmur, suffices to fix the beliefs of people for centuries. At the same moment the breath of air was felt, they believed that they heard sounds. Some declared that they had seen the word schalom, "happiness" or "peace." This was the ordinary salutation of Jesus, and the word by which he signalized his presence. It was impossible to doubt; Jesus was present; he was there, in the assembly. It was his dear voice; everyone recognized it. This idea was the more easily accepted, inasmuch as Jesus had said to them, that as often as they came together in his name, he would be in the midst of them. It was then an accepted fact, that on Sunday evening, Jesus had appeared before his assembled disciples. Some of them pretended to have distinguished the marks of the nails in his hands and his feet, and in his side the trace of the spear thrust. According to a widely-spread tradition, this was the self-same evening that he breathed upon his disciples the holy spirit. The idea, at least, that his breath had passed over them on re-assembling, was generally admitted.

Such were the incidents of that day, which has decided the fate of humanity. The opinion that Jesus had risen was, on that day, established in an irrevocable manner. The sect, which was believed to be extinguished by the death of the Master, was, from that instant, assured of a great future.

Some doubts were, nevertheless, ventilated. The apostle, Thomas, who was not present at the meeting on Sunday evening, avowed that he envied those who had seen the marks of the spear and of the nails. Eight days after, this envy, it is said, was allayed. But there has attached to him, in consequence, some slight blame and a mild reproach. By an instinctive feeling of exquisite justness, they understood that the ideal was not to be touched with hands, and that it must not be subjected to the test of experience. Noli, me tangere (touch me not) is the motto of all great affection. The sense of touch leaves nothing to faith; the eye, a purer and more noble organ than the hand, which nothing can sully, and by which nothing is sullied, became very soon a superfluous witness. A singular sentiment began to grow up; any hesitation was held to be a mark of disloyalty and lack of love; one was ashamed to remain behind hand, and one interdicted oneself from desiring to see. The dictum: "Blessed are they who have not seen and yet believed," became the key-note of the situation. It was thought to be a thing so much more generous to believe without proof. The really sincere friends denied having seen any vision. Just as, in later times, Saint Louis refused to be a witness to an eucharistic miracle, so as not to detract from the merits of faith. From that time, credulity became a hideous emulation, and a kind of out-bidding one another. The merit consisted in believing without having seen; faith at any cost; gratuitous faith; the faith which went as far as folly--was exalted, as if it were the first of the gifts of the soul. The credo quia absurdum (I believe because I cannot understand) was established. The law of Christian dogmas was to be a strange progression, which no impossibility should be able to prevent. A sort of chivalrous sentiment prevented one from even looking back. The dogmas, the most dear to piety, those to which it was to attach itself with the most heedless frenzy, were the most repugnant to reason, in consequence of that touching idea, which the moral value of faith augments in proportion to the difficulty in believing, the reason of man not being compelled to prove any love when he admits that which is clear.

The first days were hence a period of intense feverishness, in which the faithful, infatuated with one another, and imposing one's fancies each upon the other, mutually carried away, and imparting to each other the most exalted notions. Visions were multiplied without number. The evening assemblies were the most common occasions when they were produced. When the doors were closed, and when each was beset with his fixed idea, the first who was believed to hear the sweet word, schalom, "salutation," or "peace," would give the signal. All would then listen, and would soon hear the very same thing. It was hence a great joy to those unsophisticated souls to know that Jesus was in the midst of them. Each tasted of the sweetness of that thought, and believed himself to be favoured with some inward colloquy. Other visions were noised abroad of a different description, and recalled those of the sojourners to Emmaus. During meal time, Jesus was seen to appear, taking the bread, blessing it, breaking it, and offering it to him who had been honoured with a vision of himself. In a few days, a whole string of stories, greatly differing in details, but inspired by the same spirit of love, and of absolute faith, was invented and spread abroad. It is the gravest of errors to suppose that legends require any length of time to be formed. Legend is sometimes born in a day. On Sunday evening (16 of Nisan, 5th April), the resurrection of Jesus was held to be a reality. Eight days after, the character of the life of the risen one, which had been conceived for him, was determined in regard at least to three essentials.

CHAPTER II

DEPARTURE OF THE DISCIPLES FROM JERUSALEM—SECOND GALILEAN LIFE OF JESUS

THE most eager desire of those who have lost a dear friend, is to revisit the places where they have lived with them. It was, doubtless, this sentiment which, a few days after the events of the Passover, induced the disciples to return into Galilee. From the moment of the arrest of Jesus, and immediately after his death, it is probable that many of the disciples had already found their way to the northern provinces. At the time of the resurrection, a rumour was spread abroad, according to which, it was in Galilee that he would be seen again. Some of the women who had been to the sepulchre came back with the report that the angel had said to them that Jesus had already preceded them into Galilee. Others said that it was Jesus himself who had ordered them to go there. Now and then some people said that they themselves remembered that he had said so during his life time. What is certain is, that at the end of a few days, probably after the Paschal Feast of the Pass-over had been quite over, the disciples believed they had a command to return into their own country, and to it accordingly they returned. Perhaps the visions began to abate at Jerusalem. A species of melancholy seized them. The brief appearances of Jesus were not sufficient to compensate for the enormous void left by his absence. In a melancholy mood, they thought of the lake and of the beautiful mountains where they had received a foretaste of the Kingdom of God. The women, especially, wished, at any cost, to return to the country where they had enjoyed so much happiness. It must be observed that the order to depart cane especially from them. That odious city weighed them down. They longed to see once more the ground where they had possessed him whom they loved, well assured in advance of meeting him again there.

The majority of the disciples then departed, full of joy and hope, perhaps in the company of the caravan, which took back the pilgrims from the Feast of the Passover. What they hoped to find in Galilee, were not only transient visions, but Jesus himself to continue with them, as he had done before his death. An intense expectation filled their souls. Was he going to restore the Kingdom of Israel, to found definitely the Kingdom of God, and, as was said, "Reveal his justice?" Everything was possible. They already called to mind the smiling landscapes where they had enjoyed his presence. Many believed that he had given to them a rendezvous upon a mountain, probably the same to which with them there clung so many sweet recollections. Never, it is certain, had there been a more pleasant journey. All their dreams of happiness were on the point of being realized. They were going to see him once more! And, in fact, they did see him again. Hardly restored to their harmless chimeras, they believed themselves to be in the midst of the Gospel dispensation period. It was now drawing near to the end of April. The ground is then strewn with red anemones, which were probably those "lilies of the fields" from which Jesus delighted to draw his similes. At each step, his words were brought to mind, adhering, as it were, to the thousand accidental objects they met by the way. Here was the tree, the flower, the seed, from which he had taken his parables; there was the hill on which he delivered his most touching discourses; here was the little ship from which he taught. It was like the recommencement of a beautiful dream. Like a vanished illusion which had reappeared. The enchantment seemed to revive. The sweet Galilean "Kingdom of God" had recovered its sway. The clear atmosphere, the mornings upon the shore or upon the mountain, the nights passed on the lakes watching the nets, all these returned again to them in distinct visions. They saw him everywhere where they had lived with him. Of course it was not the joy of the first enjoyment. Sometimes the lake had to them the appearance of being very solitary. But a great love is satisfied with little, if all of us, while we are alive, could surreptitiously, once a year, and during a moment long enough to exchange but a few words, behold again those loved ones whom we have lost--death would not be death!

Such was the state of mind of this faithful band, in this short period when Christianity seemed to return for a moment to his cradle and bid to him an eternal adieu. The principal disciples, Peter, Thomas, Nathaniel, the sons of Zebedee, met again on the shores of the lake, and henceforth lived together; they had taken up again their former calling of fishermen, at Bethsaida or at Capernaum. The Galilean women were no doubt with them. They had insisted more than the others on that return, which was to them a heartfelt love. This was their last act in the establishment of Christianity. From that moment, they disappear. Faithful to their love, their wish was to quit no more the country in which they had tasted their greatest delight. They were quickly forgotten, and, as the Galilean Christianity possessed but little of futurity, the remembrance of them was completely lost in certain ramifications of the tradition. These touching demoniacs, these converted fisherwomen, these actual founders of Christianity, Mary Magdalene, Mary Cleophas, Joanna, Susanna, all passed into the condition of forgotten saints. St. Paul knew them not. The faith which they had created almost consigned them to oblivion. We must come down to the middle ages before we find justice done them; then, one of them, Mary Magdalene, takes her proper place in the Christian hierarchy.

The visions, at first, on the lake appear to have been pretty frequent On board these crafts where they had come in contact with God, how many times had the disciples not seen again their Divine Friend? The simplest circumstances brought him back to them. Once they had toiled all night without taking a single fish; suddenly the nets were filled; this was a miracle. It appeared that some one from the land had said to them: "Cast your nets to the right." Peter and John regarded one another. "It is the Lord," said John. Peter, who was naked, covered himself hastily with his fisher's coat, and cast himself into the sea, in order to go to the invisible councillor. At other times Jesus came and partook of their simple repasts. One day, when they had done fishing, they were surprised to find lighted coals, with fish placed upon them, and bread near by. A lively sense of their feasts of past times crossed their minds, since bread and fish had been always an essential part of their diet. Jesus was in the habit of offering these to them. After the meal they were persuaded that Jesus himself had sat by their side, and had presented to them those victuals which hail already become to them eucharistic and sacred, John and Peter were the ones who were specially favoured with those private conversations with the well-beloved phantom. One day, Peter, dreaming, perhaps (but what am I saying! their life on the shore was it not a perpetual dream?) believed that he heard Jesus ask him: "Lovest thou Me?" The question was repeated three times. Peter, wholly possessed by a tender and sad sentiment, imagined that he responded, "Yea, Lord, Thou knowest that I love thee," and each time the apparition said: "Feed my sheep." On another occasion Peter told John, in confidence, a strange dream. He had dreamt he had been walking with the Master, John was following a few steps behind. Jesus said to him, in terms most obscure, which seemed to announce to him a prison or a violent death, and repeated to him at different times: "Follow me." Peter, thereupon, pointing his finger to John, who was following him, asked: "Lord, and this man?" "If I will," said Jesus, "that he tarry till I come, what is that to thee? Follow thou me." After the execution of Peter, John remembered that dream, and saw in it a prediction of the manner of death his friend had died. He recounted it to his disciples; the latter believed to discover in it the assurance that their master would not die before the final advent of Jesus.

These grand and melancholy dreams, these never ceasing conversations, broken off and recommenced with the death of the cherished one, occupied the days and months. The sympathy of Galilee for the prophet that the Hierosolymites of Jerusalem had put to death was re-awakened. More than five hundred persons were already devoted to the memory of Jesus. In default of the lost master, they obeyed the disciples, the most authoritative--Peter--in particular. One day, when following in the suite of their spiritual chiefs, the faithful Galileans had ascended one of those mountains whither Jesus had often conducted them, and they imagined that they saw him again. The atmosphere of these heights is full of strange mirages. The same vision which formerly had occurred to the most intimate disciples was once more produced. The whole assembly believed that they saw the divine spectre displayed in the clouds; all fell on their faces and worshipped. The sentiment which the clear horizon of those mountains inspires is the idea of the extent of the world, and the desire of conquering it. On one of the neighbouring peaks Satan, pointing out to Jesus with his finger the kingdoms of the world and all their glory, offered to give them to him, it is stated, if he would only fall down and worship him On this occasion, it was Jesus who, from the tops of these sacred summits, showed to his disciples the whole world, and assured them of the future. They descended from the mountain, persuaded that the son of God had given to them the command to convert the whole human race, and promised to be with them till the end of time. A strange ardour, a divine fire, pervaded them at the close of these conversations. They regarded themselves as the missionaries of the world, capable of performing supernatural deeds. St. Paul saw several of those who had assisted at that extraordinary scene. At the end of twenty-five years the impression they left was still as strong and as lively as on the first day.

Nearly a year rolled on, during which they led this life, suspended between heaven and earth. The charm, far from diminishing, increased. It is a property of great and holy things, always to become grander and more pure of themselves. The sentiment in regard to a loved one who has been lost, is certainly keener at a distance of time, than on the morrow after the death. The greater the distance, the more the sentiment gains strength. The sorrow, which at first is a part of it and, in a sense, lessens it, is changed into a serene piety. The image of the defunct one is transfigured, idealized, becomes the soul of life, the principle of all action, the source of all joy, the oracle which is consulted, the consolation which is sought in moments of despondency. Death is a necessary, condition of every apotheosis. Jesus, so beloved during his life, was in this way more so after his last breath, or rather his last breath was the commencement of his actual life in the bosom of the church. He became the intimate friend, the confidant, the travelling companion, the one who, at the turning point of the route, joins you, follows you, sits down at table with you, and reveals himself at the moment of disappearance. The absolute lack of scientific exactitude in the minds of these new believers, made it that one could not weigh any question in regard to the nature of one's existence. They represented him as impassible, endowed with a subtle body, passing through opaque walks, now visible, now invisible, but always living. Sometimes they imagined that his body was not composed of matter; that it was pure shadow or apparition. At other times there was attributed to him a material body, with flesh and bones; through a naïve scrupulousness, as though the hallucination had inclined to take precautions against himself, he was made to drink and eat; nay, it was maintained that some of them had touched his body gently with their hands. Their ideas on this point were extremely vague and uncertain. We have not until now dreamt of putting a frivolous question; at the same time the present is one not easily of solution. Whilst Jesus had risen in this real manner, that is to say, in the hearts of those who loved him; whilst the immovable conviction of the apostles was being formed, and the faith of the world prepared, in what place did the worms consume the inanimate body which on the Saturday evening had been deposited in the tomb? People ignore always this point, for, naturally, the Christian traditions can do nothing to clear up the subject. It is the spirit which quickeneth; the flesh is nothing. The resurrection was the triumph of the idea over the reality. Now that the idea had entered upon its immortality, what mattered the body?

About the years 80 or 83, when the actual text of the first Gospel received its final additions, the Jews already had on this matter a settled opinion. If they are to be believed, the disciples might have come by night and stolen away his body. The Christian conscience was alarmed at this rumour, and in order to cut short such an objection, they invented the circumstance of the military guard, and of the seal put on the sepulchre. That circumstance, to be found only in the first gospel, mixed up with legends of doubtful authority, is wholly inadmissible. But the explanation of the Jews, although irrefutable, is far from being altogether satisfactory. It can hardly be admitted that those who had so firmly believed Jesus had risen from the dead, were the same persons who had taken away his body. Little accustomed as these men were to reflection, one can hardly imagine so singular an illusion. It must be remembered that the little church at that moment was completely dispersed. It had no expectation, no centralisation, no regular method of procedure. Beliefs sprang up on every hand, and were then amalgamated as best they might. The contradictions between the narratives, upon which we base the incidents of the Sabbath morning, prove that the rumours were spread through the most diverse channels, and that they did not care much about bringing them into accord. It is possible that the body may have been taken away by some of the disciples, and transported by them into Galilee. The others, who remained at Jerusalem, may not have been cognizant of the fact. On the other hand, the disciples, who may have carried the body into Galilee, could not at first have any knowledge of the stories which were current at Jerusalem, so that the belief in the resurrection may have been invented after they went away, and must, therefore, have surprised them. They did not reclaim, and, even had they done so, it would have unsettled nothing. When it is a question of miracles a tardy correction is not feared. No material difficulty ever impedes a sentiment from being developed and of creating the fictions it has need of. In the recent history of the miracle of Salette, the error was demonstrated by the clearest of evidence, but that did not hinder the belief from springing up, and the faith from spreading. It is allowable also to suppose that the disappearance of the body was the work of the Jews. Probably they thought by that to prevent the tumultuous scenes which might be enacted over the body of a man so popular as Jesus. Probably they wished to prevent people from making a noisy funeral display, or from raising a tomb to that just man. Finally, who knows that the disappearance of the corpse was not the work of the proprietor of the garden, or of the gardener. The proprietor, according to all accounts, was a stranger to the sect. His sepulchre was chosen because it was the nearest to Golgotha, and because they were pressed for time. Probably he was dissatisfied with the mode of taking possession of his property, and had the body removed. In good truth, the details reported in the fourth gospel, of the linen left in the sepulchre, and the napkin folded carefully away in the corner, does not accord with such an hypothesis.

This last circumstance would lead one to suppose that a woman's hand had crept in there. The five narratives of the visit of the women to the tomb are so confused and embarrassing, that it is certainly quite allowable for us to suppose that they contained some misapprehension. The female conscience, when dominated by passion, is capable of the most extravagant illusions. Often it becomes the abettor of its own dreams. To these sort of incidents, for the purpose of having them considered as marvellous, nobody deliberately deceives; but everybody, without thinking of it, is led to connive at them. Mary Magdalene, according to the language of the times, had been "possessed of seven devils." In all this it is necessary to take account of the lack of the precision of mind of the women of the East, of their absolute want of education, and of the peculiar shade of their sincerity. Exalted conviction renders any return upon herself impossible. When the sky is seen everywhere, one is led to put oneself at times in the place of the sky.

Let us draw a veil over these mysteries. In states nt religious crises, everything being regarded as divine, the greatest effects may be the results of the most trifling causes. If we were witnesses of the strange facts which are at the origin of all the works of faith, we should discover circumstances which to us would not appear proportioned to the importance of the results, and others which would make us smile. Our old cathedrals are reckoned among the most beautiful objects in the world; one cannot enter them without being in some sort inebriated with the infinite. Yet these splendid marvels are almost always the fruit of some little conceit. And what does it matter definitively. The result alone counts in such matters. Faith purifies all. The material incident which has induced belief in the resurrection was not the true cause of the resurrection. That which raised Jesus from the dead was love. That love was so powerful that a petty accident sufficed to erect the edifice of a universal faith. If Jesus had been less loved, if faith in the resurrection had had less reason for its establishment, these kind of accidents would have occurred in vain, nothing would have come out of them. A grain of sand causes the fall of a mountain, when the moment for the fall of the mountain has come. The greatest things proceed at once from the greatest and smallest causes. Great causes alone are real; little ones only serve to determine the production of an effect which has for a long time been in preparation.

CHAPTER III

RETURN OF THE APOSTLES TO JERUSALEM.--END OF THE PERIOD OF APPARITIONS

THE apparitions, in the meanwhile, as happens always in movements of credulous enthusiasm, began to abate. Popular chimeras resemble contagious maladies; they grow stale quickly and change their form. The activity of these ardent souls had already turned in another direction. What they believed to have heard from the lips of the dear risen one, was the order to go forth and preach, and to convert the world. But where should they commence? Naturally, at Jerusalem. The return to Jerusalem was then resolved upon by those who at that time had the direction of the sect. As these journeys were ordinarily made by caravan at the time of the feasts, we now suppose with all manner of likelihood, that the return in question took place at the Feast of Tabernacles at the close of the year 33, or the Paschal Feast of the year 34. Galilee was thus abandoned by Christianity, and abandoned for ever. The little church which remained there continued, no doubt, to exist; but we hear it no more spoken of. It was probably broken up, like all the rest, by the frightful disaster which then overtook the country during the war of Vespasian; the wreck of the dispersed community sought refuge beyond Jordan. After the war it was not Christianity which was brought back into Galilee; it was Judaism. In the ii., iii., and iv. centuries, Galilee was a country wholly Jewish; the centre of Judaism, the country of the Talmud. Galilee thus counted but an hour in the history of Christianity; but it was the sacred hour, par excellence; it gave to the new religion that which has made it endure--its poetry, its penetrating charms. "The Gospel," after the manner of the synoptics, was a Galilean work. But we shall attempt further on to show that "The Gospel" thus extended, has been the principal cause of the success of Christianity, and continues to be the surest guarantee of its future. It is probable that a fraction of the little school which surrounded Jesus in his last days remained at Jerusalem. At the moment of separation the belief in the resurrection was already established. That belief was thus developed from two points of view, each having a perceptibly different aspect; and such is, no doubt, the cause of the complete divergencies which are remarked in the narratives of the apparitions. Two traditions, the one Galilean, the other Hierosolymitish, were formed; according to the first, all the apparitions (except those of the first period) had taken place in Galilee; according to the second, all had taken place at Jerusalem. The accord of the two fractions of the little church on the fundamental dogma, naturally only served to confirm the common belief. They embraced each other effusively; they repeated with the same faith, "He is risen." Perhaps the joy and the enthusiasm which were the consequences of this agreement, led to some other visions. It is about this period that we can place the vision of James, mentioned by Saint Paul. James was the brother, or at least, a relation of Jesus. We do not find that he had accompanied Jesus on his last sojourn to Jerusalem. He probably went there with the apostles, when the latter gritted Galilee. All the chief apostles had had their visions; it was hard that this "brother of the Lord," should not also have his. It was, it seems, an eucharistic vision, that is to say, in which Jesus appeared taking and breaking the bread. Later, those portions of the Christian family who attached themselves to James, those that were called the Hebrews, changed this vision to the same day as the resurrection, and wanted it to be looked upon as the first of all.

In fact, it is very remarkable that the family of Jesus, some of whose members during his life had been incredulous and hostile to his mission, constituted now a part of the Church, and held in it a very exalted position. One is led to suppose that the reconciliation took place during the sojourn of the apostles in Galilee. The celebrity which had attached itself to the name of their relative, those five thousand persons who believed in him, and were assured of having seen him after he had arisen, served to make an impression on their minds. From the time of the definite establishment of the apostles at Jerusalem, we find with them Mary, the mother of Jesus, and the brothers of Jesus. In what concerns Mary, it appears that John, thinking in this to obey a recommendation of the Master, had adopted and taken her to his own home. He perhaps took her back to Jerusalem. This woman, whose personal history and character have remained veiled in obscurity, assumed hence great importance. The words that the evangelist put into the mouth of some unknown women: "Blessed is the womb that bare thee, and the babes which thou has sucked," began to be verified. It is probable that Mary survived her son a few years. As for the brothers of Jesus, their history is wrapped in obscurity. Jesus had several brothers and sisters. It seemed probable, however, that in the class of persons which were called "Brothers of the Lord," there were included relations in the second degree. The question is only of moment so far as it concerns James. This James the Just, or "brother of the Lord," whom we shall see playing a great part in the first thirty years of Christianity, was the James, the son of Alphæus, who appears to have been a cousin germain of Jesus, or a whole brother of Jesus? The data in respect of him are altogether uncertain and contradictory. What we do know of this James represents him to be such a different person from Jesus, that we refuse to believe that two men so dissimilar were born of the same mother. If Jesus was the true founder of Christianity, James was its most dangerous enemy; he nearly ruined everything by his narrow-mindedness. Later, it was certainly believed that James the Just was a whole brother of Jesus. But perhaps some confusion was mixed up with the subject.

Be that as it may, the apostles henceforth separated no more, except to make temporary journeys. Jerusalem became their head-quarters; they seemed to be afraid to disperse, while certain acts served to reveal in them the prepossession of being opposed to return again into Galilee, which latter had dissolved its little society. An express order of Jesus is supposed to have interdicted their quitting Jerusalem, before, at least, the great manifestations which were to take place. Apparitions became more and more rare. They were spoken much less of, and people began to believe that they would not see the Master again until His grand appearance in the clouds. Peoples' thoughts were turned with great force towards a promise which it was supposed Jesus had made. During his life-time, Jesus, it was said, had often spoken of the Holy Spirit, which was understood to mean a personification of divine wisdom. He had promised his disciples that the Spirit would nerve them in the combats that they would have to engage in, would be their inspirer in difficulties, and their advocate, if they had to speak in public. When the visions became rare, the brethren found compensation in this Spirit, which they looked upon as a consoler, as another self which Jesus had bequeathed to his friends. Sometimes it was supposed that Jesus suddenly presented himself in the midst of his disciples assembled, and breathed on them out of his own mouth a current of vivifying air. At other times the disappearance of Jesus was regarded as a premonition of the coming of the Spirit. It was believed that in the apparitions he had promised the descent of this Spirit. Many people established an intimate connection between this descent and the restoration of the kingdom of Israel. All the fervency of imagination which the sect had displayed in inventing the legend of Jesus risen again, was now about to be employed to create an assemblage of pious believers, in regard to the descent of the Spirit and its marvellous gifts. It seems, however, that a grand apparition of Jesus had taken place at Bethany or upon the Mount of Olives. Certain traditions annexed it to that vision of the final recommendations of Jesus, and the reiterated promise of the sending down of the Holy Spirit, the act which was to invest the disciples with the power of remitting sins. The features of these apparitions became more and more vague; they were confounded one with another; and people came not to think much about them. It was an accepted fact that Jesus was living; that he manifested himself by a number of apparitions, sufficient to prove his existence; that he would again be manifested in some partial visions, until the grand final revelation which would be the consummation of all. Thus, Saint Paul presents the vision he had on the way to Damascus, as of the same order as those we have just been speaking of. At all events, it was admitted, in an idealistic sense, that the Master was to be with his disciples and he would remain with them unto the end. In the first period the apparitions were very frequent. Jesus was conceived as dwelling permanently on the earth and fulfilling more or less the functions of terrestrial life. When the visions became rare, they were made to conform to another idea. Jesus was represented as having entered into his glory, and as being seated at the right hand of his Father. "He is ascended to Heaven," it was said. This statement rested mainly on a vague conception of the idea, or on an induction. But it was converted by many into a material scene. It was desired that it should follow the last vision common to all the apostles, and in which he gave them his supreme recommendations. Jesus was received up into Heaven. Later, the scene was developed and became a complete legend. It was recounted that some heavenly messengers, agreeably to the divine manifestations, most brilliant, appeared at the moment when a cloud enveloped him, and consoled his disciples by the assurance of his return in the clouds, resembling wholly the scene of which they had just been witnesses. The death of Moses had been surrounded in the popular imagination with circumstances of the same kind. Perhaps they also called to mind the ascension of Elias. A tradition placed the locality of this scene near Bethany, upon the summit of the Mount of Olives. That quarter remained very dear to his disciples, doubtless because Jesus had lived there.

The legend would make it appear that the disciples, after that marvellous scene, re-entered Jerusalem "with joy." For ourselves, it is with sadness that we have to say to Jesus a final adieu. To have found him living again his shadow life, has been to us a great consolation. That second life of Jesus, a pale image of the first, is yet full of charm. Now, all scent of him is lost. Raised on a cloud to the right hand of his Father, he has left us with men, but, oh, Heaven! the fall is terrible! The reign of poetry is past. Mary Magdalene, retired to her native village, buried there her recollections. In consequence of that eternal injustice which ordains that man appropriates to himself alone the work in which woman has had as great a share as he, Cephas eclipsed her, and made her to be forgotten! No more sermons on the Mount; no more of the possessed of devils healed; no more courtesans touched; no more of those strange female fellow workers in the work of redemption whom Jesus had not repelled! God has verily disappeared. No; history of the church is to be most often henceforth the history of treasons to blot out the name of Jesus. But such as it is, that history is still a hymn to his glory. The wools and the image of the illustrious Nazarene shall remain in the midst of infinite miseries as a sublime ideal. We shall comprehend better how great it was when we have seen how little were his disciples.

CHAPTER IV

DESCENT OF THE HOLY SPIRIT--ECSTATICAL, AND PROPHETICAL PHENOMENA

Mean, narrow, ignorant, inexperienced they were, as completely so as it was possible to be. Their simplicity of mind was extreme; their credulity had no limits. But they had one quality: they loved their Master to foolishness. The recollection of Jesus was the only moving power of their lives; it was perpetually with them, and it was clear that they lived only for him, who, during two or three years, had so strangely attached and seduced them. For souls of a secondary standard, who cannot love God directly, that is to say, discover truth, create the beautiful, do right of themselves, salvation consists in loving some one in whom there shines a reflection of the true, the beautiful, and the good. The great majority of mankind require a worship of two degrees. The multitude of worshippers desire an intermediary between it and God.

When a person has succeeded in attracting to himself, by an elevated moral bond, several other persons, when he dies, it always happens that the survivors, who, up to that time are often divided by rivalries and dissensions, beget a strong friendship the one for the other. A thousand cherished images of the past, which they regret, become to them a common treasure. There is .a manner of loving the dead, which consists in loving those with whom we have known him. We are anxious to meet one another, in order to re-call the happy times which are no more. A profound saying of Jesus is found then to be true to the letter: The dead one is present in the midst of those who are united again by his memory.

The affection that the disciples had the one for the other, while Jesus was alive, was thus enhanced tenfold after his death. They formed a very small and very retired society, and lived exclusively by themselves. At Jerusalem they numbered about one-hundred-and-twenty. Their piety was active, and, as yet, completely restrained by the forms of Jewish piety. The temple was then the chief place of devotion. They worked, no doubt, for a living; but at that time, manual labour in Jewish society engaged very few. Everyone had a trade, but that trade by no means hindered a man from being educated and well-bred. With us, material wants are so difficult to satisfy, that the man living by his hands is obliged to work twelve or fifteen hours a day; the man of leisure alone can follow intellectual pursuits; the acquisition of instruction is a rare and costly affair. But in those old societies (of which the East of our days gives still an idea), in those climates, where nature is so prodigal to man and so little exacting, in the life of the labourer there was plenty of leisure. A sort of common instruction puts every man au courant of the ideas of the times. Mere food and clothing satisfied their wants; a few hours of moderate labour provided these. The rest was given up to day dreaming, and to passion. Passion had attained in the minds of those people a decree of energy which is to us inconceivable. The Jews of that time appear to us to be in truth possessed, each pursuing with a blind fatality the idea with which he had been seized.

The dominant idea in the Christian community, at the moment at which we are now arrived, and when apparitions had ceased, was the coming of the Holy Spirit. People were believed to receive it in the form of a mysterious breath, which passed over the assembly. Mary pretended that it was the breath of Jesus himself. Every inward consolation, every bold movement, every flush of enthusiasm, every feeling of lively, and pleasant gaiety, which was experienced without knowing whence it came, was the work of the Spirit. These simple con-sciences referred, as usual, to some exterior cause the exquisite sentiments which were being created in them. It was in the assemblies, particularly, that these fantastic phenomena of illumination were produced. When all were assembled, and when they awaited in silence, inspiration from on high, a murmur, any noise whatever, was believed to be the coming of the Spirit. In the early times, it was the apparitions of Jesus which were produced in this manner. Now the turn of ideas had changed. It was the divine breath which passed over the little church, and filled it with a celestial effluvia.

These beliefs were strengthened by notions drawn from the Old Testament. The prophetic spirit is represented in the Hebrew books as a breathing which penetrates man and inspires him. In the beautiful vision of Elijah, God passes by in the form of a gentle wind, which produces a slight rustling noise. This ancient imagery had handed down to later ages beliefs analogous to those of the Spiritualists of our days. In the ascension of Isaiah, the coming of the Spirit is accompanied by a certain rustling at the doors. More often, however, people regarded this coming as another baptism, to wit, the "baptism of the

Spirit," far superior to that of John. The hallucinations of touch being very frequent among persons so nervous and so excited, the least current of air, accompanied by a shuddering in the midst of the silence, was considered as the passage of the Spirit. One conceived that he felt it; soon everybody felt it; and the enthusiasm was communicated from one to another. The correspondence of these phenomena with those which are to be found amongst the visionaries of all times is easily apprehended. They are produced daily, partly under the influence of the Acts of the Apostles, in the English or American sects of Quakers, Jumpers, Shakers, Irvingites; amongst the Mormons; in the camp-meetings and revivals of America; we have seen them reproduced amongst ourselves in the sect called the Spiritualists. But an immense difference ought to be made between aberrations, which are without bounds, and without a future, and the illusions which have accompanied the establishment of a new religious code for humanity.

Amongst all these "descents of the Spirit," which appear to have been frequent enough, there was one which left a profound impression on the nascent Church. One day, when the brethren were assembled, a thunder-storm burst forth. A violent wind threw open the windows: the heavens were on fire. Thunderstorms, in these countries, are accompanied by prodigious sheets of lightning; the atmosphere is, as it were, everywhere furrowed with ridges of flame. Whether the electric fluid had penetrated the room itself, or whether a dazzling flash of lightning had suddenly illuminated the faces of all, everyone was convinced that the Spirit had entered, and that it had alighted on the head of each in the form of tongues of fire. It was a prevalent opinion in the theurgic schools of Syria, that the communication of the Spirit was produced by a divine fire, and under the form of a mysterious glare. People fancied themselves to be present at the splendours of Sinai, at a divine manifestation analogous to those of former days. The baptism of the Spirit thenceforth became also a baptism of fire. The baptism of the Spirit and of fire was opposed to, and greatly preferred to, the baptism of water, the only baptism which John had known. The baptism of fire, was only prepared on rare occasions. Thy apostles and the disciples of the first guest-chamber alone were reputed to have received it. But the idea that the Spirit had alighted on them in the form of jets of flene, resembling tongues of fire, gave rise to a series of singular ideas, which took a foremost place in the thought of the period.

The tongue of the inspired man was supposed to receive a kind of sacrament. It was pretended that many prophets, before their mission, had been stammerers; that the Son of God had passed a coal over their lips, which purified them and conferred on them the gift of eloquence. In preaching, the man was supposed not to speak of his own volition. His tongue was considered as the organ of divinity which inspired it. These tongues of fire appeared a striking symbol. People were convinced that God desired to signify in this manner that he poured out upon the apostles his most precious gifts of eloquence, and of inspiration. But they did not stop there. Jerusalem was, like the majority of the large cities of the East, a city in which many languages were spoken. The diversity of tongues was one of the difficulties which one found there in the way of propagating a universal form of faith. One of the things, moreover, which alarmed the apostles, at the commencement of a ministry destined to embrace the world, was the number of languages which was spoken there: they were asking themselves incessantly how they could learn so many tongues. "The gift of tongues" became thus a marvellous privilege. It was believed that the preaching of the Gospel would clear away the obstacle which was created by the diversity of idioms. It was imagined that, in some solemn circumstances, the auditors had heard the apostle preaching each in his own tongue: in other words, that the apostolic preaching translated itself to each of the listeners. At other times, this was understood in a somewhat different manner. To the apostles was attributed the gift of knowing, by divine inspiration, all tongues, and of speaking them at will. There was in this a liberal idea; they meant to imply that the Gospel should have no language of its own; that it should be translatable into every tongue; and that the translation should be of the came value as the original. Such was not the sentiment of orthodox Judaism. Hebrew was for the Jews of Jerusalem the holy tongue; no language could be compared to it. Translations of the Bible were lightly esteemed, whilst the Hebrew text was scrupulously guarded. In translations, changes and modifications were permitted. The Jews of Egypt, and the Hellenists of Palestine, practised, it is true, a more tolerant system. They employed Greek in prayer, and perused constantly Greek translations of the Bible. But the first Christian idea was even broader. According to that idea the word of God has no language of its own: it is free and unhampered by idiomatic fetters; it is delivered to all spontaneously, and needs no interpreter. The facility with which Christianity was detached from the Semetic tongue which Jesus had spoken, the liberty which it left at first each nation to create its own liturgy, and its versions of the Bible in its natural tongue, served as a sort of emancipation of tongues. It was generally admitted that the Messiah would gather into one all tongues as well as all peoples. Common usage and the promiscuity of languages were the first steps towards that great era of universal pacification.

For the rest, the gift of tongues soon underwent a considerable transformation, and resulted in more extraordinary effects. Brain excitement led to ecstacy and prophecy. In these ecstatic moments the faithful, impelled by the Spirit, uttered inarticulate and incoherent sounds, which were taken for the words of a foreign language, and which they innocently sought to interpret. At other times it was believed that the ecstatically possessed spoke new and hitherto unknown languages, or even the language of the angels. These extravagant scenes, which led to abuses, did not become habitual until a later period. Yet it is probable that from the earliest years of Christianity they were produced. The visions of the ancient prophets had often been accompanied by phenomena of nervous excitation. The dythyrambic state amongst the Greeks produced the same kind of occurrences; the Pythia used by preference foreign or obsolete words, which were called, as in the apostolic phenomena, glosses. Many of the passwords of primitive Christianity, which were properly bilingual, or formed by anagrams, such as Abba pater, anathema, maran-atha, were probably derived from these strange paroxysms, intermingled with sighs, stifled groans, ejaculations, prayers, and sudden transports, which were taken for prophecies. It resembled a vague music of the soul, uttered in indistinct sounds, and which the auditors sought to transform into images and determinate words, or rather as the prayers of the Spirit addressed to God, in a language known to God only, and which God knew how to interpret. No ecstatic person, in short, understood anything of what he uttered, and had not even any cognizance of it. People listened with eagerness and attributed to the incoherent utterances the thoughts which there and then occurred to them. Each referred to his own tongue and ingenuously sought to explain the unintelligible sounds by what little he actually knew of languages. In this they always more or less succeeded, the auditor filling in between the broken sentences the thoughts he had in mind.

The history of fanatical sects is fruitful in instances of the same kmd. The preachers of the Cevennes displayed similar instances of "glossolaly." The most striking instance, however, is that of the "readers" of Sweden, about the years 1841-43. Involuntary utterances, enunciations, having no meaning to those who uttered them, and accompanied by convulsions and fainting fits, were for a long time practised daily in that little sect. The thing became perfectly contagious, and occasioned a considerable popular movement. Amongst the Irvingites the phenomenon of tongues has been produced with features which reproduce in the most striking manner the stories of the Acts and of Saint Paul. Our own century has witnessed illusive scenes of the same kind, which we will not recount here; for it is always unjust to compare the inseparable credulity of a great religious movement with the credulity which results from dulness of intellect.

These strange phenomena were sometimes produced out of doors. The ecstatic persons, at the very moment when they were a prey to their extravagant illuminations, had the hardihood to go out and show themselves to the multitude. They were taken for drunken persons. Although sober-minded in point of mysticism, Jesus had more than once presented in his own person the ordinary phenomena of the ecstatic state. The disciples, for two or three years, were beset with these ideas. Prophesying was frequent and considered as a gift analogous to that of tongues. Prayers, accompanied by convulsions, rhythmic modulations, mystic sighs, lyrical enthusiasm, songs with graceful attitudes, were a daily exercise. A rich vein of "canticles," "psalms," "hymns," in imitation of those of the Old Testament, was thus found to be open to them. Sometimes the mouth and heart mutually accompanied one another; sometimes the heart sang alone, accompanied inwardly by grace. No language being able to render the new sensations which were produced, they indulged in an indistinct muttering, at once sublime and puerile, in which what one might call "the Christian language," was wafted in a state of embryo. Christianity, not finding in the ancient languages an appropriate instrument for its needs, has shattered them. But whilst the new religion was forming a language suited to its use, centuries of obscure effort and, so to speak, of childish prattle, were required. The style of Saint Paul, and, in general, that of the authors of the New Testament, what is its characteristic, if it be not stifled, halting, informal, improvisation of the "glossolalist"? Language failed them. Like the prophets, they aped the a, a, a, of the infant. They did not know how to speak. The Greek and the Semetic tongues equally betrayed them. Hence that shocking violence which nascent Christianity inflicted on language. It might be compared to a stutterer, in whose mouth the tones being stifled, clash with and against each other, and terminate in a confused medley, but yet marvellously expressive.

All this was very far from the sentiment of Jesus; but for minds penetrated with a belief in the supernatural, these phenomena possessed great importance. The gift of tongues, in particular, was considered as an essential sign of the new religion, and as a proof of its truth. In any case, there resulted from it much fruit for edification. Many Pagans were converted in this way. Up to the third century "glossolaly" was manifested in a manner analogous to that described by St. Paul, and was considered as a perpetual miracle. Many of the sublime words of Christianity are derived from these incoherent sighs. The general effect was touching and penetrating. Their manner of offering in common their inspirations and of handing them over to the community for interpretation established in time amongst the faithful a strong bond of fraternity.

As in the case of all mystics, the new sectaries led fasting and austere lives. Like the majority of Orientals, they ate little, which contributed to maintain them in a state of excitement. The sobriety of the Syrian, the cause of his physical weakness, keeps him in a perpetual state of fever and of nervous susceptibility. Our severe, continuous, intellectual efforts, are impossible under such a regimen. But this cerebal debility and muscular laxity, produces, apparently without cause, lively alternations of sorrow

31

and joy, and puts the soul in constant relationship with God. That which was called "Godly sorrow" passed for a Heavenly gift. All the teachings of the Fathers concerning the life spiritual, such as John Climacus, as Basil, as Nilus, as Arsenius,--all the secrets of the grand art of the inward life, one of the most glorious creations of Christianity--were in germ in the peculiar state of mind which possessed, in their mouths of ecstatic expectation, those illustrious ancestors of all "The men of longings." Their moral condition was peculiar; they lived in the supernatural. They acted only upon visions, dreams, and the most insignificant circumstances appeared to them to be admonitions from heaven. Under the name of gifts of the Holy Spirit were thus concealed the rarest and most exquisite effusions of soul, love, piety, respectful fears, objectless sighings, sudden languors, and spontaneous tenderness. All the good that is born in man, without man having any part in it, was attributed to a breathing from on high. Tears, above all, were regarded as a heavenly favour. This charming gift, the exclusive privilege of souls most good and most pure, was produced with infinite sweetness. We know what power, delicate natures, especially in women, find in the divine faculty of being able to weep much. It is to them prayer, and, assuredly, the most holy of prayers. We must come down quite to the middle ages to that piety, drenched with the tears of St. Bruno, St. Bernard and St. Francis de Assisi, to find again the chaste melancholy of those early days, when they truly sowed in tears in order that they might reap with joy. To weep became a pious act. Those who were not qualified to preach, work, speak languages, nor to perform miracles, wept. It might, indeed, be said that their souls were melted, and that they desired, in the absence of a language which would interpret their sentiments, to display themselves outwardly, by a vivid and brief expression of their whole inner being.

CHAPTER V

FIRST CHURCH OF JERUSALEM; IT IS ENTIRELY CENOBITICAL

The custom of living together, holding the same faith, and indulging the same expectation, necessarily produced many common habits. Very soon rules were framed, which made that primitive church resemble, to some extent, the establishments of the cenobitical life, rules with which Christianity subsequently became acquainted. Many of the precepts of Jesus conduced to this; the true ideal of evangelical life is a monastery, not a monastery enclosed with iron bars, a prison after the type of the Middle Ages, with the separation of the sexes, but an asylum in the midst of the world, a place set apart for spiritual life, a free association or little private confraternity, surrounded by a barrier, which may serve to ward off the cares which are prejudicial to the liberty of the Kingdom of God.

All, then, lived in common, having but one heart and one mind. No one possessed anything which was his own. On becoming a disciple of Jesus, one sold one's goods and made a gift of the proceeds to the society. The chiefs of the society then distributed the common possessions to each, according to his needs. They lived in the same quarter, They took their meals together, and continued to attach to them the mystic sense that Jesus had prescribed. They passed long hours in prayers. Their prayers were sometimes improvised aloud, but more often meditated in silence. Trances were frequent, and each one believed oneself to be constantly favoured with divine inspiration. The concord was perfect; no dogmatic quarrels, no disputes in regard to precedence. The tender recollection of Jesus effaced all dissensions. Joy, lively and deep-seated, was in every heart. Their morals were austere, but pervaded by a soft and tender sentiment. They assembled in houses to pray, and to devote themselves to ecstatic exercises. The recollection of these two or three first years remained and seemed to them like a terrestrial paradise, which Christianity will pursue henceforth in all its dreams and to which it will vainly endeavour to return. Who does not see, in fact, that such an organisation could only be applicable to a very small church? But, subsequently, the monastic life will resume on its own account that primitive ideal which the church universal will hardly dream of realising.

That the author of the Acts, to whom we are indebted for the picture of this primitive Christianity at Jerusalem, has laid on his colours a little too thickly, and, in particular, exaggerated the community of goods which obtained in the sect, is certainly possible. The author of the Acts is the same as the author of the third gospel, who, in his life of Jesus, had the habit of adapting his facts to suit his theories, and with whom a tendency to the doctrine of ebonism, that is to say, of absolute poverty, is very perceptible. Nevertheless, the narrative of the Acts cannot here be destitute of some foundation. Although Jesus himself would not have given utterance to any of the communistic axioms which one reads in the third gospel, it is certain that a renunciation of worldly goods and of the giving of alms pushed to the length of self-despoilment, were perfectly conformable to the spirit of his preaching. The belief that the world is coming to an end has always produced a distaste for worldly goods, and a leaning to the communistic life. The narrative of the Acts is, however, perfectly conformable to that which we know of the origin of other ascetic religions--of Buddhism for example. These sorts of religion commence always with monastical life. Their first adepts are some species of mendicant monks. The layman does not appear in them until later, and when these religions have conquered entire societies, in which monastic life can only exist under exceptional circumstances.

We admit, then, in the Church of Jerusalem a period of cenobitical life. Two centuries later Christianity produced still on the Pagans the effect of a communistic sect. It must be remembered that the Essenians or Therapeutians had already given the model of this species of life, which sprang very legitimately from Mosaism. The Mosaic code being essentially moral and not political, its natural product was a social Utopia (church, synagogue and convent) not a civil state, nation or city. Egypt had had for many centuries recluses, both male and female, maintained by the state, probably in fulfilment of charitable legacies, near the Serapeum at Memphis. It must especially be remembered that such a life in the East is by no means what it has been in our West. In the East, one can very well enjoy nature and existence without possessing anything. Man, in these countries, is always free, because he has few wants; the slavery of toil is there unknown. We readily admit that the communism of the primitive church was neither so rigorous nor so universal as the author of the Acts would have. What is certain is, that there was at Jerusalem a large community of poor, governed by the apostles, and to whom were sent gifts from every quarter of Christendom. This community was obliged, no doubt, to establish some rather seven rules, and some years later, it was even necessary, in order to enforce these rules, to employ terror. Some frightful legends were circulated, according to which the mere fact of having retained anything beyond that which one gave to the community, was looked upon as a capital crime and punished by death.

The porticoes of the temple, especially the portico of Solomon, which looked down on the Valley of Cedron, was the place where the disciples usually met during the day. There they could recall the hours Jesus had spent in the same place. In the midst of the extreme activity which reigned all about the Temple, they were little noticed. The galleries, which formed a part of the edifice, were the resort of numerous schools and sects, the theatre of endless disputations. The faithful followers of Jesus were, however, regarded as extreme devotees; for they still, without scruple, observed the Jewish customs, praying at the appointed hours, and observing all the precepts of the Law. They were Jews, differing only from others in believing that the Messiah had already come. The common people who were not informed as to their concerns, and they were an immense majority, regarded them as a sect of Hasidim, or pious people. One needed not to be either a schismatic or a heretic, in order to affiliate oneself with them, any more than one need cease to be a Protestant in order to be a disciple of Spencer, or a Catholic, in order to belong to the sect of Saint Francis or of Saint Bruno. The people loved them, because of their piety, their simplicity, their kindly disposition. The aristocrats of the Temple looked upon them, no doubt, with displeasure. But the sect made little noise; it was tranquil, thanks to its obscurity.

At eventide, the brethren returned to their quarters, and partook of the meal, being divided into groups, in sign of paternity, and in remembrance of Jesus, whom they always believed to be present in the midst of them. The one at the head of the table broke the bread, blessed the cup, and sent them round as a symbol of union in Jesus. The most common act of life became in this way the most sacred and the most holy. These meals en famille, which were always enjoyed by the Jews, were accompanied by prayers, pious raptures, and pervaded by a sweet cheerfulness. They believed themselves once more to be in the time when Jesus animated them by his presence: they imagined they saw him, and it was not long before the rumour went abroad that Jesus had said: "As often as ye break the bread, do it in remembrance of Me." The bread itself became in some sort Jesus, conceived to be the only source of strength for those who had loved him, and who still lived by him. These repasts, which were always the chief symbol of Christianity, and the soul of its mysteries, took place at first every evening. Usage, however, soon restricted them to Sunday evenings. Later on, the mystic repast was changed to the morning. It is probable that at the period of the history which we have now reached, the holy day of each week was still, with the Christians, the Saturday.

The apostles chosen by Jesus, and who were supposed to have received from him a special mandate to announce to the world the Kingdom of God, had, in the little community, an incontestable superiority. One of the first cares, as soon as they saw the sect settle quietly down at Jerusalem, was to fill the vacancy that Judas of Kerioth had left in its ranks. The opinion that the latter had betrayed his master, and had been the cause of his death, became more and more general. The legend was mixed up with him, and every day one heard of some new circumstance which enhanced the black-heartedness of his deed. He had bought a field near the old necropolis of Hakeldama, to the south of Jerusalem, and there he lived retired. Such was the state of artless excitation in which the little Church found itself, that, in order to replace him, it was resolved to have recourse to a vote of some sort. In general, in great religious agitations we decide upon this method of coming to a determination, since it is admitted on principle that nothing is fortuitous, that the question in point is the chief object of divine attention, and that God's part in an action is so much the more greater in proportion as that of man's is the more feeble. The sole condition was, that the candidate should be chosen from the groups of the oldest disciples, who had been witnesses of the whole series of events, from the time of the baptism of John. This reduced considerably the number of those eligible. Two only were found in the ranks, Joseph Bar-Saba, who bore the name of Justus, and Matthias. The lot fell upon Matthias, who was accounted as one of the Twelve. But this was the sole instance of such a replacing. The apostles were hitherto regarded as having been nominated, once for all, by Jesus, and not as having successors. The danger of a permanent college, reserving to itself all the life and the strength of the association, was, with extraordinary instinct, discarded for a time. The concentration of the Church into an oligarchy did not happen until later.

For the rest, it is necessary to guard against the misunderstandings, which the name of "apostle" might provoke, and which it has not failed to occasion. From a very early period, people were led by some passages in the Gospel, and, above all, by the analogy of the life of Saint Paul, to regard the apostles as essentially wandering missionaries, distributing in a kind of way the world in advance, and traversing as conquerors all the kingdoms of the earth. A cycle of legends was founded upon that data, and imposed upon ecclesiastical history. Nothing could be more contrary to the truth. The body of Twelve lived, generally, permanently at Jerusalem. Till about the year 60 the apostles did not leave the holy city except upon temporary missions. This explains the obscurity in which the majority of the members of the central council remained. Very few of them had a rôle. This council was a kind of sacred college or senate, destined only to represent tradition, and a spirit of conservatism. It finished by being relieved of every active function, so that its members had nothing to do but to preach and pray; but as yet the brilliant feats of preaching had not fallen to their lot. Their names were hardly known outside Jerusalem, and about the year 70 or 80 the lists which were given of these chosen Twelve, agreed only in the principal names.

The "brothers of the Lord" appear often by the side of the "apostles," although they were distinct from them. Their authority, however, was equal to that of the apostles. Here two groups constituted, in the nascent Church, a sort of aristocracy, founded solely on the more or less intimate relations that their members had had with the Master. These were the men whom Paul denominated "the pillars" of the Church at Jerusalem. For the rest, we see that no distinctions in the ecclesiastical hierarchy yet existed. The title was nothing; the personal authority was everything. The principle of ecclesiastical celibacy was already established, but it required time to bring all these germs to their complete development. Peter and Philip were married, and had sons and daughters.

The term used to designate the assembly of the faithful was the Hebrew Kahal, which was rendered by the essentially democratic word Ecclesia, which is the convocation of the people in the ancient Grecian cities, the summons to the Pnyx or the Agora. Commencing with the second or the third century before Jesus Christ, the words of the Athenian democracy became a sort of common law in Hellenic language; many of these terms, on account of their having been used in the Greek confraternities, entered into the Christian vocabulary. It was, in reality, the popular life, which; restrained for centuries, resumed its power under forms altogether different. The Primitive Church was, in its way, a little democracy. Even election by lot, a method an dear to the ancient Republics, had sometimes found its way into it. Less harsh, and less suspicious, however, than the ancient cities, the Church voluntarily delegated its authority. Like all theocratic societies, it inclined to abdicate its functions into the hands of a clergy, and it was easy to foresee that one or two centuries would not roll over before all this democracy would resolve itself into an oligarchy.

The power which was ascribed to the Church assembled and to its chiefs was enormous. The Church conferred every mission, and was guided solely in its choice by the signs given by the Spirit. Its authority went as far as decreeing death. It is recorded that at the voice of Peter, several delinquents had fallen back and expired immediately. Saint Paul, a little later, was not afraid, in excommunicating a fornicator "to deliver him to Satan for the destruction of the flesh, that the spirit may be saved in the day of the Lord Jesus" (1 Cor., v. vii.). Excommunication was held to be equivalent to a sentence of death. It was not doubted that any person whom the apostles or the elders of the Church had cut off from the body of the Saints, and delivered over to the power of evil, was not lost. Satan was considered as the author of diseases. To deliver over to him the corrupted member was to deliver over the latter to the natural executor of the sentence. A premature death was ordinarily held to be the result of these occult sentences, which, according to the expressive Hebrew phrase, "cut off a soul from Israel." The apostles were believed to be invested with supernatural powers. In pronouncing such condemnations, they thought that their anathemas could not fail but be effectual. The terrible impression which their excommunications produced, and the hatred manifested by the brethren against all the members thus cut off, were sufficient, in fact, in many cases, to bring about death, or at least to compel the culprit to expatriate himself. The same terrible ambiguity was found in the ancient law. "Extirpation" implied at once death, expulsion from the community, exile, and a solitary and mysterious demise. So with the apostate, or blasphemer. To destroy his body in order to save his soul came to be looked on as legitimate. It must be remembered that we are treating of the times of zealots, who regarded it as an act of virtue to poignard anyone who failed to obey the Law; and it must not be forgotten that certain Christians were or had been zealots. Accounts like those of the death of Ananias and Saphira did not excite any scruple. The idea of the civil power was so foreign to all that world placed without the pale of the Roman law, people were so persuaded that the Church was a complete society, sufficient in itself, that no person saw, in a miracle leading to death or the mutilation of an individual, an outrage punishable by the civil law. Enthusiasm and faith covered all, excused everything. But the frightful danger which these theocratic maxims laid up in store for the future is readily perceived. The Church is armed with a sword; excommunication is a sentence of death. There was henceforth in the world a power outside that of the state, which disposed of the life of citizens. Certainly, if the Roman authority had limited itself to repressing amongst the Jews precepts so condemnatory, it would have been a thousand times in the right. Only, in its brutality, it confounded the most legitimate of liberties, that of worshipping in one's own manner, with abuses which no society has ever been able to support with impunity.

Peter had amongst the apostles a certain precedence, derived directly from his zeal and his activity. In these first years, he was hardly ever separate from John, son of Zebedee. They went almost always together, and their amity was doubtless the corner stone of the new faith. James, the brother of the Lord, almost equalled them in authority, at least amongst a fraction of the Church. In regard to certain intimate friends of Jesus, like the Galilean women, and the family of Bethany, we have already remarked that no more mention is made of them. Less solicitous of organizing and of establishing a society, the faithful companions of Jesus were content with loving in death him whom they had loved in life. Absorbed in their expectation, these noble women, who have formed the faith of the world, were almost unknown to the important men of Jerusalem. When they died, the most important elements of the history of nascent Christianity were put into the tomb with them. Only those who played active parts earned renown. Those who were content to love in secret, remained obscure but assuredly they chose the better part.

It is needless to remark that this little group of simple people had no speculative theology. Jesus wisely kept himself far removed from all metaphysics. He had only one dogma, his own divine sonship and the divinity of his mission. The whole symbol of the primitive church might be embraced in one line: "Jesus is the Messiah, the Son of God." This belief rested upon a peremptory argument--the fact of the resurrection, of which the disciples claimed to be witnesses. In reality nobody (not even the Galilean women) said they had seen the resurrection. But the absence of the body and the apparitions which had followed, appeared to be equivalent to the fact itself. To attest the resurrection of Jesus was the task which all considered as being specially imposed upon them. It was, however, very soon put forth that the master had predicted this event. Different sayings of his were recalled, which were represented as having not been well understood, and in which was seen, on second thoughts, an announcement of the resurrection. The belief in the near glorious manifestation of Jesus was universal. The secret word which the brethren used amongst themselves, in order to be recognized and confirmed, was maran-atha, the "Lord is at hand." They believed to remember a declaration of Jesus, according to which their preaching would not have time to go over all the cities of Israel, before that the Son of Man appeared in his majesty. In the meanwhile the risen Jesus had seated himself at the right hand of his Father. Here he is to remain until the solemn day on which he shall conic, seated upon the clouds, to judge the quick and the dead.

The idea which they had of Jesus was the one which Jesus had given them of himself. Jesus had been "a prophet, mighty in deed and word," a man chosen of God, having received a special mission on behalf of humanity, a mission which he had proved by his miracles, and especially by his resurrection. God had anointed him with the Holy Spirit and had clothed him with power; he passed his time in doing good, and in healing those who were under the power of the devil, for God was with him He is the Son of God; that is to say, a perfect man of God, a representation of God upon earth; he is the Messiah, the Saviour of Israel, announced by the prophets (Acts x. 38). The reading of the books of the Old Testament, especially of the Prophets and the Psalms, was habitual in the sect. They carried into that reading a fixed idea--that of discovering everywhere the type of Jesus. They were persuaded that the ancient Hebrew books were full of him, and from the very first years they formed a collection of texts drawn from the Prophets, the Psalms, and from certain apocryphal books, wherein they were convinced that the life of Jesus was predicted and described in advance. This method of arbitrary interpretation belonged at that time to all the Jewish schools. The Messianic missions were a sort of jeu d'esprit, analogous to the allusions which the ancient preachers made of passages of the Bible, diverted from their natural sense and accepted as the simple ornaments of sacred rhetoric.

Jesus with his exquisite tact in religious matters had instituted no new ritual. The new sect had not yet any special ceremonies. The practices of piety were Jewish. The assemblies had, in a strict sense, nothing liturgic. They were the meetings of confraternities, at which prayers were offered up, devoted themselves to glossolaly or prophecy, and the reading of correspondence. There was nothing yet of sacerdotalism. There was no priest (cohen); the presbyter was the "elder," nothing more. The only priest was Jesus: in another sense, all the faithful were priests. Fasting was considered a very meritorious practice. Baptism was the token of admission to the sect. The rite was the same as administered by John, but it was administered in the name of Jesus. Baptism was, however, considered an insufficient initiation. It had to be followed by the gifts of the Holy Spirit, which were effected by means of a prayer, offered up by the apostles, upon the head of the new convert, accompanied by the imposition of hands.

This imposition of hands, already as familiar to Jesus, was the sacramental act par excellence. It conferred inspiration, universal illumination, the power to produce prodigies, prophesying, and the speaking of languages. It was what was called the Baptism of the Spirit. It was supposed to recall a saying of Jesus: "John baptised you with water, but as for you, you shall be baptised by the Spirit." Gradually, all these ideas became amalgamated, and baptism was conferred "in the name of the Father, and of the Son, and of the Holy Ghost." But it is not probable that this formula, in the early days in which we now are, was yet employed. We see the simplicity of this primitive Christian worship. Neither Jesus nor the apostles had invented it. Certain Jewish sects had adopted, before them, these grave and solemn ceremonies, which appeared to have come in part from Chaldea, where they are still practised with special liturgies by the Sabæans or Mendaïtes. The religion of Persia embraced also many rites of the same description.

The beliefs in popular medicine, which constituted a part of the force of Jesus, were continued in his disciples. The power of healing was one of the marvellous gifts conferred by the Spirit. The first Christians, like almost all the Jews of the time, looked upon diseases as the punishment of a transgression, or the work of a malignant demon. The apostles passed, just as Jesus did, for powerful exorcists. People imagined that the anointings of oil administered by the apostles, with imposition of hands, and invocation of the name of Jesus, were all powerful to wash away the sins which were the cause of disease, and to heal the afflicted one. Oil has always been in the East the medicine par excellence. For the rest, the simple imposition of the hands of the apostles was reputed to have the same effect. This imposition was made by immediate contact. Nor is it impossible that, in certain cases, the heat of the hands, being communicated suddenly to the head, insured to the sick person a little relief.

The sect being young and not numerous, the question of deaths was not taken into account until later on. The effect caused by the first demises which took place in the ranks of the brethren was strange. People were troubled by the manner of the deaths. It was asked whether they were less favoured than those who were reserved to see with their eyes the advent of the Son of Man. They came generally to consider the interval between death and the resurrection as a kind of blank in the consciousness of the defunct. The idea set forth in the Phædon, that the soul existed before and after death, that death was a boon, that it was the philosophical state par excellence, inasmuch as the soul was then free and disengaged; this idea, I say, was by no means settled in the minds of the first Christians. More often it would seem that man, to them, could not exist without the body. This conception endured for a long time, and was only given up when the doctrine of the immortality of the soul, in the sense of the Greek philosophy, made its entry into the Church, and united in itself so much good and bad with the Christian dogma of the resurrection and with the universal renovation. At the time of which we speak, belief in the resurrection almost alone prevailed. The funeral rite was undoubtedly the Jewish rite. No importance was attached to it; no inscription indicated the name of the dead. The great resurrection was near; the bodies of the faithful had only to make in the rock a very short sojourn. It did not require much persuasion to put people in accord on the question as to whether the resurrection was to be universal, that is to say, whether it would embrace the good and the bad, or whether it would apply to the elect only. One of the most remarkable phenomena of the new religion was the reappearance of prophecy. For a long time people had spoken but little of prophets in Israel. That particular species of inspiration seemed to revive in the little sect. The primitive Church had several prophets and prophetesses analogous to those of the Old Testament. The psalmists also reappeared. The model of our Christian psalms is without doubt given in the canticles which Luke loved to disseminate in his gospel, and which were copied from the canticles of the Old Testament. These psalms and prophesies are, as regards form, destitute of originality, but an admirable spirit of gentleness and of piety animates and pervades them. It is like a faint echo of the last productions of the sacred lyre of Israel. The Book of Psalms was in a measure the calyx from which the Christian bee sucked its first juice. The Pentateuch, on the contrary, was, as it would seem, little read and little studied; there was substituted for it allegories after the manner of the Jewish midraschim in which all the historic sense of the books was suppressed.

The music which was sung to the new hymns was probably that species of sobbing, without distinct notes, which is still the music of the Greek Church, of the Maronites, and in general of the Christians of the East. It is less a musical modulation than a manner of forcing the voice and of emitting by the nose a sort of moaning in which all the inflexions follow each other with rapidity. That odd melopoeia was executed standing, with the eyes fixed, the eyebrows crumpled, the brow knit, and with an appearance of effort. The word amen, in particular, was given out in a quivering, trembling voice. That word played a great part in the liturgy. In imitation of the Jews, the new adherents employed it to mark the assent of the multitude to the words of the prophet or the precentor. People, perhaps, already attributed to it some secret virtues and pronounced it with a certain emphasis. We do not know whether that primitive ecclesiastical song was accompanied by instruments. As to the inward chant, by which the faithful "made melody in their hearts," and which was but the overflowing of those tender, ardent, pensive souls, it was doubtless executed like the catilenes of the Lollards of the middle ages, in medium voice. In general, it was joyousness which was poured out in these hymns. One of the maxims of the sages of the sect was: "Is any afflicted among you, let him pray. Is any merry, let him sing psalms" (James v. 13). Moreover, this Christian literature being destined purely for the edification of the assembled brethren, was not written down. To compose books was an idea which had occurred to nobody. Jesus had spoken; people remembered his words. Had he not promised that the generation to whom he had spoken should not pass away, until he appeared again?

CHAPTER VI

THE CONVERSION OF HELLENISTIC JEWS AND OF PROSELYTES

Till now, the Church of Jerusalem presents itself to the outside world as a little Galilean colony. The friends whom Jesus had made at Jerusalem, and in its environs, such as Lazarus, Martha, Mary of Bethany, Joseph of Arimathea, and Nicodemus, had disappeared from the scene. The Galilean group, who pressed around the Twelve, alone remained compact and active. The preachings of these zealous disciples were incessant, and subsequently, after the destruction of Jerusalem, and far away from Judea, the sermons of the apostles were represented as public occasions, being delivered in presence of assembled multitudes. Such a construction appears to have been put upon a number of those convenient images of which legend is so prodigal. The authorities who had caused Jesus to be put to death would not have permitted the renewal of such scandals. The proselytism of the faithful was chiefly carried on by means of struggling conversions, in which the fervour of their souls was communicated to their neighbours. Their preachings under the porticoes of Solomon were addressed to circles, not at all numerous. But the effect of this was only the more profound. Their discourses consisted principally of quotations from the Old Testament, by which it was sought to prove that Jesus was the Messiah. The reasoning was at once subtle and feeble, but the entire exegesis of the Jews of that time was of the same kind, while the deductions which the doctors of the Mischna drew from the texts of the Bible were no more convincing.

More feeble still was the proof invoked in support of their arguments, which was drawn from pretended prodigies. It was impossible to doubt that the apostles did not believe that they could work miracles. Miracles were regarded as the sign of every divine mission. Saint Paul, imbued with much of the spirit the most ripe of the first Christian school, believed he wrought them. It was held as certain that Jesus had performed them. It was but natural that the series of these divine manifestations should be continued. In fact, thaumaturgy was a privilege of the apostles until the end of the first century. The miracles of the apostles were of the same character as those of Jesus, and consisted principally, but not exclusively, in the healing of the sick, and in exorcising the possessed of devils. It was pretended that their shadows alone sufficed to operate these marvellous cures. These prodigies were accounted to be the regular gifts of the Holy Spirit, and held the same rank as the gifts of knowledge, preaching and prophesy. In the third century the Church believed itself still to be in possession of the same privileges, and to exercise as a sort of right the power of healing diseases, of casting out devils, and of predicting the future. Ignorance rendered everything possible in this respect. Do we not see in our day, honest men, who, however, lack scientific knowledge, deceived in an enduring manner by the chimeras of magnetism and other illusions?

It is not by reason of innocent errors, or by the pitiful discourses we read in the Acts, by which we are to judge of the means of conversion which laid the foundations of Christianity. The real preaching was the private conversations of these good and sincere men; it was the reflection always noticeable in their discourses, of the words of Jesus; it was above all their piety, their gentleness. The attraction of communistic life carried with it also a great deal of force. Their houses were a sort of hospitals, in which all the poor and the forsaken found asylum and succour.

One of the first to affiliate himself with the rising society was a Cypriote, named Joseph Hallevi, or the Levite. Like the others, he sold his land and carried the price of it to the feet of the Twelve. He was an intelligent man, with a devotion proof against everything, and a fluent speaker. The apostles attached him closely to themselves and called him Bar-naba, that is to say, "the son of prophesy," or of "preaching." He was accounted, in fact, of the number of the prophets, that is to say, of the inspired preachers. Later on we shall see him play a capital part. Next to Saint Paul, he was the most active missionary of the first century. A certain Mnason, his countryman, was converted about the same time. Cyprus possessed many Jews. Barnabas and Mnasou were undoubtedly Jewish by race. The intimate and prolonged relations of Barnabas with the Church at Jerusalem, induces the belief that Syro-Chaldaic was familiar to him.

A conquest, almost as important as that of Barnabas was that of one John, who bore the Roman surname of Marcus. He was a cousin of Barnabas, and was circumcised. His mother, Mary, enjoyed an easy competency; she, was likewise converted, and her dwelling was more than once made the rendezvous of the apostles. These two conversions appear to have been the work of Peter. In any case, Peter was very intimate with mother and son; he regarded himself as at home in their house. Even admitting the hypothesis that John-Mark was not identical with the real or supposed author of the second Gospel, his rôle was, nevertheless, a very considerable one. Later, we shall see him accompanying Paul, Barnabas, and even Peter himself, in their apostolic journeys.

The first flame was thus spread with great rapidity. The men, the most celebrated of the apostolic century, were almost all gained over to the cause in two or three years, by a sort of simultaneous attraction. It was a second Christian generation, similar to that which had been formed five or six years previously, upon the shores of Lake Tiberias. This second generation had not seen Jesus, and could not equal the first in authority. But it was destined to surpass it in activity and in its love for distant missions. One of the best known among the new converts was Stephen, who, before his conversion, appears to have been only a simple proselyte. He was a man full of ardour and of passion. His faith was of the most fervent, and he was considered to be favoured with all the gifts of the Spirit. Philip, who, like Stephen, was a zealous deacon and evangelist, attached himself to the community abort the sane time. He was often confounded with his namesake, the apostle. Finally, there were converted it this epoch, Andronicus and Junia, probably husband and wife, who, like Aquila and Priscilla, later on, were the model of an apostolic couple, devoted to all the duties of missionary work. They were of the blood of Israel, and were in the closest relations with the apostles.

The new converts, when touched by grace, were all Jews by religion, but they belonged to two very different classes of Jews. The one class was the Hebrews; that is to say, the Jews of Palestine, speaking Hebrew or rather Armenian, reading the Bible in the Hebrew text; the other class was "Hellenists," that is to say, Jews speaking Greek, and reading the Bible in Greek. These last were further sub-divided into two classes, the one being of Jewish blood, the other being proselytes, that is to say, people of non-Israelitish origin, allied in divers degrees to Judaism. These Hellenists, who almost all came from Syria, Asia Minor, Egypt, or Cyrene, lived at Jerusalem in distinct quarters. They had their separate synagogues, and formed thus little communities apart. Jerusalem contained a great number of these special synagogues. It was in these that the words of Jesus found the soil prepared to receive it and to make it fructify.

The primitive nucleus of the Church at Jerusalem had been composed wholly and exclusively of Hebrews; the Aramaic dialect, which was the language of Jesus, was alone known and employed there. But we see that from the second or third years after the death of Jesus, Greek was introduced into the little community, where it soon became dominant. In consequence of their daily relations with the new brethren, Peter, John, James, Jude, and in general the Galilean disciples, acquired the Greek with much more facility than if they had already known something of it. An incident, of which we are soon to speak, shows that this diversity of tongues caused at first some divisions in the community, and that the relations of the two factions were not of the most agreeable kind. After the destruction of Jerusalem, we shall see the "Hebrews," retire to beyond Jordan, to the heights of Lake Tiberias, and form a separate Church, which had a separate destiny. But in the interval, between these two events, it does not appear that the diversity of languages was of any consequence in the Church. The Orientals have a great facility for learning languages; in the cities everybody invariably speaks two or three tongues. It is then probable that those of the Galilean apostles who played an active part, acquired the practise of speaking Greek; and came even to make use of it in preference to the Syro-Chaldaic, when the faithful, speaking Greek, became the much more numerous. The Palestinian dialect came, therefore, to be abandoned from the day in which people dreamed of a wide-spread propaganda. A provincial patois, which was rarely written, and which was not spoken beyond Syria, was as little adapted as could be to such an object. Greek, on the contrary, was necessarily imposed on Christianity. It was at the time the universal language, at least for the eastern basin of the Mediterranean. It was, in particular, the language of the Jews who were dispersed over the Roman empire. At that time, as in our day, the Jews adopted with great facility the tongues of the countries in which they resided. They did not pique themselves on purism; and this is the reason that the Greek of primitive Christianity is so bad. The Jews, even the most instructed, pronounced badly the classic tongue. Their sentences were always modelled upon the Syriac; they never got rid of the unwieldiness of the gross dialects which the Macedonian conquest had imported.

The conversions to Christianity became soon much more numerous amongst the "Hellenists" than amongst the "Hebrews." The old Jews at Jerusalem were but little drawn towards a sect of provincials, moderately advanced in the single science that a Pharisee appreciated--the science of the law. The position of the little Church in regard to Judaism was, as with Jesus himself, rather equivocal. But every religious or political party carries in itself a force that dominates it, and obliges it, despite itself, to revolve in its own orbit. The first Christians, whatever their apparent respect for Judaism was, were in reality only Jews by birth or by exterior customs. The true spirit of the sect came from another source. That which grew out of official Judaism was the Talmud; but Christianity has no affinity with the Talmudic school. This is why Christianity found special favour amongst the parties, the least Jewish belonging to Judaism. The rigid orthodoxists took to it but little; it was the new corners, people scarcely catechised, who had not been to any of the great schools, free from routine, and not initiated into the holy tongue, which lent an ear to the apostles and the disciples. Lightly considered by the aristocracy of Jerusalem, these parvenues of Judaism took in this way a sort of revenge. It is always the young and newly formed portions of a community that have the least respect for tradition, and who are the most carried away by novelties.

In these classes so little subject to the doctors of the law, credulity was also, it seems, more naive and more complete. That which distinguished the Talmudic Jews was not credulity. The credulous Jew, the lover of the marvellous, whom the Latin satirists knew, was not the Jew of Jerusalem; he was the Hellenist Jew, at once very religious and little instructed, and, consequently, very superstitious. Neither the half-incredulous Sadducee, nor the rigorous Pharisee, could be much affected by the theurgy popular in the apostolic circle. But the Judæus Apella, at whom the epicurean Horace laughed, was easy to convince. Social questions, besides, interested particularly those not benefited by the wealth which the temple and the central institutions of the nation caused to flow into Jerusalem. Yet it was in allying itself to the desires so very analogous to what is now called "socialism" that the new sect laid the solid foundation upon which was to be reared the edifice of its future.

CHAPTER VII

THE CHURCH CONSIDERED AS AN ASSOCIATION OF POOR PEOPLE.--INSTITUTION OF THE DIACONATE--DEACONESSES AND WIDOWS

A general truth is revealed to us in the comparative history of religions; to wit: all those which have had a beginning, and have not been contemporary with the origin of language itself, were established rather on account of social than theological reasons. This was assuredly the case with Buddhism. That which was the cause of the enormous success of that religion was not the nihilistic philosophy which served it as a basis; it was its social element. It was in proclaiming the abolition of castes, in establishing, to use his own words, "a law of grace for all," that Cakya-Mouni and his disciples drew after them first India, then the greater part of Asia. Like Christianity, Buddhism was a movement proceeding from the common people. The great attraction which it had was the facility it afforded the disinherited classes to rehabilitate themselves by the profession of a religion which bettered their condition, and offered infinite resources of assistance and sympathy.

The number of the poor, at the beginning of the first century of our era, was very considerable in Judea. The country is materially destitute of the resources which procure luxury. In these countries, where there is no industry, fortunes almost always originate either in richly endowed religious institutions, or in favours shown by She Government. The wealth of the temple had for a long time been the exclusive appanage of a limited number of nobles. The Asmoneans had formed around their dynasty a circle of rich families; the Herods augmented lunch the luxury and well-being of a certain class of society. But the true theocratic Jew, when turning his back on the Roman civilization, became only the poorer. There was formed a class of holy rocs, pious, fanatical, rigid observers of the Law, and outwardly altogether miserable. It was from this class that the sects and the fanatical parties, so numerous at this period, were recruited. The universal dream was the reign of the proletariat Jew, who remained faithful, and the humiliation of the rich, who were esteemed as renegades and traitors, given up to a profane life, and to a foreign civilization. Never did hatred equal that of these poor children of God against the splendid edifices which began to cover the country, and against the works of the Romans. Being obliged, so as not to die of hunger, to toil at these edifices, which appeared to them monuments of pride and of forbidden luxury, they believed themselves to be the victims of wicked, rich, corrupt men, and infidels, before the Law.

We can conceive how, in such a social state, an association for mutual assistance would be eagerly welcomed. The small Christian Church must have seemed a paradise. This family of simple and united brethren drew associates from every quarter. In return for that which these brought, they obtained an assured future, the society of a congenial brotherhood, and precious hopes. The general custom, before entering the sect, was for each one to convert his fortune into specie. These fortunes ordinarily consisted of small rural, semi-barren properties, and difficult of cultivation. It had one advantage, especially for unmarried people; it enabled them to exchange these plots of land against funds sunk in an assurance society, with a view to the Kingdom of God. Even some married people came to the fore in that arrangement; and precautions were taken to insure that the associates brought all that they really possessed, and did not retain anything outside the common fund. Indeed, seeing that each one received out of the latter a share, not in proportion to what one put in, but in proportion to one's needs, every reservation of property was actually a theft made upon the community. We see in such attempts at organisation on the part of the proletariat, a wonderful resemblance to certain Utopias, which have been introduced at a period not very distant from the present. Yet there is an important difference, arising out of the fact that the Christian communism had religion for a basis, whilst modern socialism has nothing of the kind. It is clear that an association in which the dividend was made in virtue of the needs of each person, and not by reason of the capital put in, could only rest upon a very exalted sentiment of self-abnegation, and upon an ardent faith in a religious ideal.

Under such a social constitution, the administrative difficulties were necessarily very numerous, whatever might be the degree of fraternal feeling which prevailed. Between two factions of a community, whose language was not the same, misapprehensions were inevitable. It was difficult for well-descended Jews not to entertain some contempt for their co-religionists, who were less noble. In fact, it was not long before murmurs began to be heard. The "Hellenists," who each day became more numerous, complained because their widows were not so well-treated at the distributions as those of the "Hebrews." Till now, the apostles had presided over the affairs of the treasury. But in face of these protestations, they felt the necessity of delegating to others this part of their powers. They proposed to the community to confide these administrative cares to seven experienced and considerate men. The proposition was accepted. The seven chosen were Stephanas, or Stephen, Philip, Prochorus, Nicanor, Timon, Parmenas and Nicholas. The last was from Antioch, and was a simple proselyte. Stephen was perhaps of the same condition. It appears that contrary to the method employed in the election of the apostle Matthias it was decided not to choose the seven administrators from the group of primitive disciples, but from amongst the new converts, and especially from amongst the Hellenists. Every one of them, indeed, bore purely Greek names. Stephen was the most important of the seven, and, in a sense, their chief. The seven were presented to the apostles, who, in accordance with a rite already consecrated, prayed over them, while imposing their hands upon their heads.

To the administrators thus designated were given the Syriac name of Schammaschin. They were also sometimes called "The Seven," to distinguish them from "The Twelve." Such, then, was the origin of the Diaconate, which is found to be the most ancient ecclesiastical function, the most ancient of sacred orders. Later, all the organised churches, in imitation of that of Jerusalem, had deacons. The growth of such an institution was marvellous. It placed the claims of the poor on an equality with religious services. It was a proclamation of the truth that social problems are the first which should occupy the attention of mankind. It was the foundation of political economy in the religious sense. The deacons were the first preachers of Christianity. We shall see presently what part they played as evangelists. As organisers, financiers, and administrators, they filled a yet more important part. These practical men, is constant contact with the poor, the sick, the women, went everywhere, observed everything, exhorted, and were most efficacious in converting people. They accomplished more than the apostles, who remained on their seats of honour at Jerusalem. They were the founders of Christianity, in respect of that which it possessed which was most solid and enduring.

At an early period, women were admitted to this office. They were designated, as in our day, by the name of "sisters." At first widows were selected; later, virgins were preferred. The tact which guided the primitive church in all this was admirable. These simple and good men, with the most profound skill, because it proceeded only from the heart, laid the basis of that grand Christian feature, par excellence--charity. They had no models of similar institutions to go upon. A vast ministry of benevolence and reciprocal succour, into which the two sexes threw their diverse talents and concentrated their efforts with a view to the alleviation of human misery, was the holy creation which resulted from the labour of these two or three first years--years the most fruitful in the history of Christianity. We feel that the thoughts of Jesus still lived in the bosoms of his disciples, and directed them, with marvellous lucidity, in all their acts. To be just, it is indeed to Jesus to whom must be referred the honour of that which the apostles did which was great. It is probable that, during his life, he had laid the basis of these establishments which were developed with such marvellous success immediately after his death.

The women were naturally drawn towards a community in which the weak were surrounded by so many guarantees. Their position in the society was then humble and precarious; the widow in particular, despite several protective laws, was the most often abandoned to misery, and the least respected. Many of the doctors advocated the not giving of any religious education to women. The Talmud placed in the same category with the pests of the world the gossiping and inquisitive widow, who passed her life in chattering with her neighbours, and the virgin who wasted her time in praying. The new religion created for these disinherited unfortunates an honourable and sure asylum. Some women held most important places in the church, and their houses served as places for meeting. As for those women who had no houses, they were formed into a species of order, or feminine presbyterial body, which also comprised virgins, who played so capital a role in the collection of alms. Institutions, which are regarded as the later fruit of Christianity--congregations of women, nuns, and sisters of charity--were its first creations, the basis of its strength, the most perfect expression of its spirit. In particular, the grand idea of consecrating by a sort of religious character and of subjecting to a regular discipline the women who were not in the bonds of marriage, is wholly Christian. The term "widow" became synonymous with religious person, consecrated to God, and, by consequence, a "deaconess." In those countries where the wife, at the age of twenty-four, is already faded, where there is no middle state between the infant and the old woman, it was a kind of new life, which was created for that portion of the human species, the most capable of devotion.

The times of the Seleucidæ had been a terrible epoch for female depravity. Never were so many domestic dramas seen, or such a series of poisonings and adulteries. The sages of that time came to consider woman as a pest to humanity, as the origin of baseness, and of shame, as an evil genius, whose only object in life was to destroy every noble germ in the opposite sex. Christianity changed all this. At that age which seems to us still youth, but at which the life of Oriental woman is so gloomy, so fatally prone to evil suggestions, the widow could, by covering her head with a black shawl, become a respectable person, be worthily employed, a deaconess, the equal of men, the most highly esteemed. This position, so distressing for a childless widow, Christianity elevated, rendered it holy. The widow became almost the equal of the maiden. She was calogrie, "beautiful in old age, venerated, useful, treated as a mother." These women, constantly going to and fro, were admirable missionaries of the new religion. Protestants are mistaken in carrying into the recognition of these facts our modern ideas of individuality. As a mere question of Christian history, socialism and cenobitism are its primitive features.

The bishop and the priest, as we now know them, did not yet exist. Still, the pastoral ministry, that intimate familiarity of souls, not bound by ties of blood, had already been established. This latter has ever been the special gift of Jesus, and a kind of heritage from him. Jesus had often said, that to everyone he was more than a father and a mother, and that in order to follow him, it was necessary to forsake those the most dear to us. Christianity placed soma things above family; it instituted brotherhood, and spiritual marriage. The ancient form of marriage, which placed the wife unreservedly in the power of the husband, was pure slavery. The moral liberty of the woman began when the Church gave to her in Jesus a guide and a confidant, who should advise and console her, listen always to her, and on occasion, council resistance on her part. Woman needs to be governed, and is happy in so being; but it is necessary that she should love him who governs her. This is what neither ancient societies, nor Judaism, nor Islamism, have been able to do. Woman has never had, up to the present time, a religious conscience, a moral individuality, an opinion of her own, except in Christianity. Thanks to the bishops and monastic life, Radegonda could find means to escape from the arms of a barbarous husband. The life of the soul being all which is of account, it is just and reasonable that the pastor who knows how to make the divine chords of the heart vibrate, the secret counsellor who holds the key of consciences, should be more than father, more than husband.

In a sense, Christianity was a re-action against the too narrow domestic economy of the Aryan race. The old Aryan societies did not only admit but few besides married men, but also interpreted marriage in the strictest sense. It was something analogous to an English family, a narrow, exclusive, contracted circle, an egotism of several, as withering for the soul, as the egotism of the individual. Christianity, with its divine conception of the liberty of the Kingdom of God, corrected these exaggerations. It first guarded itself against imposing upon everyone the duties of the generality of mankind. It discovered that family was not the sole thing in life, that the duty of reproducing the species did not devolve on everyone, and that there should be persons freed front these duties--duties undoubtedly sacred but not designed for all.

The exception which Greek society made in favour of the hetærae, like Aspasia, and of the cortigiana, like Imperia, in consequence of the necessities of polite society, Christianity made for the priest, the nun and the deaconess, with a view to the general good. It recognised different classes in society. There are souls who find more sweetness in the love of five or six hundred people than in that of five or six; for such the ordinary conditions of family seem insufficient, cold and wearisome. Why extend to all, the exigences of our dull and mediocre societies? The temporal family suffices not for man. He requires brothers and sisters not of the flesh.

By its hierarchy of different social functions, the primitive church appeared to conciliate these opposing requirements. We shall never comprehend how happy these people were, under these holy restrictions, which maintained liberty, without restraining it, rendering at once possible the pleasures of communistic life, and those of private life. It was altogether different from the hurly-burly of our modern societies, artificial, and without love, in which the sensitive soul is sometimes so cruelly isolated. In these little refuges, which are called churches, the atmosphere was genial and sweet. People lived together in the same faith and in the same hope. But it is clear also that these conditions would be inapplicable to a large society. When entire countries embraced Christianity, the rules of the first churches became a Utopian idea, and sought refuge in monasteries. The monastic life is, in this sense, but the continuation of the primitive churches. The convent is the necessary consequence of the Christian spirit. There is no perfect Christianity without the convent, seeing that the evangelical idea can be realized there only.

A large allowance of credit, ought certainly to be made to Judaism in these great creations. Each of the Jewish communities scattered along the coasts of the Mediterranean, was already a sort of church, possessing its funds for mutual succour. Almsgiving, always recommended by the sages, had become a precept: it was done in the Temple, and in the synagogues: it was regarded as the first duty of the proselyte. In all times Judaism has been distinguished by its care for its poor, and for the fraternal sentiment of charity which it inspires.

There is a supreme injustice in opposing Christianity to Judaism by way of reproach, since all which Primitive Christianity possesses came bodily from Judaism. It is while thinking of the Roman world that one is struck by the miracles of charity and free association undertaken by the Church. Never did profane society, recognizing reason alone for its basis, produce such admirable results. The law of every profane, or, if I may say so, philosophical society, is liberty, sometimes equality; never fraternity.

Charity, viewed from the point of right, has nothing about it obligatory; it concerns only individuals; it is even found to possess certain inconveniences, on which account it is distrusted. Every attempt to apply the public funds for the benefit of the poor savours of communism. When a man dies of hunger, when entire classes languish in misery, profane policy limits itself to finding out the cause of the misfortune. It points out at once that there can be no civil or political order without liberty; but the consequence of that liberty is that he who has nothing, and can earn nothing, must die of hunger. That is logical; but nothing can withstand the abuse of logic. The wants of the most numerous class always prevail in the long run. Institutions purely political and civil do not suffice; social and religious aspirations have also a right to a legitimate satisfaction.

The glory of the Jewish people is that they have loudly proclaimed this principle, from which emanated the ruin of the ancient empires, but which will never be eradicated. The Jewish law is social and non-political; the prophets, the authors of the apocalypses, were the promoters of social revolutions. In the first half of the first century, in the presence of profane civilization, the Jews had but one idea, which was to refuse the benefits of the Roman law, that philosophical and Atheistic law, which placed everyone on an equality, and to proclaim the excellence of their theocratic law, which formed a religious and moral society. "The Law is Happiness": this was the idea of all Jewish thinkers, such as Philo and Josephus. The laws of other peoples were designed that justice should have its course; it mattered little whether men were good or happy. The Jewish law took account of the minutest details of moral education. Christianity is due to the development of the same idea. Each church is a monastery, in which all possess equal rights, in which there ought to be neither poor nor wicked, in which, consequently, each watches over and commands each other. Primitive Christianity may be defined as a great association of poor people, a heroic struggle against egotism, based upon the idea that each has a right to no more than is necessary for him, that all superfluity belongs to those who have nothing. We can at once see that between such a spirit and the Roman spirit, would be established a war to the death, and that Christianity, on its part, will never attain to dominating over the world, except on the condition of making important modifications in its inherent tendencies and in its original programme.

But the wants which it represents will always endure. The communistic life, commencing with the second half of the Middle Ages, having served for the abuses of an intolerant Church, the monastery having too often become but a feudal fief, or the barracks of a dangerous and fanatical military, the modern mind evinced a most bitter opposition in regard to cenobitism. But we forget that it was in the communistic life that the soul of man tasted its fullest joy. The canticle, "Behold, how good and joyful a thing it is for brethren to dwell together in unity," has ceased to be our refrain. But when modern individualism shall have borne its latest fruits; when humanity, shrunken, saddened, and become impotent, will return to these grand institutions, and stern disciplines; when our pitiful bourgeois society--I speak unadvisedly, our world of pigmies--shall have been scourged with whips by the heroic and idealistic portions of mankind, then the communistic life will regain all its value. Many great things, science, for example, will be organized under a monastic form, with hereditary rights, but not those of blood. The importance which our century attributes to family will diminish. Egotism, the essential rule of civil society, will not be sufficient for great minds. All, proceeding from the most opposite points of view, will league themselves against vulgarity. We shall return again to the words of Jesus, and the ideas of the Middle Ages in regard to poverty. We will comprehend how that to possess anything could have been regarded as a mark of inferiority, and how that the founders of the mystic life could have disputed for centuries in order to discover whether Jesus owned even so much as the things which were necessary for his daily wants. These Franciscan subtleties will become once more great social problems. The splendid ideal, traced by the author of the Acts, will be inscribed as a prophetic revelation on the gates of the paradise of humanity. "And the multitude of them that believed were of one heart and of one soul; neither said any of them, that the things which he possessed were his own, but they had all things in common, neither was there any of them that lacked; fur as many as were possessors of land or houses sold them, and brought the price of things that were sold, and laid them down at the apostles feet, and distribution was made to every man according as he had need. And they, continuing with one daily accord in the temple, and breaking bread from house to house, did eat their meat with gladness and singleness of heart." (Acts ii., 44-47.)

But let us not anticipate events. It was now about the year 36. Tiberius, at Caprea, has little idea of the enemy to the empire which is growing up. In two or three years the sect had made surprising progress. It numbered several thousand of the faithful. It was already easy to forsee that its conquests would be effected chiefly amongst the Hellenists and proselytes. The Galilean group which had listened to the master, though preserving always its precedence, seemed as if swamped by the floods of new corners speaking Greek. One could already perceive that the principal parts were to be played by the latter. At the time at which we are arrived, no Pagan, that is to say, no man without some anterior connection with Judaism, had entered into the Church. Proselytes, however, performed very important functions in it. The circle de provenance of the disciples had likewise largely extended; it is no longer a simple little college of Palestineans; we can count in it people from Cyprus, Antioch, and Cyrene, and from almost all the points of the eastern coasts of the Mediterranean, where Jewish colonies had been established. Egypt alone was wanting in the primitive Church, and for a long time continued to be so. The Jews of that country were almost in a state of schism with Judea. They lived after their own fashion, which was superior in many respects to the life in Palestine, and scarcely felt the shock of the religious movements at Jerusalem

CHAPTER VIII

FIRST PERSECUTION.--DEATH OF STEPHEN.--DESTRUCTION OF THE FIRST CHURCH OF JERUSALEM

It was inevitable that the preachings of the new sect, although delivered with so much reserve, should revive the animosities which had accumulated against its founder, and eventually brought about his death. The Sadducee family of Hanan, who had caused the death of Jesus, was still reigning. Joseph Caiaphas occupied, up to 36, the sovereign Pontificate, the effective power of which he gave over to his father-in-law Hanan, and to his relatives, John and Alexander. These arrogant and pitiless men viewed with impatience a troop of good and holy people, without official title, winning the favour of the multitude. Once or twice, Peter, John, and the principal members of the apostolic college, were put in prison and condemned to flagellation. This was the chastisement inflicted on heretics. The authorization of the Romans was not necessary in order to apply it. As we might indeed suppose, these brutalities only served to inflame the ardour of the apostles. They came forth from the Sanhedrim where they had just undergone flagellation, rejoicing that they were counted worthy to suffer shame for him whom they loved. Eternal puerility of penal repressions applied to things of the soul! They were regarded, no doubt, as men of order, as models of prudence and wisdom; these blunderers, who seriously believed in the year 36, to gain the upper hand of Christianity by means of a few strokes of a whip!

These outrages proceeded chiefly from the Sadducees, that is to say, from the upper clergy, who crowded the Temple and derived from it immense profits. We do not find that the Pharisees exhibited towards the sect the animosity they displayed to Jesus. The new believers were strict and pious people, somewhat resembling in their manner of life the Pharisees themselves. The rage which the latter manifested against the founder arose from the superiority of Jesus--a superiority which he was at no pains to dissimulate. His delicate railleries, his wit, his charm, his contempt for hypocrites, had kindled a ferocious hatred. The apostles, on the contrary, were devoid of wit; they never employed irony. The Pharisees were at times favourable to them; many Pharisees had even become Christians. The terrible anathemas of Jesus against Pharisaism had not yet been written, and the accounts of the words of the Master were neither general nor uniform. These first Christians were, besides, people so inoffensive, that many persons of the Jewish aristocracy, who did not exactly form part of the sect, were well disposed towards them. Nicodemus and Joseph of Arimathea, who had known Jesus, remained no doubt with the Church in the bonds of brotherhood. The most celebrated Jewish doctor of the age, Rabbi Gamaliel the elder, grandson of Hillel, a man of broad and very tolerant ideas, spoke, it is said, in the Sanhedrim in favour of permitting gospel preaching. The author of the Acts credits him with some excellent reasoning, which ought to be the rule of conduct of governments, on all occasions when they find themselves confronted with novelties of an intellectual or moral order. "If this work is frivolous," said he, "leave it alone, it will fall of itself; if it is serious, how dare you resist the work of God? In any case, you will not succeed in stopping it." Gamaliel's words were hardly listened to. Liberal minds in the midst of opposing fanaticisms have no chance of succeeding. A terrible commotion was produced by the deacon Stephen. His preaching had, as it would appear, great success. Multitudes flocked around him, and these gatherings resulted in acrimonious quarrels. It was chiefly Hellenists, or proselytes, habitues of the synagogue, called Libertini, people of Cyrene, of Alexandria, of Cilicia, of Ephesus, who took an active part in these disputes. Stephen passionately maintained that Jesus was the Messiah, that the priests had committed a crime in putting him to death, that the Jews were rebels, sons of rebels, people who rejected evidence. The authorities resolved to dispatch this audacious preacher. Several witnesses were suborned to seize upon some words in his discourses against Moses. Naturally they found that for which they sought. Stephen was arrested and led into the presence of the Sanhedrim. The sentence with which they reproached him was almost identical with the one which led to the condemnation of Jesus. They accused him of saying that Jesus of Nazareth would destroy the Temple and change the traditions attributed to Moses. It is quite possible, indeed, that Stephen had used such language. A Christian of that epoch could not have had the idea of speaking directly against the Law, inasmuch as all still observed it; as for traditions, however, Stephen might combat them as Jesus had himself done; nevertheless, these traditions were foolishly ascribed by the orthodox to Moses, and people attributed to them a value, equal to that of the written Law.

Stephen defended himself by expounding the Christian thesis, with a wealth of citations from the written Law, from the Psalms, from the Prophets, and wound up by reproaching the members of the Sanhedrim with the murder of Jesus. "Ye stiff-necked and uncircumcised in heart," said he to them, "you will then ever resist the Holy Ghost as your fathers also have done. Which of the prophets have not your fathers prosecuted? They have slain those who announced the coming of the Just One, whom you have betrayed, and of whom you have been the murderers. This law that you have received from the mouth of angels you have not kept." At these words a scream of rage interrupted him. Stephen, his excitement increasing more and more, fell into one of those transports of enthusiasm which were called the inspiration of the Holy Spirit. His eyes were fixed on high; he witnessed the glory of God and Jesus by the side of his Father, and cried out: "Behold, I see the heavens opened, and the Son of Man sitting on the right hand of God." The whole assembly stopped their ears, and threw themselves upon him, gnashing their teeth. He was dragged outside the city and stoned. The witnesses, who, according to the law, had to cast the first stones, divested themselves of their garments and laid them at the feet of a young fanatic named Saul, or Paul, who was thinking with secret joy of the renown he was acquiring in participating in the death of a blasphemer.

In all this there was an observance to the letter of the prescriptions of Deuteronomy, chapter xiii. But viewed from a civil law point, this tumultuous execution, carried out without the sanction of the Romans, was not regular. In the case of Jesus, we have seen that it was necessary to obtain the ratification of the Procurator. It may be that this ratification was obtained in the case of Stephen and that the execution did not follow his sentence quite so closely as the narrator of the Acts would have us believe. It may have happened also that the Roman authority was at this time somewhat relaxed. Pilate had been, or was about to be, suspended from his functions. The cause of this disgrace was simply the too great firmness which he had shown in his administration. Jewish fanaticism had rendered his life insupportable. Possibly he was tired of refusing the outrages these frantic people demanded of him, and the proud family of Hanan had reached the point that they no longer required the sanction of the Procurator to pronounce sentences of death. Lucius Vetellius (the father of him who was emperor) was then imperial legate at Syria. He sought to win the good graces of the population; and he restored to the Jews the pontifical vestments, which, since the time of Herod the Great, had been deposited in the tower of Antonia. Instead of sustaining the rigorous acts of Pilate, he lent an ear to the complaints of the natives and sent Pilate back to Rome, to answer the accusations of his subordinates (commencement of the year 36). The chief grievance of the latter was that the Procurator would not lend himself with sufficient complacency to their intolerant behests. Vitellius replaced him provisionally by his friend Marcellus, who was undoubtedly more careful not to displease the Jews, and, consequently, more willing to indulge them in their religious murders. The death of Liberius (16 March, 37) only encouraged Vitellius in this policy. The two first years of the reign of Caligula was an epoch of general relaxation of the Roman authority in Syria. The policy of that prince, before he lost his reason, was to restore to the peoples of the East their autonomy and their native chiefs. It was thus that he established the kingdoms or principalities of Comagene, of Herod Agrippa, of Soheym, of Cotys, of Polemon II., and permitted that of Harêth to aggrandise itself. When Pilate arrived at Rome, the new reign had already begun. It is probable that Caligula held him to be in the wrong, inasmuch as he confided the government of Jerusalem to a new functionary, Marcellus, who appears not to have excited, on the part of the Jews, the violent recriminations which overwhelmed poor Pilate with embarrassment, and filled him with disgust.

At all events, that which is important to remark is, that in that epoch the persecutors of Christianity were not Romans; they were orthodox Jews. The Romans preserved in the midst of this fanaticism a principle of tolerance and of reason. If we can reproach the imperial authority with anything, it is with being too lenient, and with not having cut short with a stroke the civil consequences of a sanguinary law which visited with death religious derelictions. But as yet the Roman domination was not so complete as it became later; it was only a sort of protectorate or suzerainty. Its condescension even went the length of not putting the head of the emperor on the coins struck during the rule of procurators, so as not to shock Jewish ideas. Rome did not yet, in the East at least, seek to impose upon vanquished peoples her laws, her gods, her manners; she left them, outside the Roman laws, their local customs. Their semi-independence was simply a further indication of their inferiority. The imperial power in the East, at that epoch, resembled somewhat the Turkish authority, and the condition of the native population, that under the Rajahs. The notion of equal rights and equal protection for all did not exist. Each provincial group had its jurisdiction, just as at this day the various Christian Churches and the Jews have in the Ottoman Empire. In Turkey, a few years ago, the patriarchs of the different communities of Rajahs, provided that they had some sort of understanding with the Porte, were sovereigns as far as their subordinates were concerned, and could sentence them to the most cruel punishments.

As Stephen's death may have taken place at any time during the years 36, 37, 38, we cannot, therefore, affirm whether Caiaphas ought to be held responsible for it. Caiaphas was deposed by Lucius Vitellius, in the year 36, shortly after the time of Pilate; but the change was inconsiderable. He had for a successor his brother-in-law, Jonathan, son of Hanan. The latter, in turn, was succeeded by his brother Theophilus, son of Hanan, who continued the Pontificate in the house of Hanan till the year 42. Hanna was still alive, and, possessed of the real power, maintained in his family the principles of pride, severity, hatred against innovators which were, so to speak, hereditary.

The death of Stephen produced a great impression. The proselytes solemnized his funeral with tears and groanings. The separation of the new secretaries from Judaism was not yet absolute. The proselytes and the Hellenists, leas strict in regard to orthodoxy than the pure Jews, considered that they ought to render public homage to a man who respected their constitution, and whose peculiar beliefs did not put him without the pale of the Law.

Thus began the era of Christian martyrs. Martyrdom was not an entirely new thing. Not to mention John the Baptist and Jesus, Judaism at the time of Antiochus Epiphanus, had had its witnesses, faithful even to the death. But the series of courageous victims, beginning with Saint Stephen, has exercised a peculiar influence upon the history of the human mind. It introduced into the western world an element which it lacked, to wit, absolute and exclusive faith, the idea that there is but one good and true religion. In this sense, the martyrs began the era of intolerance. It may be avouched with great assurance, that he who can give his life for his faith would, if he were master, be intolerant. Christianity, when it had passed through three centuries of persecution, and became, in its turn, dominant, was more persecuting than any religion had ever been. When people have shed their blood for a cause they are too prone to shed the blood of others, so as to conserve the treasure they have gained.

The murder of Stephen, moreover, was not an isolated event. Taking advantage of the weakness of the Roman functionaries, the Jews brought to bear upon the Church a real persecution. It seems that the vexations pressed chiefly on the Hellenists and the proselytes whose free behaviour exasperated the orthodox. The Church of Jerusalem, which though already strongly organized, was compelled to disperse. The apostles, according to a principle which seems to have seized strong hold of their minds, did not quit the city. It was probably so, too, with the whole purely Jewish group, those who were denominated the "Hebrews." But the great community with its common table, its diaconal services, its varied exercises, ceased from that time, and was never re-formed upon its first model. It had endured for three or four years. It was for nascent Christianity an unequalled good fortune that its first attempts at association, essentially communistic, were so soon broken up. Essays of this kind engender such shocking abuses, that communistic establishments are condemned to crumble away in a very short time, or to ignore very soon the principle upon which they are founded. Thanks to the persecution of the year 37 the cenobitic Church of Jerusalem was saved from the test of time. It was nipped in the bud, before interior difficulties had undermined it. It remained like a splendid dream, the memory of which animated in their life of trial all those who had formed part of it, like an ideal to which Christianity incessantly aspires without ever succeeding in reaching its goal. Those who know what an inestimable treasure the memory of Menilmontant is to the members still alive of the St. Simonian Church, what friendship it creates between them, what joy kindles in their eyes, when they speak of it, will comprehend the powerful bond which was established between the new brethren, from the fact of having first loved and then suffered together. It is almost always a principle of great lives, that during several months they have realised God, and the recollection of this suffices to fill up the entire after-years with strength and sweetness.

The leading part in the persecution we have just related belonged to that young Saul, whom we have above found abetting, as far as in him lay, the murder of Stephen. This hot-headed youth, furnished with a permission from the priests, entered houses suspected of harbouring Christians, laid violent hold on men and women and dragged them to prison, or before the tribunals. Saul boasted that there was no one of his generation so zealous as himself for the traditions. True it is, that often the gentleness and the resignation of his victims astonished him; he experienced a kind of remorse; he fancied he heard these pious women, whom, hoping for the Kingdom of God, he had cast into prison, saying during the night, in a sweet voice: "Why persecutest thou us?" The blood of Stephen, which had almost smothered him, sometimes troubled his vision. Many things that he had heard said of Jesus went to his heart. This superhuman being, in his ethereal life, whence he sometimes emerged, revealing himself in brief apparitions, haunted him like a spectre. But Saul shrunk with horror from such thoughts; he confirmed himself with a sort of frenzy in the faith of his traditions, and meditated new cruelties against those who attacked him. His name had become a terror to the faithful; they dreaded at his hands the most atrocious outrages, and the most sanguinary treacheries.

CHAPTER IX

FIRST MISSIONS.--PHILIP THE DEACON

The persecution of the year 37 had for its result, as is always the case, the spread of the doctrine which it was wished to arrest. Till now, the Christian preaching had not extended far beyond Jerusalem; no mission had been undertaken; enclosed within its exalted but narrow communison, the mother Church had spread no haloes around herself, or formed any branches. The dispersion of the little circle scattered the good seed to the four winds of heaven. The members of the Church of Jerusalem, driven violently from their quarters, spread themselves over every part of Judæ and Samaria, and preached everywhere the Kingdom of God. The deacons, in particular, freed from their administrative functions by the destruction of the community, became excellent evangelists. They constituted the young and active element of the sect, in contradistinction to the somewhat heavy element formed by the apostles, and the "Hebrews." One single circumstance, that of language, would have sufficed to create in the latter an inferiority as regards preaching. They spoke, at least as their habitual tongue, a dialect which was not used by the Jews themselves more than a few leagues from Jerusalem. It was to the Hellenists that belonged all the honour of the great conquest, the account of which is to be now our main purpose.

The scene of the first of these missions, which was soon to embrace the whole basin of the Mediterranean, was the region about Jerusalem, within a radius of two or three days' journey. Philip, the Deacon, was the hero of this first holy expedition. He evangelized Samaria most successfully. The Samaritans were schismatics; but the young sect, following the example of the Master, was less susceptible than the rigorous Jews in regard to questions of orthodoxy. Jesus, it was said, had shown himself at different times to be quite favourable to the Samaritans. Philip appeared to have been one of the apostolical men most pre-occupied with theurgy. The accounts which relate to him transport us into a strange and fantastic world. The conversions which he made in Samaria, and in particular in the capital, Sebaste, are explained by prodigies. This country was itself wholly given up to superstitious ideas in regard to magic. In the year 36, that is to say, two or three years before the arrival of the Christian preachers, a fanatic had excited among the Samaritans quite a serious commotion by preaching the necessity of a return to primitive Mosaism, the sacred utensils of which he pretended to have found. A certain Simon, of the village of Gitta or Gitton, who obtained later a great reputation, began about that time to gain notoriety by means of his enchantments. One feels at seeing the gospel finding a preparation and a support in such chimeras. Quite a large multitude were baptized in the name of Jesus. Philip had the power of baptizing, but not that of conferring the Holy Ghost. That privilege was reserved to the apostles. When people learned at Jerusalem of the formation of a group of believers at Sebaste, it was resolved to send Peter and John to complete their initiation. The two apostles came, laid their hands on the new converts, prayed over their heads; the latter were immediately endowed with the marvellous powers attached to the conferring of the Holy Spirit. Miracles, prophecy, all the phenomena of illusionism were produced, and the Church of Sebaste had nothing in this respect to envy the Church of Jerusalem for.

If the tradition about it is to be credited, Simon of Gitton found himself from that time in relations with the Christians. According to their accounts, he, being converted by the preaching and miracles of Philip, was baptized, and attached himself to this evangelist. Then when the apostles Peter and John had arrived, and when he saw the supernatural powers procured by the imposition of hands, he came, it is said, and offered them money, in order that they might impart to him the faculty of conferring the Holy Spirit. Peter is then reported to have made to him this admirable response: "Thy money perish with thee, because thou hast thought that the gift of God may be bought! Thou hast neither part nor lot in this matter, for thy heart is not right in the sight of God."

Whether these words were or were not pronounced, they seem to picture exactly the situation of Simon regard to the nascent sect. We shall see, in fact, that according to all appearances, Simon of Gitton was the chief of a religious movement, similar to that of Christianity, which might be regarded as a sort of Samaritan counterfeit of the work of Jesus. Had Simon already commenced to dogmatize and to perform prodigies when Philip arrived at Sebaste? Did he enter thereupon into relations with the Christian Church? Has the anecdote, which made of him the father of all "Simony," any reality? Must it be admitted that the world one day saw face to face two thaumaturgists, one of which was a charlatan.

the other the "corner-stone," which has been made the base of the faith of humanity? Was a sorcerer able to counter-balance the destinies of Christianity? This is what, for lack of documentary evidence, we do not know; for the narrative of the Acts is here but a feeble authority; and, from the first century, Simon became for the Christian church a subject of legends. In history, the general idea alone is pure. It would be unjust to dwell on that, which is shocking in this sad page of the origin of Christianity. To vulgar auditors, the miracle proves the doctrine; to us, the doctrine makes us forget the miracle. When a belief has consoled and ameliorated humanity, it is excusable to employ proofs proportioned to the weakness of the public to which it is addressed. But when error after error has been proved, what excuse can be alleged? This is not a condemnation which we intend to pro. pounce against Simon of Gitton. We shall have to explain later on his doctrine, and the part he played which was only made manifest under the reign of Claudius. It is of moment only to remark here, that an important principle seems to have been introduced by him into the Christian theurgy. Compelled to admit that some impostors could also perform miracles, orthodox theology attributed these miracles to the Evil One. For the purpose of conserving some demonstrative value in prodigies, it was necessary to invent rules for distinguishing the true from the false miracles. In order to this, they descended to a species of ideas utterly childish.

Peter and John, after confirming the Church of Sebaste, departed again for Jerusalem, evangelizing on their tray the villages of the country of Samaria. Philip the Deacon, continued his evangelizing journeys, directing his steps towards the south, into the ancient country of the Philistines. This country, since the advent of the Maccabees had been much encroached upon by the Jews; Judaism, however, had not succeeded in becoming dominant there. During this journey Philip accomplished a conversion which made some noise and which was much talked about because of a singular circumstance. One day, as he was journeying along the route, a very lonely route, from Jerusalem to Gaza, he encountered a rich traveller, evidently a foreigner, for he was riding in a chariot, which was a mode of locomotion that has at all times been unknown to the inhabitants of Syria and of Palestine. He was returning from Jerusalem, and, gravely seated, was reading the Bible in a loud voice, according to a custom quite common at that time. Philip, who in everything was believed to act on inspiration from on high, felt himself drawn towards the chariot. He came up alongside of it, and quietly entered into conversation with the opulent personage, offering to explain to him the passages, which the latter did not comprehend. This was a rare occasion for the evangelist to develop the Christian thesis upon the figures employed in the Old Testament. He proved that in the books of prophecy everything there related to Jesus; that Jesus was the solution of the great enigma; that it was of him in particular that the All-Seeing had spoken in this beautiful passage: "He was led as a sheep to the slaughter; as a lamb that is dumb before its shearers, he opened not his mouth." The traveller listened, and at the first water to which they came he said: "Behold, here is water, why could I not be baptized." The chariot was stopped: Philip and the traveller descended into the water, and the latter was baptized.

Now this traveller was a powerful personage. He was a eunuch of the Candace of Ethiopia, her finance minister, the keeper of her treasures, who had come to worship at Jerusalem, and was now returning to Napata by the Egyptian route. Candace or Condaoce was the title of feminine royalty in Ethiopia, about the period of which we are now speaking. Judiasm had already penetrated into Nubia and Abyssinia; many of the natives had been converted, or at least were counted among those proselytes, who, without being circumcised, worshipped the one God. The eunuch probably be-longed to the latter class, a simple pious Pagan, like the centurion Cornelius who will figure presently in this history. In any case, it is impossible to suppose that he was completely initiated into Judaism. From this time we hear no more said about the eunuch. But Philip recounted the incident, and at a later period much importance was attached to it. When the question of admitting Pagans into the Christian Church became an affair of moment, there was found here a precedent of great weight. In all this affair, Philip was believed to have acted under divine inspiration. This baptism, administered by order of the Holy Spirit to a man scarcely a Jew. assuredly not circumcised, who had believed in Christianity, only for a few hours, possessed a high dogmatic value. It was an argument for those who thought that the doors of the new church should be open to all.

Philip, after that adventure, betook himself to Ashdod or Azote. Such was the artless state of enthusiasm in which these missionaries lived, that at each step they believed they heard the voice of Heaven, and received directions from the Spirit. Each of their steps seemed to them to be regulated by a superior power, and when they went from one city to another, they thought they were obeying a supernatural inspiration. Sometimes they fancied they made ærial trips. Philip was in this respect one of the most privileged. It was, as he believed, on the indication of an angel, that he had come from Samaria to the place where he had encountered the eunuch; after the baptism of the latter he was persuaded that the Spirit had lifted him bodily, and transported him with one swoop to Azote.

Azote and the Gaza route were the limits of the first evangelical preachings towards the south. Beyond were the desert and the nomadic life upon which Christianity has never taken much hold. From Azote, Philip the Deacon turned towards the north and evangelized all the coast as far as Cesarea. It is probable that the Church of Joppa and of Gydda, which we shall soon find flourishing, were founded by him. At Cesarea he settled and founded an important Church. We shall encounter him there again twenty years later. Cesarea was a new city and the most considerable of Judea. It had been built on the site of a Sidonian fortress, called Abdastartes or Shato's Tower, by Herod the Great, who gave to it, in honour of Augustus, the name which its ruins bear still to-day. Cesarea was much the best part in all Palestine, and tended day by day to become its capital. Tired of living at Jerusalem, the Judean Procurators were soon to repair thence, to make it their permanent residence. It was principally peopled by Pagans; the Jews, however, were somewhat numerous there; cruel strifes had often taken place between the two classes of the population. The Greek language was alone spoken there, and the Jews themselves had come to recite certain parts of their liturgy in Greek. The austere Rabbis of Jerusalem regarded Cesarea as a dangerous and profane abode, and in which one became nearly a Pagan. From all the facts which have just been cited, this city will occupy an important place in the sequel of this history. It was in a kind of way the port of Christianity, the point by which the Church of Jerusalem communicated with all the Mediterranean.

Many other missions, the history of which is unknown to us, were conducted simultaneously with that of Philip. The very rapidity with which this first preaching was done, was the reason of its success. In the year 38, five years after the death of Jesus, and probably one year after the death of Stephen, all this side of Jordan had heard the glad tidings from the mouths of missionaries hailing from Jerusalem. Galilee, on its part, guarded the holy seed and probably scattered it around her, although we know of no missions issuing from that quarter. Perhaps the city of Damascus, from the period at which we now are, had also some Christians, who received the faith from Galilean preachers.

CHAPTER X

CONVERSION OF ST. PAUL.--RIDICULOUS TO PUT PAUL'S CONVERSION A.D. 38--ARETAS SETTLES THE DATE AS ABOUT 34

The year 38 is marked in the history of the nascent Church by a much more important conquest. During that year we may safely place the conversion of that Saul whom we witnessed participating in the stoning of Stephen, and as a principal agent in the persecution of 37, but who now, by a mysterious act of grace, becomes the most ardent of the disciples of Jesus.

Saul was born at Tarsus, in Cilicia, in the year 10 or 12 of our era. Following the custom of the times, his name was latinized into that of Paul; he did not, however, regularly adopt this last name until he became the apostle of the Gentiles. Paul was of the purest Jewish blood. His family, who probably hailed originally from the town of Gischala, in Galilee, pretended to belong to the tribe of Benjamin; while his father enjoyed the title of a Roman citizen, a title no doubt inherited from ancestors who had obtained that honour, either by purchase or by services rendered to the state. His grandfather may have obtained it for aid given to Pompey during the Roman conquest (63 B.C.) His family, like most of the good old Jewish houses, belonged to the sect of Pharisees. Paul was brought up according to the strictest principles of this sect, and though he afterwards repudiated its narrow dogmas, he always retained its exaltation, its asperity, and its ardent faith.

During the epoch of Augustus, Tartus was a very flourishing city. The population, though composed chiefly of the Greek and Aramaic races, included, as was common in all the commercial towns, a large number of Jews. A taste for letters and the sciences was a marked characteristic of the place; and no city in the world, not even excepting Athens and Alexandria, had so many scientific institutions and schools. The number of learned men which Tarsus produced, or who prosecuted their studies there, was truly extraordinary; but it must not hence be imagined that Paul received a careful Greek education. The Jews rarely frequented the institutions of secular instruction. The most celebrated schools of Tarsus were those of rhetoric, where the Greek classics received the first attention. It seems hardly probable that a man who had taken even elementary lessons in grammar and rhetoric, could have written in the incorrect non-Hellenistic style of that of the Epistles of St. Paul. He talked constantly and even fluently in Greek, and wrote or rather dictated in that language; but his Greek was that of the Hellenistic Jews, bristling with Hebraisms and Syriacisms, scarcely intelligible to a lettered man of that period, and which can only be understood by trying to discover the Syriac turn of mind which influenced Paul, at the time he was dictating his epistles. He was himself cognizant of the vulgar and detective character of his style. Whenever it was possible he spoke Hebrew--that is to say, the Syro-Chaldaic of his time. It was in this language that he thought, it was in this language he was addressed by the mysterious voice on the way to Damascus.

His doctrine, moreover, shows us no direct adaptation from Greek philosophy. The verse quoted from the Thais of Menander, which occurs in his writings, is one of those monostich-proverbs that were familiar to the public, and could easily have been quoted by one who was not acquainted with the original. Two other quotation--one from Epimenides, the other from Aratus--which appear under his name, though it is by no means certain that he used them, may also be understood as having been borrowed at second-hand. The literary training of Paul was almost exclusively Jewish, and it is in the Talmud rather than in the Greek classics that the analogies of his modes of thought must be sought. A few general ideas of popular philosophy, which one could learn without opening a single book of the philosophers, alone reached him. His manner of reasoning is most singular. He knew nothing certainly of the peripatetic logic. His syllogism is not that of Aristotle; on the contrary, his dialectics greatly resemble those of the Talmud. Paul, in general is carried away by words rather than by thought. When a word took possession of his mind it suggested a train of thought wholly irrelevant to the subject in hand. His transitions were sudden, his treatment disjointed, his periods frequently suspended. No writer could be more unequal. We would seek in vain throughout the realm of literature for a phenomenon as capricious as that of the sublime passage in the thirteenth chapter of the First Epistle to the Corinthians, placed by the side of such feeble arguments, painful repetitions, and fastidious subtleties.

His father at the outset intended that he should be a rabbi; and following the general custom, gave him a trade. Paul was an upholsterer, or rather a manufacturer of the heavy cloths of Cilicia, called

Cilicium. At various times he had to work at this trade, having no patrimonial fortune. It seems quite certain that he had a sister, whose son lived at Jerusalem. As regards a brother and other relatives, who it is said embraced Christianity, the testimony is vague and uncertain.

Refinement of manners being, according to the modern ideas of the middle-classes, in direct proportion to personal wealth, it might be imagined, from what has just been said that Paul was badly brought up and undistinguished amongst the proletariat. This idea would, however, be quite erroneous. His politeness, when he chose, was extreme, and his manners, exquisite. Despite the defects in his style, his letters show that he was a man of uncommon intelligence, who could find for the expression of his lofty sentiments, language of rare felicity; and no correspondence displays more careful attention, finer shades of meaning, and more charming hesitancy and timidity. Some of his pleasantries shock us. But what animation! What a fund of charming sayings! What simplicity! One can easily see that his character, when his passions did not make him irascible and fierce, was that of a polite, earnest, and affectionate man, susceptible at times, and a trifle jealous. Inferior as such men are in the eyes of the general public, they yet possess within small Churches, immense advantages, because of the attachments they inspire, their practical aptitude, and their skill in escaping from the greatest difficulties.

Paul had a sickly appearance, which did not correspond with the greatness of his soul. He was uncomely, short, squat, and stooping, his broad shoulders awkwardly sustaining a little bald pate. His sallow countenance was half concealed in a thick beard; his nose was aquiline, his eyes piercing, while his black, heavy eye-brows met across his forehead. Nor was there anything imposing about his speech; his timid and embarassed air, and incorrect language, gave at first but a poor idea of his eloquence. He gloried, however, in his exterior defects, and even shrewdly extracted advantage from them. The Jewish rare possesses the peculiarity of presenting at once types of the greatest beauty, and of the most utter ugliness; but this Jewish ugliness is something quite unique. Some of the strange visages which at first excite a smile, assume, when lighted up by emotion, a rare brilliance and majesty.

The temperament of Paul was not less peculiar than his exterior. His constitution was sickly, yet its singular endurance was tested by the way in which he supported an existence full of fatigues and sufferings. He makes constant allusions to his bodily weakness. He speaks of himself as a sick man, exhausted, and nigh unto death; add to this, that he was timid, without any appearance or prestige, without any of those personal advantages, calculated to produce an impression, so much so, that it was a marvel people were not repelled by such uninviting an exterior. Elsewhere, he mysteriously hints at a secret affliction, "a thorn in the flesh," which he compares to a messenger of Satan sent, with God's permission, to buffet him, "lest he should be exalted above measure." Thrice he besought the Lord to deliver him, and thrice the Lord replied, "My grace is sufficient for thee." This was evidently some bodily infirmity; for it is not to be supposed that he refers to the allurements of carnal delights, since he himself informs us in another place that he was insensible to these. It would seem he was never married: the thorough coldness of his temperament, the result of the intense ardour of his brain, manifests itself throughout his life, and he boasts of it with an assurance savouring of affectation, to an extent which is disagreeable.

At an early age he came to Jerusalem, and entered, as it is said, the school of Gamaliel the Elder. This Gamaliel was the most cultured man in Jerusalem. As the name of Pharisee was applied to every prominent Jew who was not of a priestly family, Gamaliel was taken for a member of that sect. Yet he had none of its narrow and exclusive spirit. He was a liberal, intelligent man, acquainted with Greek, and understood the heathen. It is possible that the broad ideas professed by Paul after he received Christianity, were a reminiscence of the teachings of his first master; yet it must be admitted that at first he had not learned much moderation from him. Breathing the heated atmosphere of Jerusalem, he became an ardent fanatic. He was the leader of a young, unbending, and enthusiastic Pharisee party, which carried to extremes their keen attachment for the national traditions of the past. He had not known Jesus, and was not present at the bloody scene of Golgotha; but we have seen him take an active part in the murder of Stephen, and among the foremost of the persecutors of the Church. He breathed only threatenings and slaughter, and went up and down Jerusalem bearing a mandate which authorized and legalized all his brutalities. He went from synagogue to synagogue, compelling the more timid to deny the name of Jesus, and subjecting others to scourging or imprisonment. When the Church of Jerusalem was dispersed, his persecutions were extended to the neighbouring cities. Exasperated by the progress of the new faith, and learning that there was a group of the faithful at Damascus, he obtained from the high-priest Theophilus, son of Hanan, letters to the synagogue of that city, which conferred on him the power of arresting all evil-thinking persons, and of bringing them bound to Jerusalem.

The confusion of Roman authority in Judea, explains these arbitrary vexations. The insane Caligula was in power, and the administrative service was everywhere distracted. Fanaticism had gained all that the civil power had lost. After the dismissal of Pilate, and the concessions made to the natives by Lucius Vitellius, the country was permitted to govern itself according to its own laws. A thousand local tyrannies profited by the weakness of an indifferent authority. In addition , Damascus had just passed into the hands of Hartat, or Hâreth, whose capital was at Petra. This bold and powerful prince, having beaten Herod Antipas, and withstood the Roman forces, commanded by the imperial legate, Lucius Vitellius, had been marvellously aided by fortune. The news of the death of Tiberius (16th March, 37), had suddenly arrested the march of Vitellius. Hâreth seized Damascus, and established there an ethnarch or governor. The Jews at the time of this new occupation formed a numerous party at Damascus, where they carried on an extensive system of proselytizing, especially among the females. It was thought advisable to seek to make them contented; and the best method of doing so was to grant concessions to their autonomy, and every concession was simply a permission to commit further religious violences. To punish and even kill those who did not think with them, was their idea of independence and liberty.

Paul, in leaving Jerusalem, followed doubtless the usual road, and crossed the Jordan at the "Bridge of the Daughters of Jacob." His mental excitement was now at its greatest height, and he was at times troubled and shaken in his faith. Passion is not a rule of faith. The passionate man flies from one extreme creed to another, but always retains the same impetuosity. Now, like all strong minds, Paul almost loved that which he hated. Was he sure, after all, that he was not thwarting the designs of God? Perhaps he remembered the calm, dispassionate views of his master Gamaliel. Often these ardent souls experienced terrible revulsions. He felt a liking for those whom ho had tortured. The more these excellent sectarians were known, the better they were liked; and none had greater opportunities of knowing them better than their persecutor. At times he fancied he saw the sweet face of the Master who inspired his disciples with no much patience, regarding him with an air of pity and tender reproach. He was also much impressed by the accounts of the apparitions of Jesus, describing him as an ariel being who was at times visible; for at the epochs and in the countries when and where there is a tendency to the marvellous, miraculous recitals influence equally each opposing party. The Mahommedans, for instance, are afraid of the miracles of Elias; and, like the Christians, pray to St. George and St. Anthony for supernatural cures.

Having crossed Ithuria, and while in the great plain of Damascus, Paul, with several companions, all, as it appears, journeying on foot, approached the city, and had probably already reached the beautiful gardens which surrounded it The time was noon. The road from Jerusalem to Damascus has in nowise changed. It is the one, which, leaving Damascus in a south-westerly direction, crosses the beautiful plain watered by the streams flowing into the Abana and the Pharpar, and upon which are now marshalled the villages of Dareya, Kaukab, and Sasa. The exact locality of which we speak, which was the scene of one of the most important facts in the history of humanity, could not have been beyond Kaukab (four hours from Damascus). It is even probable that the point in question was much nearer the city, perhaps about Dareya (an hour and a half from Damascus), or between Dareya and Meidan. The great city lay before Paul, and the outlines of several of its edifices could be dimly traced through the thick foliage: behind him towered the majestic dome of Hermon, with its ridges of snow, making it resemble the bald head of an old man; upon his right were the Hauran, the two little parallel chains which enclose the lower course of the Pharpar, and the tumuli of the region of the lakes; and upon his left were the outer spurs of the Anti-Libanus stretching out to Mt Hermon. The impression produced by these richly-cultivated fields and beautiful orchards, separated from one another by trenches and laden with the most delicious fruits, is that of peace and happiness. Let one imagine to himself a shady road, passing through rich soil, crossed at intervals by irrigating canals, bordered by declivities and serpentining through forests of olives, walnuts, apricots, and prunes; trees draped by graceful festoons of vines; and then will be presented to the mind the image of the scene of that remarkable event which has exerted so great an influence upon the faith of the world. In the environs of Damascus one can scarcely believe oneself in the East; especially after leaving the arid and burning regions of the Gaulonitide and of Ithuria. It is joy indeed to meet once more the works of man and the blessings of Heaven. From the most remote antiquity until the present time this zone, which surrounds Damascus with freshness and health, has had but one name, has inspired but one dream,--that of the "Paradise of God."

if Paul experienced these terrible visions, it was because he carried them in his heart. Every step in his journey towards Damascus awakened in him painful perplexities. The odious part of executioner, which he was about to undertake, became insupportable. The houses which he saw through the trees were, perhaps, those of his victims. This thought beset him and delayed his steps; he did not wish to advance; he seemed to be resisting a mysterious impulse which pressed him forward. The fatigue of the journey, joined to this pre-occupation of mind, overwhelmed him. He had, it would seem, inflamed eyes, probably the beginning of ophthalmia. In these prolonged journeys, the last hours are the most trying. All the debilitating effects of the days just past accumulate, the nerves relax their power, and a re-action sets in. Perhaps, also, the sudden passage from the sun-smitten clam to the cool shades of the gardens enhanced his suffering condition and seriously excited the fanatical traveller. Dangerous fevers, accompanied by delirium, are quite sudden in these latitudes, and in a few minutes the victim is prostrated as by a thunder-stroke. When the crisis is over, the sufferer retains only the impression of a period of profound darkness, relieved at intervals by dashes of light in which he has seen images outlined against a dark background. It is quite certain that a sudden stroke instantly deprived Paul of his remaining consciousness, and threw him senseless on the ground. From the accounts which we have of this singular event, it is impossible to say whether any exterior fact led to the crisis to which Christianity owes its most ardent apostle. But in such cases, the exterior fact is of little importance. It was the state of St. Paul's mind; it was his remorse on his approach to the city in which he was to commit the most signal of his misdeeds, which were the true causes of his conversion. For my part, I much prefer the hypothesis of an affair personal to Paul, and experienced by him alone. It is not, however, improbable that a thunder-storm suddenly burst forth. The flanks of Mount Hermon are the point of formation for thunder-showers which are unequalled in violence. The most unimpressionable person cannot observe without emotion these terrible hurricanes of fire. It ought to be remembered that in ancient times accidents from lightning were considered divine revelations; that with the ideas regarding providential interference then prevalent, nothing was fortuitous; and that every man was accustomed to view the natural phenomena around him as having a direct relation to himself. The Jews in particular always considered that thunder was the voice of God, and that lightning was the fire of God. Paul at this juncture was in a state of great excitement, and it was but natural that he should interpret as the voice of the storm the thoughts which were passing in his mind. That a delirious fever, resulting from a sun-stroke or an attack of ophthalmia, had suddenly seized him; that a flash of lightning blinded him for a time; that a peal of thunder had produced a cerebral commotion, temporarily depriving him of sight--it matters little. The recollections of the apostle on this point appear to be rather confused; he was persuaded that the incident was supernatural, and such a conviction would not permit him to entertain any clear consciousness of material circumstances. Such cerebral commotions produce sometimes a sort of retroactive effect, and completely perturb the recollections of the moments immediately preceding the crisis. Paul, moreover, elsewhere informs us that he was subject to visions; and a circumstance, insignificant as it might appear to others, was sufficient to make him beside himself.

And what did he see, what did he hear, while he was a prey to these hallucinations? He saw the countenance which had haunted him for several days; he saw the phantom of which so much had been told. He saw Jesus himself, who spoke to him in Hebrew, saying, "Saul, Saul, why persecutest thou me? "Impetuous natures pass instantaneously from one extreme to the other. For them there exists solemn moments which change the course of a lifetime, which colder natures never experience. Reflective men do not change, but are transformed; ardent men, on the contrary, change and are not transformed. Dogmatism is a shirt of Nessus which they cannot tear off. They must have a pretext for loving and hating. Our western races alone have been able to produce those minds--large yet delicate, strong yet flexible--which no empty affirmation can mislead, no momentary illusion carry away. The East has never produced men of this stamp. Instantly, the most thrilling thoughts rushed in upon the soul of Paul. Awakened to the enormity of his conduct, he saw himself stained with the blood of Stephen, and this martyr appeared to him as his father, his initiator into the new faith. Touched to the quick, his sentiments experienced a revulsion as complete as it was sudden; still, all this was but a new phase of fanaticism. His sincerity and his need of an absolute faith precluded any middle course; it was already clear that he would one day exhibit in the cause of Jesus the same fiery zeal he had shown in persecuting him.

With the assistance of his companions, who led him by the hand, Paul entered Damascus. His friends took him to the house of a certain Judas, who lived in the street called Straight, a grand colonnaded avenue over a mile long and a hundred feet broad, which crossed the city from east to west, and the line of which yet forms, with a few deviations, the principal artery of Damascus. The blindness and delirium had not yet subsided. For three days Paul, a prey to fever, neither ate nor drank. It is easy to imagine what passed during this crisis in that burning brain maddened by violent disease. Mention was made in his hearing of the Christians of Damascus, and in particular of a certain Ananias, who appeared to be the chief of the community. Paul had often heard of the miraculous powers of new believers over maladies, and he became impressed by the idea that the imposition of hands would cure him of his disease. His eyes all this time were highly inflamed, and in his delirious imaginings he thought he saw Ananias enter the room and make to him the sign familiar to Christians. From that moment he felt convinced he should owe his recovery to Ananias. The latter, informed of this, visited the sick man, spoke kindly, addressed him as his "brother," and laid his hands upon his head; and from that hour peace returned to the soul of Paul. He believed himself cured; and as his ailment had been purely nervous, he was indeed cured. Little crusts or scales, it is said, fell from his eyes; he partook of food and recovered his strength.

Almost immediately after this he was baptized. The doctrines of the Church were so simple that he had nothing new to learn, and became at once a Christian and a perfect one., And from whom else did he need instruction? Had not Jesus himself appeared to him? He too, like James and Peter, had had his vision of the risen Jesus. He had learned everything by direct revelation. Here the fierce and unconquerable nature of Paul was again made manifest. Smitten down on the public highway, he was willing to submit, but only to Jesus, to that Jesus who had left the right hand of the Father to convert and instruct him. Such was the foundation of his faith; and such will be the starting point of his pretensions.

He will maintain that it was by design that he did not go to Jerusalem immediately after his conversion, and place himself in relations with those who had been apostles before him; he will main-tam that he has received a special revelation, for which he is indebted to no human agency; that, like the Twelve, he is an apostle by divine institution and by direct commission from Jesus; that his doctrine is the true one, although an angel from heaven should say to the contrary.

An immense danger found entrance through this proud man into the little society of the poor in spirit who until now had constituted Christianity. It will be a real miracle if his violence and his inflexible personality do not overthrow everything. But at the same time his boldness, his initiative force, his prompt decision, will be precious elements when brought into contact with the narrow, timid, and indecisive spirit of the saints of Jerusalem! Certainly, if Christianity had remained confined to these good people, shut up in a conventicle of elect, leading a communistic life, it would, like Essenism, have faded away, leaving scarcely a trace behind. It is this ungovernable Paul who will secure its success, and who at the risk of every peril will boldly launch it on the high seas. By the side of the obedient faithful, accepting his creed from his superior without questioning him, there will be a Christian disengaged from all authority who will believe only from personal conviction. Protestantism thus existed five years after the death of Jesus, and St. Paul was its illustrious founder. Surely Jesus had not anticipated such disciples; and it was such as these who would most largely contribute to the vitality of his work and insure its eternity.

Violent natures disposed to proselytism only change the object of their passion. As ardent for the new faith as he had been for the old, St. Paul, like Omar, dropped in one day his part of persecutor for that of apostle. He did not return to Jerusalem, where his position towards the Twelve would have been peculiar and delicate. He tarried at Damascus and in the Hauran for three years (38-41), preaching that Jesus was the Son of God. Herod Agrippa I. held the sovereignty of the Hauran and of the neighbouring countries; but his power was at several points superseded by that of a Nabatian king, Hâreth. The decay of the Roman power in Syria had delivered to the ambitious Arab the great and rich city of Damascus, besides a part of the countries beyond Jordan and Mount Hermon, then just being opened up to civilization. Another emir, Soheyn, perhaps a relative or lieutenant of Hâreth, had received from Caligula the command of Ithuria. It was in the midst of this great awakening of the Arab nation, upon this strange soil, where an energetic race manifested with great success its feverish activity, that Paul first displayed the ardour of his apostolic soul. Perhaps the material and so remarkable a movement which revolutionized the country was prejudicial to a theory and to a preaching wholly idealistic, and founded on a belief of a near approach of the end of the world. Indeed, there exists no traces of an Arabian Church founded by St. Paul. If the region of the Hauran became, towards the year 70, one of the most important centres of Christianity, it was owing to the emigration of Christians from Palestine; and it was the Ebonites, the enemies of St. Paul, who had in this region their principal establishment.

At Damascus, where there were many Jews, the teachings of Paul received more attention. In the synagogues of that city he entered into warm arguments to prove that Jesus was the Christ. Great indeed was the astonishment of the faithful on beholding him who had persecuted their brethren at Jerusalem, and who had come to Damascus "to bring themselves bound unto the chief-priests," now appearing as their chief defender. His audacity and personal peculiarities almost alarmed them. He was alone; he sought no counsel; he established no school; and the emotions he excited were those of curiosity rather than those of sympathy. The faithful felt that he was a brother, but a brother distinguished by singular peculiarities. They believed him to be incapable of treachery; but amiable and mediocre natures always experience sentiments of mistrust and alarm when brought in contact with powerful and original minds, who they know must one day supersede them.

CHAPTER XI

PEACE AND INTERIOR DEVELOPMENTS OF THE CHURCH OF JUDEA

From the year 38 to the year 44 no persecution seems to have been directed against the Church. The faithful were, no doubt, far more prudent than before the death of Stephen, and avoided speaking in public. Perhaps, too, the troubles of the Jews who, during all the second part of the reign of Caligula, were at variance with that prince, contributed to favour the nascent sect. The Jews, in fact, became active persecutors in proportion to the good understanding they maintained with the Romans. To buy or to recompense their tranquility, the latter were led to augment their privileges, and in particular the one to which they clung most closely--the right of killing persons whom they regarded as inimical to their law. But the period at which we have arrived was one of the most stormy in the turbulent history of this singular people.

The antipathy which the Jews, in consequence of their moral superiority, their odd customs, as well as their harshness, excited in the populations among which they lived, was at its height, especially at Alexandria. This accumulated hatred, for its own satisfaction, took advantage of the coming to the imperial throne of one of the most dangerous lunatics that ever wore a crown. Caligula, at least after the malady which completed his mental derangement (October, 37), presented the frightful spectacle of a maniac governing the world endowed with the most enormous powers ever put into the hands of any man. The atrocious law of Cæsarism rendered such horrors possible, and left the governed without remedy. This lasted three years and three mouths. One cannot without shame set down in a serious history that which is now to follow. Before entering upon the recital of these saturnalia we cannot but exclaim with Suetonius: Reliqua ut de monstro narranda sunt.

The most inoffensive pastime of this madman was the care of his own divinity. In order to do this he used a sort of bitter irony, a mixture of the serious and the comic (for the monster was not wanting in wit), a sort of profound derision of the human race. The enemies of the Jews were not slow to perceive the advantage they might gain from this mania. The religious abasement of the world was such that not a protest was heard against the sacrilege of the Cæsar; every cult hastened to bestow upon him the titles and the honours which it had reserved for its gods. It is to the eternal glory of the Jews that, amidst this ignoble idolatry, they uttered the cry of outraged conscience. The principle of intolerance which was in them, and which led them to so many cruel acts, exhibited here its bright side. Alone in affirming their religion to be the absolute religion, they would not bend to the odious caprice of the tyrant. This was the source of endless troubles for them. It needed only that there should be in a city some person discontented with the synagogue, spiteful, or simply mischievous, to bring about frightful consequences. At one time people would insist on erecting an altar to Caligula in the very place where the Jews could least of all suffer it? At another, a troupe of the rag-tags would collect, and cry out against the Jews for being the only people who refused to place the statue of the emperor in their houses of prayer. Anon, people would run to the synagogues and the oratories; they would install there the bust of Caligula; and the unfortunate Jews were placed in the alternative of either renouncing their religion, or be guilty of high treason. Thence followed frightful vexations.

Such pleasantries had been several times repeated when a still more diabolical idea was suggested to the emperor. This was to place a colossal golden statue of himself in the sanctuary of the temple at Jerusalem, and to have the temple itself dedicated to his own divinity. This odious design very nearly hastened by thirty years the revolt and the ruin of the Jewish nation. The moderation of the imperial legate, Publius Petronius, and the intervention of King Herod Agrippa, a favourite of Caligula, averted the catastrophe. But until the moment in which the sword of Chæræa delivered the earth from the most execrable tyrant it had as yet endured, the Jews lived everywhere in terror. Philo has preserved for us the monstrous scene which occurred when the deputation of which he was the chief was admitted to see the emperor. Caligula received them during a visit he was paying to the villas of Mæcenas and of Lamia, near the sea, in the environs of Pozzuoli. On that day he was in a vein of gaiety. Helicon, his favourite joker, had been relating to him all sorts of buffooneries about the Jews. "Ah, then, it is you," said he to them, with a bitter smile, and showing his teeth, "who alone will not recognize me for a god, and who prefer to adore one whose name you cannot even utter!" He accompanied these words with a horrible blasphemy. The Jews trembled; their Alexandrian enemies were the first to take up speech:

"You would still more, O Sire, detest these people and all their nation, if you knew the aversion they have for you; for they alone have refused to offer sacrifices for your health when all the other peoples have done so!" At these words, the Jews exclaimed that it was a calumny, and that they had three times offered for the prosperity of the emperor the most solemn sacrifices their religion would allow. "Yes," said Caligula, with comical seriousness, "you have sacrificed; so far, good; but it was not to me that you sacrificed. What advantage do I derive therefrom?" Thereupon, turning his back upon them, he strode through the apartments, giving orders for repairs, going up and down stairs incessantly. The unfortunate deputies, and among them Philo, eighty years of age, the most venerable man of the time, perhaps-- Jesus being no longer living--followed him up and down, trembling and out of breath, the object of derision to the assembled company. Caligula turning suddenly, said to them: "By the by, why will you not eat pork?" The flatterers burst into laughter! some of the officers, in a severe tone, reminded them that in laughing immoderately they offended the majesty of the emperor. The Jews were stunned; one of them awkwardly said: "There are some persons who do not eat lamb." "Ah!" said the emperor, "such people are right; lamb is insipid." Some time after, he made a show of inquiring into their business; then, when they had just begun to inform him of it, he left them and went off to give orders about the decorations of a hall which he wanted to have adorned with specular stones. Returning, he affected an air of moderation, and asked the deputation if they had anything to add; and as the latter resumed their interrupted discourse, he turned his back upon them to go and see another hall which he was ornamenting with paintings. This game of tiger sporting with its prey lasted for hours. The Jews were expecting death; but at the last moment the monster withdrew his fangs. "Well," said Caligula, while repassing "these folks are decidedly less guilty than pitiable for not believing in my divinity." Thus could the gravest questions be treated under the horrible regime created by the baseness of the world, cherished by a soldiery and a populace about equally vile, and maintained by the dissoluteness of nearly all.

We can easily understand how so painful a situation must have taken from the Jews of the time of Marullus much of that audacity which made them speak so boldly to Pilate. Already almost entirely detached from the temple, the Christians must have been much less alarmed than the Jews at the sacrilegious projects of Caligula. Their numbers were, moreover, too few for their existence to be known at Rome. The storm at the time of Caligula, like that which resulted in the taking of Jerusalem by Titus, passed over their heads, and was in many regards serviceable to them. Everything which weakened Jewish independence was favourable to them, since it was so much taken away from the power of a suspicious orthodoxy, which maintained its pretensions by severe penalties.

This period of peace was fruitful in interior developments. The nascent church was divided into three provinces; Judea, Samaria, Galilee, to which Damascus was no doubt attached. The primacy of Jerusalem was uncontested. The church of this city, which had been dispersed after the death of Stephen, was quickly reconstituted. The apostles had never quitted the city. The brothers of the Lord continued to reside there, and to wield a great authority. It does not seem that this new church of Jerusalem was organized in so strict a manner as the first: the community of goods was not strictly re-established in it. But there was founded a large fund for the poor, to which was added the contributions sent by minor churches to the mother church, which latter was the origin and permanent source of their faith.

Peter undertook frequent apostolical journeys in the environs of Jerusalem. He had always a great reputation as a thaumaturgist. At Lydda in particular he was reputed to have cured a paralytic named Æneas, a miracle which is said to have led to numerous conversions in the plain of Saron. From Lydda he repaired to Joppa, a city which appears to have been a centre for Christianity. Cities of workmen, of sailors, of poor people, where the orthodox Jews were not dominant, were those in which the new sect found people the best disposed towards them. Peter made a long sojourn at Joppa, at the house of a tanner named Simon, who dwelt near the sea. Working in leather was an industry regarded as unclean, according to the Mosaic code; it was not lawful to associate with those who carried it on, so that the curriers had to reside in a district by themselves. Peter, in selecting such a host, gave a proof of his indifference to Jewish prejudices, and worked for that ennoblement of petty callings which constitutes a grand feature of the Christian spirit.

The organization of works of charity was soon actively entered upon. The church of Joppa possessed a woman most appropriately named in Aramaic, Tabitha (gazelle), and in Greek, Dorcas, who consecrated all her time to the poor. She was rich, it seems, and distributed her wealth in alms. This worthy lady had formed a society of pious widows, who passed their days with her in weaving clothes for the poor. As the schism between Christianity and Judaism was not yet consummated, it is probable that the Jews participated in the benefit of these acts of charity. The "saints and widows" were thus pious persons, doing good to all, a sort of friars and nuns, whom only the most austere devotees of a pedantic orthodoxy could suspect, fraticelli, loved by the people, devout, charitable, full of pity.

The germ of those associations of women, which are one of the glories of Christianity, thus existed in the first churches of Judea. At Jaffa commenced those societies of veiled women, clothed in linen, who were destined to continue through centuries the tradition of charitable secrets. Tabitha was the mother of a family which will have no end as long as there are miseries to be relieved and feminine instincts to be gratified. It is related further on, that Peter raised her from the dead. Alas! death, however unmindful and revolting, in such a case, is inflexible. When the most exquisite soul has sped, the decree is irrevocable; the most excellent woman can no more respond to the invitation of the friendly voices which would fain recall her, than can the vulgar and frivolous. But ideas are not subject to the conditions of matter. Virtue and goodness escape the fangs of death. Tabitha had no need to be resuscitated. For the sake of a few days more of this sad life, why disturb her sweet and eternal repose? Let her sleep in peace; the day of the just will come!

In these very mixed cities, the problem of the admission of Pagans to baptism was propounded with much persistency. Peter was strongly pre-occupied by it. One day while he was praying at Joppa, on the terrace of the tanner's house, having before him the sea that was soon going to bear the new faith to all the empire, he had a prophetic ecstasy. Plunged into a state of reverie, he thought he experienced a sensation of hunger, and asked for something to eat. And while they were making it ready for him, he saw the heavens opened, and a cloth tied at the four corners descend. Looking inside the cloth he saw there all sorts of animals, and thought he heard a voice saying to him: "Kill and eat" On his objecting that many of these animals were impure, he was answered: "Call not that unclean which God has cleansed." This, as it appears, was repeated three times. Peter was persuaded that these animals represented the mass of the Gentiles, which God himself had just rendered fit for the holy communion of the Kingdom of God.

An occasion was soon presented for applying these principles. From Joppa, Peter went to Cesarea. There he came in contact with a centurion named Cornelius. The garrison of Cesarea was formed, at least in part, of one of those cohorts composed of Italian volunteers which were called Italicæ. The complete name which this term represented may have been cohors prima Augustus Italica civium Romamorum. Cornelius was a centurion of this cohort, consequently an Italian and a Roman citizen. He was a man of probity, who had long felt himself drawn towards the monotheistic worship of the Jews. He prayed; gave alms; practised, in a word, those precepts of natural religion which are taken for granted by Judaism; but he was not circumcised; he was not a proselyte in any sense whatever; he was a pious Pagan, an Israelite in heart, nothing more. His whole household and some soldiers of his command were, it is said, in the same state of mind. Cornelius applied for admission into the new Church. Peter, whose nature was open and benevolent, granted it to him, and the centurion was baptized.

Perhaps Peter at first saw no difficulty in this; but on his return to Jerusalem he was severely reproached for it. He had openly violated the Law; he had gone amongst the uncircumcized and had eaten with them. The question was an important one; it was no other than whether the Law was abolished; whether it was permissible to violate it in proselytism; whether Gentiles could be freely received into the Church. Peter related in self defence the vision he had at Joppa. Subsequently the fact of the centurion served as an argument in the great question of the baptism of the uncircumcized. To give it more importance it was pretended that each phase of this important business had been marked by a revelation from heaven. It was related that after long prayers Cornelius had seen an angel who ordered him to go and inquire for Peter at Joppa; that the symbolical vision of Peter took place at the very hour of the arrival of the messengers from Cornelius; that, moreover, God himself had undertaken to legitimize all that had been done, seeing that the Holy Ghost had descended upon Cornelius, and upon his household the latter having spoken strange tongues and sung psalms after the fashion of the other believers. Was it natural to refuse baptism to persons who had received the Holy Ghost?

The Church of Jerusalem was still exclusively composed of Jews and of proselytes. The Holy Ghost being shed upon the uncircumcized before baptism, appeared an extraordinary fact. It is probable that there existed thenceforward a party opposed in principle to the admission of Gentiles, and that all did not accept the explanations of Peter. The author of the Acts would have us believe that the approbation was unanimous. But in a few years we shall see the question revived with much greater intensity. This matter of the good centurion was, perhaps, like that of the Ethiopian eunuch, accepted as an exceptional case, justified by a revelation and an express order from God. Still the matter was far from being settled. This was the first controversy which had taken place in the bosom of the Church; the paradise of interior peace had lasted for six or seven years.

About the year 40, the great question upon which depended all the future of Christianity appears thus to have been propounded. Peter and Philip took a very just view of what was the true solution, and baptized Pagans. It is difficult, no doubt, in the two accounts given us by the author of the Acts on this subject, and which are partly borrowed one from the other, not to recognize an argument. The author of the Acts belonged to a party of conciliation, favourable to the introduction of Pagans into the Church, and who was not willing to confess the violence of the divisions to which the affair gave rise. One feels strongly that in writing the account of the eunuch, of the centurion, and even of the conversion of the Samaritans, this author means not only to narrate facts, but also seeks special precedents for an opinion.

On the other hand, we cannot admit that he invents the facts which he narrates. The conversions of the eunuch of Candace, and of the centurion Cornelius, are probably real facts, which are presented and transformed according to the needs of the thesis in view of which the book of the Acts was composed.

Paul, who was destined, some ten or twelve years later, to give to this discussion so decisive a bearing, had not yet meddled with it. He was in the Hauran, or at Damascus, preaching, refuting the Jews, placing at the service of the new faith the same ardour he had shown in combatting it. The fanaticism, of which he had once been the instrument, was not long in pursuing him in turn. The Jews resolved to kill him. They obtained from the ethnarch, who governed Damascus in the name of Hâreth, an order to arrest him. Paul hid himself. It was known that he was to leave the city; the ethnarch, who wanted to please the Jews, placed detachments at the gates to seize his person; but the brethren secured his escape by night, letting him down in a basket from the window of a house which over-looked the ramparts.

Having escaped this danger, Paul turned his eyes towards Jerusalem. He had been a Christian for three years, and had not yet seen the apostles. His stern, unyielding character, prone to isolation, had made him at first turn his back as it were upon the great family into which he had just entered in spite of himself, and prefer for his first apostolate a new country, in which he would find no colleague. There was awakened in him, how. ever, a desire to see Peter. He recognized his authority, and designated him, as every one did, by the name of Cephas, "the stone." He repaired then to Jerusalem, taking the same road, whence he had come three years before in a state of mind so different.

His position at Jerusalem was extremely false and embarrassing. It had, no doubt, been understood there that the persecutor had become the most zealous of evangelists, and one of the first defenders of the faith which he had formerly sought to destroy. But there remained great prejudices against him. Many dreaded on his part some horrible plot. They had seen him so enraged, so cruel, so zealous in entering houses and tearing open family secrets in order to find victims, that he was believed capable of playing an odious farce in order to destroy those whom he hated. He resided, as it seems, in the house of Peter. Many disciples remained deaf to his advances, and shrank from him. Barnabas, a man of courage and will, took at this moment a decisive part. As a Cypriote and a new convert, he understood better than the Galilean disciples the position of Paul. He came to meet him, took him by the hand, introduced him to the most suspicious, and became his surety. By this sagacious and far-seeing act, Barnabas earned at the hands of the Christian worlds the highest degree of merit. It was he who appreciated Paul; it is to him that the Church owes the most extraordinary of her founders. The advantageous friendship of these two apostolic men, a friendship that no cloud ever tarnished, notwithstanding many differences in opinion, afterwards led to their association in the work of missions to the Gentiles. This grand association dates, in one sense, from Paul's first sojourn at Jerusalem. Amongst the sources of the faith of the world, we must count the generous movement of Barnabas, who stretched out his hand to the suspected and forsaken Paul; the profound intuition which led him to discover the soul of an apostle under that downcast mien; the frankness with which be broke the ice and levelled the obstacles raised between the convert and his new brethren by the unfortunate antecedents of the former, and perhaps, also, by certain traits in his character.

Paul, however, systematically avoided seeing the apostles. He himself says so, and he takes the trouble to affirm it with an oath; he saw only Peter, and James the brother of the Lord. His sojourn lasted but two weeks. It is certainly possible that at the time in which he wrote the Epistle to the Galatians (towards 56), Paul may have found himself constrained by the exigencies of the moment, to alter a little the nature of his relations with the apostles; to represent them as more harsh, more imperious, than they were in reality. Towards 56 the essential point for him to prove was that he had received nothing from Jerusalem--that he was in no wise the mandatory of the Council of the Twelve established in this city. His attitude at Jerusalem would have been the proud and lofty bearing of a master, who avoids relations with other masters in order not to have the air of subordinating himself to them, and not the humble and repentant mien of a sinner ashamed of the past, as the author of the Acts represents. We cannot believe that from the year 41 Paul was animated by this jealous care to preserve his own individuality, which he showed at a later day. The few interviews he had with the apostles, and the briefness of his sojourn at Jerusalem, arose probably from his embarrassment in the presence of people, whose nature was different from his own, and who were full of prejudices against him, rather than from a refined policy, which would have revealed to him fifteen years in advance the disadvantages there might be in his frequenting their society.

In reality, that which must have erected a sort of wall between the apostles and Paul, was the difference of their character and of their education. The apostles were all Galileans; they had not been at the great Jewish school; they had seen Jesus; they remembered his words; they were good and pious folk, at times a little solemn and simple-hearted. Paul was a man of action, full of fire, only moderately mystical, enrolled, as by a superior power, in a sect which was not that of his first adoption. Revolt, protestation, were his habitual sentiments. His Jewish education was much superior to that of all his new brethren. But not having heard Jesus, not having been appointed by him, he was, according to Christian ideas, greatly inferior.

Now Paul was not the man to accept a secondary place. His haughty temperament required a position for itself. It was probably about this time that there sprang up in him the singular idea that after all he had nothing to envy those who had known Jesus, and had been chosen by him, since he also had seen Jesus, and had received from Jesus a direct revelation and the commission of his apostleship. Even those who had been honoured by the personal appearance of the risen Christ were no better than he was. Although the last apostle, his vision had been none the less remarkable. It had taken place under circumstances which gave it a peculiar stamp of importance and of distinction. A signal error! The echo of the voice of Jesus was found in the discourses of the humblest of his disciples. With all his Jewish science, Paul could not make up for the immense disadvantage under which he was placed in consequence of his tardy initiation. The Christ whom he had seen on the road to Damascus was not, whatever he might say, the Christ of Galilee; it was the Christ of his imagination, of his own conception. Although he may have been most industrious in learning the words of the Master, it is clear that he was only a disciple at second-hand. If Paul had met Jesus during his life, it is doubtful whether he would have attached himself to him. His doctrine must be his own, not that of Jesus; the revelations of which he was so proud were the fruit of his own brain.

These ideas, which he dared not as yet communicate, rendered his stay at Jerusalem disagreeable. At the end of a fortnight he took leave of Peter, and went away. He had seen so few people that he ventured to say that no one in the Churches of Judea knew him by sight, or knew aught of him, save by hearsay. At a subsequent period he attributed this sudden departure to a revelation. He related that being one day in the temple praying, he was in an ecstasy, and saw Jesus in person, and received from him the order to quit Jerusalem immediately, "because they were not inclined to receive his testimony." As a compensation for these hard hearts, Jesus had promised him the Apostolate of distant nations, and an auditory who would listen more willingly to his words. Those who would fain hide the traces of the many ruptures caused by the coming of this intractable disciple into the church, pretended that Paul remained a long while at Jerusalem, living with the brethren on a footing of the most complete amity; but that, having begun to preach to the Hellenic Jews, he was nearly killed by them, so that the brethren had to protect him, and to send him safely to Cæsarea.

It is probable, indeed, that from Jerusalem he did repair to Cæsarea. But he stayed there only a short time, and then set out to traverse Syria, and afterwards Cilicia. He was, no doubt, already preaching, but it was on his own account, and without any understanding with anybody. Tarsus, his native place, was his habitual sojourn during this period of his apostolic life, which we may reckon as having lasted about two years. It is possible that the Churches of Cilicia owed their origin to him. Still, the life of Paul was not at this epoch that which we see it to be subsequently. He did not assume the title of an apostle, which latter was then strictly reserved to the Twelve. It was only from the time of his association with Barnabas (in 45) that he entered upon that career of sacred peregrinations and preachings which were to make of him the typical travelling missionary.

CHAPTER XII

FOUNDATION OF THE CHURCH OF ANTIOCH

The new faith was spread from place to place with marvellous rapidity. The members of the church of Jerusalem, who had been dispersed immediately after the death of Stephen, pushing their conquests along the coast of Phoenicia, reached Cyprus and Antioch. They were at first guided by the sole principle of preaching the Gospel to the Jews only.

Antioch, "the metropolis of the East," the third city of the world, was the centre of this Christian movement in northern Syria. It was a city with a population of more than 500,000 souls, almost as large as Paris before its recent extensions, and the residence of the Imperial Legate of Syria. Suddenly advanced to a high degree of splendour by the Seleucidæ, it reaped great benefit from the Roman occupation. In general, the Seleucidæ were in advance of the Romans in the taste for theatrical decorations, as applied to great cities. Temples, aqueducts, baths, basilicas, nothing was wanting at Antioch in what constituted a grand Syrian city of that period. The streets, flanked by colonnades, their cross-roads being decorated with statues, had more of symmetry and regularity than anywhere else. A Corso, ornamented with four rows of columns, forming two covered galleries, with a wide avenue in the midst, traversed the city from one side to the other, the length of which was thirty-six stadia (more than a league). But Antioch not only possessed immense edifices of public utility; it had also that which few of the Syrian cities possessed--the noblest specimens of Grecian art, beautiful statues, classical works of a delicacy of detail which the age was no longer capable of imitating. Antioch, from its foundation, had been wholly a Grecian city. The Macedonians of Antigone and Seleucus had brought with them into that country of the Lower Orontes their most lively recollections, their worship, and the names of their country. The Grecian mythology was there adopted as it were in a second home; they pretended to show in the country a crowd of "holy places" forming part of this mythology. The city was full of the worship of Apollo and of the nymphs. Daphne, an enchanting place two short hours from the city, reminded the conquerors of the pleasantest fictions. It was a sort of plagiarism, a counterfeit of the myths of the mother country, analogous to that which the primitive tribes carried with them in their travels--their mythical geography, their Berecyntha, their Arvanda, their Ida, their Olympus. These Greek fables was for them an antiquated religion, scarcely more serious than the Metamorphoses of Ovid. The ancient religions of the country, particularly that of Mount Cassius, contributed a little seriousness to it. But Syrian levity, Babylonian charlatanism, and all the impostures of Asia, mingling at this border of the two worlds, had made Antioch the capital of all lies, and the sink of every description of infamy.

In fact, besides the Greek population, which in no part of the East (with the exception of Alexandria) was as numerous as here, Antioch counted amongst its population a considerable number of native Syrians, speaking Syriac. These natives were a low class, inhabiting the suburbs of the great city, and the populous villages which formed a vast suburb all around it--Charandama, Ghisira, Gandigura, and Apate (chiefly Syrian names). Marriages between the Syrians and the Greeks were common: Seleucus had made naturalization a legal obligation binding on every stranger establishing himself in the city, so that Antioch, at the end of three centuries and a half of its existence, became one of the places in the world where race was most blended with race. The degradation of the people was awful. The peculiarity of these centres of moral putrefaction is to reduce all the race of mankind to the same level. The depravity of certain Levantine cities, which are dominated by the spirit of intrigue and delivered up entirely to low cunning, can scarcely give us an idea of the degree of corruption reached by the human race at Antioch. It was an inconceivable medley of mountebanks, quacks, buffoons, magicians, miracle-mongers, sorcerers, false priests; a city of races, games, dances, processions, fetes, revels, of unbridled luxury, of all the follies of the East, of the most unhealthy superstitions and of the fanaticism of the orgy. By turns servile and ungrateful, cowardly and insolent, the people of Antioch were the perfect model of peoples devoted to Cæsarism, without fatherland, without nationality, without family honour, without a name to guard. The great Corso which traversed the city was like a theatre, where rolled, day after day, the waves of a trifling, light-headed, changeable, insurrection-loving populace--a populace sometimes witty, occupied with songs, parodies, squibs, impertinence of all kinds. The city was very literary, but literary only in the literature of rhetoricians. The sights were strange; there were some games in which bands of naked young girls took part, with nothing but a mere fillet around them; at the celebrated festival of Maiouma, troops of courtesans swam in public in basins filled with limpid water. It was like an intoxication, like a dream of Sardanapalus, where all the pleasures, all the debaucheries, not excluding, however, some of a most delicate kind, were unrolled pell-mell. The river of filth, which, making its exit by the mouth of the Orontes, was invading Rome, had here its principal source. Two hundred decurions were employed in regulating the religious ceremonies and celebrations. The municipality possessed great public domains, the rents of which the decemvirs divided amongst the poor citizens. Like all cities of pleasure, Antioch had a lowest class living on the public or on sordid gains.

The beauty of works of art, and the infinite charm of nature, prevented this moral degradation from sinking entirely into hideousness and vulgarity. The site of Antioch is one of the most picturesque in the world. The city occupied the space between the Orontes and the slopes of Mount Silpius, one of the spurs of Mount Cassius. Nothing could equal the abundance and limpidness of the waters. The fortified portion, climbing up perpendicular rocks, by a master-piece of military architecture, enclosed the summit of the mountains, and formed, with the rocks at a tremendous height, an indented crown of marvellous effect. This disposition of ramparts, uniting the advantages of the ancient acropolis with those of the great walled cities, was in general preferred by the generals of Alexander, as one sees in the Pierian Seleucia, in Ephesus, in Smyrna, in Thessalonica. The result was astonishing perspectives. Antioch had within its walls mountains seven hundred feet in height, perpendicular rocks, torrents, precipices, deep ravines, cascades, inaccessible caves; and, in the midst of all these, delightful gardens. A thick wood of myrtles, of flowering box, of laurels, of evergreen plants --and of the richest green-- rocks carpeted with pinks, with hyacinths, and cyclamens, gave to these wild heights the aspect of gardens suspended in the air. The variety of the flowers, the freshness of the turf, composed of an incredible number of delicate grasses, the beauty of the plane trees which border the Orontes, inspire the gaiety, the tinge of sweet odour, with which the fine genius of Chrysostom, Libanius, and Julian was, as it were, intoxicated. On the right bank of the river stretches a vast plain bounded on one side by the Amanus, and the oddly-shaped mountains of Pieria; on the other side by the plateaus of Cyrrhestica, behind which is concealed the dangerous neighbourhood of the Arab and the desert. The valley of the Orontes, which opens to the west, puts this interior basin into communication with the sea, or rather with the vast world, in the bosom of which the Mediterranean has constituted from all time a sort neutral highway and federal bond.

Amongst the different colonies which the liberal ordinances of the Seleucidæ had attracted to the capital of Syria, that of the Jews was one of the most numerous; it dated from the time of Seleucus Nicator, and enjoyed the same rights as the Greeks. Although the Jews had an ethnarch of their own, their relations with the Pagans were very frequent. Here, as at Alexandria, these relations often degenerated into quarrels and aggressions. On the other hand, they afforded a field for an active religious propagandism. The official polytheism becoming more and more insufficient to meet the wants of serious minds, the Grecian philosophy and Judaism attracted all those whom the vain pomps of Paganism could not satisfy. The number of proselytes was considerable. From the first days of Christianity, Antioch had furnished to the Church of Jerusalem one of its most influential members, viz. Nicholas, one of the deacons. There existed there promising germs, which only waited for a ray of grace to cause thorn to burst forth into bloom and to bear the most excellent fruits which had hitherto been produced.

The Church of Antioch owed its foundation to some believers originally from Cyprus and Cyrene, who had already been much engaged in preaching. Up to this time they had only addressed themselves to the Jews. But in a city where pure Jews--Jews who were proselytes, "people fearing God"--or half-Jewish Pagans and pure Pagans, lived together, exclusive preaching restricted to a group of houses, became impossible. That feeling of religious aristocracy on which the Jews of Jerusalem so much prided themselves, did not exist in those large cities, where civilization was altogether of the profane sort, where the scope was greater, and where prejudices were less firmly rooted The Cypriot and Cyrenian missionaries were then constrained to depart from their rule. They preached to the Jews and to the Greeks indifferently.

The dispositions of the Jewish and of the Pagan population appeared at this time to have been very unsatisfactory. But circumstances of another kind probably subserved the new ideas. The earthquake, which had done serious damage to the city on 23rd March, of the year 37, still occupied their minds. The whole city was talking about an impostor named Debborius, who pretended to be able to prevent the recurrence of such accidents by silly talismans. This sufficed to direct preoccupied minds towards supernatural matters. But, be this as it may, the success of the Christian preaching was great. A young, innovating, and ardent Church, full of the future, because it was composed of the most diverse elements, was quickly founded. All the gifts of the Holy Spirit were there poured out, and it was easy to perceive that this new church, emancipated from the strict Mosaism which erected an insuperable barrier around Jerusalem, would become the second cradle of Christianity. Assuredly, Jerusalem must remain for ever the capital of the Christian world; nevertheless, the point of departure of the Church of the Gentiles, the primordial focus of Christian missions, was, in truth, Antioch. It was there that for the first time, a Christian Church was established, freed from the bonds of Judaism; it was there that the great propaganda of the Apostolic age was established; it was there that St. Paul assumed a definite character. Antioch marks the second halting-place of the progress of Christianity and in respect of Christian nobility, neither Rome, nor Alexandria, nor Constantinople can be at all compared with it.

The topography of ancient Antioch is so effaced that we should search in vain over its site, nearly destitute as it is of any vestiges of the antique, for the spot to which to attach such grand recollections. Here, as everywhere, Christianity was, doubtless, established in the poor quarters of the city and among the petty tradespeople. The basilica, which is called "the old" and "apostolic" in the fourth century, was situated in the street called Singon, near the Pantheon. But no one knows where this Pantheon was. Tradition and certain vague analogies would induce us to search the primitive Christian quarter near the gate, which even to-day is still called Paul's gate, Bâb-bolos, and at the foot of the mountain, named by Procopius Stavrin, on which stands the south-east side of the ramparts of Antioch. It was one of the quarters of the town which least abounded in Pagan monuments. There, are still to be seen the remains of ancient sanctuaries dedicated to St. Peter, St. Paul and St. John. These appear to have been the quarter where Christianity was longest maintained after the Mohammedan conquest. There, too, as it appeared, was the quarter of "the saints," in opposition to the profane Antioch. The rock is honey-combed, like a beehive, with grottoes which seem to have been used by the Anchorites. When one walks on these sharp-cut declivities, where, about the fourth century, the good Stylites, disciples at once of India and of Galilee, of Jesus and of Cakya-Mouni, disdainfully contemplated the voluptuous city from the summit of their pillar or from their flower-adorned cavern, it is probable that one is not far from the very spot where Peter and Paul dwelt. The Church of Antioch is the one whose history is most authentic, and least encumbered with fables. Christian tradition, in a city where Christianity was perpetuated with so much vigour, must possess some value.

The prevailing language of the Church of Antioch was the Greek. It is, however, very probable that the suburbs where Syriac was spoken, furnished a great number of converts to the sect. Hence, Antioch already contained the germ of two rival, and, at a later, period, hostile Churches; the one speaking Greek, and now represented by the Syrian Greeks, whether orthodox or Catholics; the other, whose actual representatives are the Maronites, who previously spoke Syriac and guard it still as if it were a sacred tongue. The Maronites, who under their entirely modern Catholicism conceal a high antiquity, are probably the last descendants of those Syrians anterior to Seleucus, of those suburbans, pagani of Ghisra, Charandama, &c., who from the first ages became a separate church, were persecuted by the orthodox emperors as heretics, and escaped into the Libanus, where, from hatred of the Grecian Church and in consequence of deeper sympathies, they allied themselves with the Latins.

As for the converted Jews at Antioch, they too were very numerous. But we are bound to believe that they accepted from the very first a fraternal alliance with the Gentiles. It was then on the shores of the Orontes that the religious fusion of races, dreamed of by Jesus, or to speak more fully, by six centuries of prophets, became a reality.

CHAPTER XIII

THE IDEA OF AN APOSTOLATE TO THE GENTILES.--SAINT BARNABAS

Great was the excitement at Jerusalem when it was learned what had taken place at Antioch. Notwithstanding the kindly wishes of some of the principal members of the Church of Jerusalem, Peter in particular, the Apostolic College continued to be influenced by the meanest ideas. On every occasion when it was told that the glad tidings had been announced to the heathen, some of the elders manifested signs of disappointment. The man who at this time triumphed over this miserable jealously, and who prevented the narrow exclusiveness of the "Hebrews" from ruining the future of Christianity, was Barnabas. He was the most enlightened member of the Church at Jerusalem. He was the chief of the liberal party, which desired progress, and wished the Church to be open to all. He had already powerfully contributed towards removing the mistrust with which Paul was regarded; and he now, also, exercised a marked influence. Sent as a delegate of the apostolical body to Antioch, he inquired into and approved of all that had been done, and declared that the new Church had only to continue in the course upon which it had entered. Conversions were effected in great numbers. The vital and creative force of Christianity appeared to be centred at Antioch. Barnabas, whose zeal sought every occasion to display itself with the utmost vigour, remained there. Antioch thenceforth was his Church, and it was there that he exercised his most influential and important ministry. Christianity has always done injustice to this great man in not placing him in the first rank of her founders. Barnabas was the patron of all good and liberal ideas. His discriminating boldness often served to counterbalance the obstinacy of the narrow-minded Jews who formed the conservative party of Jerusalem.

A magnificent idea sprung up in this noble heart at Antioch. Paul was at Tarsus in forced repose, which, to an active man like him, must have been perfect torture. His false position, his haughtiness, and his exaggerated pretensions, were sapping many of his other and better qualities. He was fretting himself, and remained almost useless. Barnabas knew how to apply to its true work that force which was wasting away in this unhealthy and dangerous solitude. For the second time, Barnabas held out the hand of friendship to Paul, and led this intractable character into the society of those brethren whom he wished to avoid. He went himself to Tarsus, sought him out, and brought him to Antioch. He did that which those obstinate old brethren of Jerusalem would never have brought themselves to do. To win over this great shrinking and susceptible soul; to accommodate oneself to the caprices and whims of a man full of ardour, and at the same time most personal; to take a secondary place to him, and forgetful of oneself, to prepare the field of operations for the most favourable display of his abilities--all this is certainly the very climax of virtue; and this is what Barnabas did for Paul. Most of the glory, which has accrued to the latter, is really due to the modest man, who excelled him in everything, brought his merits to light, prevented more than once his faults from resulting deplorably to himself and his cause, and the illiberal views of others from exciting him to revolt; and also prevented mean personalities from interfering with the work of God.

During an entire year Barnabas and Paul worked together. This was a most brilliant, and, without doubt, the most happy year in the life of Paul. The prolific originality of these two great men raised the Church of Antioch to a degree of grandeur to which no Christian Church had previously attained. Few places in the world had experienced more intellectual activity than the capital of Syria. During the Roman epoch, as in our time, social and religious questions were brought to the surface principally at the centres of population. A sort of reaction against the general immorality, which made Antioch later, the special abode of Stylites and hermits, was already felt; and the true doctrine thus found in this city, more favourable conditions for success than it had yet met.

An important circumstance proves, besides, that it was at Antioch that the sect for the first time felt the full consciousness of its existence; for it was in this city that it received a distinct name. Hitherto its adherents had called themselves "believers," "the faithful," "saints," "brothers," "the disciples;" but the sect had no public and official name. It was at Antioch that the title of Christianus was devised. The termination of the work is Latin, not Greek, which would indicate that it was selected by the Roman authority as a police designation, like Herodiani, Pompeiana, Cæsariani. In any event it is certain that such a name was formed by the heathen population. It included an error, for it implied that Christus, a translation of the Hebrew Maschiah (the Messiah), was a proper name. Not a few of those who were unfamiliar with Jewish or Christian ideas, were by this name led to believe that Christus or Chrestus was a sectarian leader yet living. The vulgar pronunciation of the name indeed was Chrestiani.

The Jews did not adopt, in a regular manner, at least, the name given by the Romans to their schismatic co-religionist. They continued to call the new converts "Nazarenes" or "Nazorenes," because no doubt they were accustomed to call Jesus Han-nasri or Han-nosri, "the Nazarene;" and even unto the present day, this name is still applied to them throughout the entire East.

This was a most important moment. Solemn indeed is the hour when the new creation receives its name, for that name is the direct symbol of its existence. It is by its name that a being, individual or collective, really becomes itself, and is distinct from others. The formation of the word "Christian" marks thus the precise date of the separation from Judaism of the Church of Jesus. For a long time to come the two religions were still confounded; but this confusion could only take place in those countries where the spread of Christianity was slow and backward. The sect quickly accepted the appelation which was applied to it, and viewed it as a title of honour. It is really astonishing to reflect that ten years after the death of Jesus, his religion had already, in the capital of Syria, a name in the Greek and Latin tongues. Christianity was now completely weaned from its mother; the true sentiments of Jesus had triumphed over the indecision of his first disciples; the Church of Jerusalem was left behind; the Aramaic language, in which Jesus spoke, was unknown to a portion of his followers; Christianity spoke Greek, and was finally launched into that great vortex of the Greek and Roman world, whence it has never departed.

The feverish activity of ideas manifested by this young Church must have been truly extraordinary. Great spiritual manifestations were frequent. All believed themselves to be inspired in various ways. Some were "prophets," others "teachers." Barnabas, as his name indicates, was no doubt among the prophets. Paul had no special title. Among the leaders of the Church at Antioch are also mentioned Simeon, surnamed Niger, Lucius of Cyrene, and Menahem, who had been the foster-brother of Herod Antipas, and was consequently rather old. All these personages were Jews. Among the converted heathen was, perhaps, already that Evhode, who, at a certain period, seems to have occupied the first place in the church of Antioch. Undoubtedly the heathen who heard the first preaching were slightly inferior, and did not shine in the public exercises of using unknown tongues, of preaching, and prophecy.

In the midst of the congenial society of Antioch, Paul quickly adapted himself to the order of things. Later, he manifested opposition to the use of tongues, and it is probable that he never practised it; but he had many visions and immediate revelations. It was apparently at Antioch where occurred that ecstatic trance which he describes in these terms: "I knew a man in Christ above fourteen years ago (whether in the body I cannot tell; or whether out of the body I cannot tell--God knoweth); such an one was caught up to the third heaven. And I knew such a man (whether in the body, or out of the body, I cannot tell--God knoweth); how that he was caught up into paradise, and heard unspeakable words which it is not lawful for a man to utter." Paul, though in general, prudent and practical, shared the prevalent ideas of the day in regard to the supernatural. Like so many others, he believed that he was working miracles, like everybody; it was impossible that the gifts of the Holy Sprit, which were acknowledged to be the common right of the church, should be denied to him.

But men permeated with so lively a faith could not content themselves with merely exuberant piety, so they panted soon for action. The idea of great missions, destined to convert the heathen, beginning in Asia Minor, seized hold of the public mind. Had such an idea been formed at Jerusalem, it could not have been realized, because the church there was without pecuniary resources. An extensive undertaking of propagandism requires a certain capital to work on. Now, the common treasury at Jerusalem was entirely devoted to the support of the poor, and was frequently insufficient for that purpose; and to save these noble mendicants from dying from hunger, it was necessary to obtain help from all quarters. Communism had created at Jerusalem an irremediable poverty and a total incapacity for great enterprises. The church at Antioch was exempt from such a calamity. The Jews in these profane cities had attained to affluence, and in some cases had accumulated vast fortunes. The faithful were wealthy when they entered the church. Antioch furnished the capital for the founding of Christianity, and it is easy to imagine the total difference in manner and spirit which this circumstance alone would create between the two churches. Jerusalem remained the city of the poor of God, of the ebionim, of those simple Galilean dreamers, intoxicated, as it were, with the expectation of the kingdom of Heaven. Antioch, almost a stranger to the words of Jesus, whom it had never heard, was the church of action and of progress. Antioch was the city of Paul; Jerusalem was the seat of the old apostolic college, wrapped up in its dreamy fantasies, and unequal to the new problems which were opening, but dazzled by its incomparable privileges, and rich in its unsurpassed events.

A certain circumstance soon brought all these traits into bold relief. So great was the lack of forethought in this half-starved Church of Jerusalem, that the least accident threw the community into distress. Now, in a country destitute of economic organization, where commerce was but little developed, and where the sources of welfare were limited, famines were inevitable. A terrible famine occurred in the reign of Claudius, in the year 44. When its threatening symptoms became apparent, the elders of Jerusalem decided to seek succour from the members of the richer churches of Syria. An embassy of prophets was sent from Jerusalem to Antioch. One of them, named Agab, who was in high repute for his prophetic powers, was suddenly inspired, and announced that the famine was now at hand. The faithful were deeply moved at the evils which menanced the mother Church, to which they still deemed themselves tributary. A collection was made, at which every one gave according to his means, and Barnabas was selected to carry the funds thus obtained to the brethren in Judea. Jerusalem for a long time remained the capital of Christianity. There were centred the objects peculiar to the faith, and there only were the apostles. But a great forward step had been taken. For several years there had been only one completely organised Church, that of Jerusalem--the absolute centre of the faith, the heart from which all life proceeded and to which it flowed back again; such was no longer the case. The Church at Antioch was now a perfect Church. It possessed all the hierarchy of the gifts of the Holy Ghost. It was the starting-point of the missions, and their head-quarters. It was a second capital, or rather a second heart, which had its own proper action, exercising its force and influence in every direction.

It was now easy to forsee that the second capital must soon eclipse the first. The decay of the Church at Jerusalem was, indeed, rapid. It is natural that institutions founded on communism should enjoy at the beginning a period of brilliancy, for communism involves always high mental exaltation; but it is equally natural that such institutions should very quickly degenerate, because communism is contrary to the instincts of human nature. In his virtuous fits, man readily believes that he can entirely sacrifice his selfish instincts and his peculiar interests; but egotism has its revenge, by proving that absolute disinterestedness engenders evils more serious than those it is hoped to avoid by the renunciation of personal rights to property.

CHAPTER XIV

PERSECUTION BY HEROD AGRIPPA THE FIRST

Barnabas found the church of Jerusalem in great trouble. The year 44 was perilous to it. Besides the famine, the fires of persecution, which had been smothered since the death of Stephen, were rekindled.

Herod Agrippa, grandson of Herod the Great, had succeeded, since the year 41, in reconstructing the kingdom of his grandfather. Thanks to the favour of Caligula, he had reunited under his sway Batanea, Trachonitis a part of the Hauran, Abilene, Galilee, and the Perea. The ignoble part he played in the tragi-comedy which raised Claudius to the empire, completed his fortune. This vile Oriental, in return for the lessons of baseness and perfidy he had given at Rome, obtained for himself Samaria and Judea, and for his brother Herod, the kingdom of Chalcis. He had left at Rome the worst memories, and the cruelties of Caligula were in part attributed to his counsels. His army, and the Pagan cities of Sebaste and Cesarea, which he sacrificed to Jerusalem, were averse to him. But the Jews found him generous, munificient, and sympathetic. He sought to make himself popular with them, and pursued a policy quite different from that of Herod the Great. The latter was much more mindful of the Greek and Roman world than of the Jewish. Herod Agrippa, on the contrary, loved Jerusalem, rigorously observed the Jewish religion, affected scrupulousness, and never let a day pass without attending to his devotions. He went so far as to receive good naturedly the advice of the rigorists, and was at the pains to justify himself against their reproaches. He returned to the inhabitants of Jerusalem the tribute which each family owed him. The orthodox, in a word had in him a king after their own heart.

It was inevitable that a prince of this character should persecute the Christians. Sincere or not, Herod Agrippa was, in the strictest sense of the word, a Jewish Sovereign. The house of Herod, as it became weaker, took to devotion. It held no longer to that broad profane idea of the founder of the dynasty, which sought to make the most diverse religions live together under the common empire of civilization. When Herod Agrippa, for the first time after he had become king, set foot in Alexandria, it was as a King of the Jews that he was received: it was this title which irritated the population and gave rise to endless buffooneries. Now what was a King of the Jews, if he did not become the guardians of the laws and the traditions, a sovereign theocrat and persecutor? From the time of Herod the Great, under whom fanaticism was entirely suppressed, until the breaking out of the war which led to the destruction of Jerusalem, there was thus a constantly increasing process of religious ardour. The death of Caligula (24th Jan., 41) had produced a reaction favourable to the Jews. Claudius was generally benevolent towards them, as a result of the favourable ear he lent to Herod Agrippa and Herod King of Chalcis. Not only did he decide in favour of the Jews of Alexandria in their quarrels with the inhabitants and allow them the right of choosing an ethnarch, but he published, it is said, an edict by which he granted to the Jews, throughout the whole empire, that which he had granted to those of Alexandria; that is to say, the freedom of living according to their own laws, on the sole condition of not abusing other worships. Some attempts at vexations, analagous to those which were inflicted under Caligula, were repressed. Jerusalem was greatly enlarged: the suburb of Bezetha was added to the city. The Roman authority scarcely made itself felt, although Vibius Marsus, a prudent man, of wide public experience, and of a very cultivated mind, who had succeeded Publius Petronius in the function of imperial legate of Syria, drew the attention of the authorities at Rome from time to time to the danger of these semi-independent Eastern Kingdoms.

The species of feudality which, since the death of Tiberius, tended to establish itself in Syria and the neighbouring countries, was in fact an interruption in the imperial policy and had almost uniformly injurious results. The "Kings" coming to Rome were great personages, and exercised there a detestable influence. The corruption and abasement of the people, especially under Caligula, proceeded in great part from the spectacle furnished by these wretches, who were seen successively dragging their purple at the theatre, at the palace of the Cæsar, and in the prisons. So far as concerns the Jews, we have seen that autonomy meant intolerance. The Sovereign Pontificate quitted for a moment the family of Hanan, only to enter that of Boëthus, a family no less haughty and cruel. A sovereign anxious to please the Jews could not fail, but to grant them what they most desired; that is to say, severities against everything which diverged from rigorous orthodoxy.

Herod Agrippa, in fact, became towards the end of his reign a violent persecutor. Some time before the Passover of the year 44, he cut off the head of one of the principal members of the apostolical college, James, son of Zebedee, brother of John. The offence was not re-presented as a religious one; there was no inquisitorial trial before the Sanhedrim: the sentence, as in the case of John the Baptist, was pronounced by virtue of the arbitrary power of the sovereign. Encouraged by the good effect which this execution produced upon the Jews, Herod Agrippa was unwilling to stop upon so easy a road to popularity. It was the first days of the Feast of the Passover, which were ordinarily marked by redoubled fanaticism. Agrippa ordered the imprisonment of Peter in the Tower of Antonia, and sought to have him judged and put to death in the most ostentations manner before the multitude of people then assembled.

A circumstance with which we are unacquainted, and which was regarded as miraculous, opened Peter's prison. One evening, as many of the disciples were assembled in the house of Mary, mother of John-Mark, where Peter constantly resided, there was suddenly a knock heard at the door. The servant, named Rhoda, went to listen. She recognised Peter's voice. Transported with delight, instead of opening the door she ran back to announce that Peter was there. They regarded her as mad. She avowed she spoke the truth. "It is his angel," said some of them. The knocking was continued; it was indeed he. Their delight was infinite. Peter immediately announced his deliverance to James, brother of the Lord, and to the other disciples. It was believed that the angel of God had entered into the prison of the apostle and made the chains drop from his hands, and the bolts of the doors fall. Peter related, in fact, all that had passed while he was in a sort of ecstasy; that after he had passed the first and second guard, and gone through the iron gate which led into the city, the angel accompanied him the distance of a street, then quitted him; that then he came to himself and recognized the hand of God, who had sent a celestial messenger to deliver him.

Agrippa survived these violences but a short time. In the course of the year 44, he went to Cesarea to celebrate games in honour of Claudius. The concourse of people was very great; and many from Tyre and Sidon, who had difficulties with him, came thither to sue for pardon. These festivals were very displeasing to the Jews, both because they took place in the city of Cæsarea, and because they were held in the theatre. Previously, on one occasion, the king having quitted Jerusalem under similar circumstances, a certain rabbi Simeon had proposed to declare him an alien to Judaism, and to exclude him from the temple. Herod Agrippa had carried his condescension so far as to place the rabbi beside him in the theatre in order to prove to him that nothing passed there contrary to the law, and thinking he had thus satisfied the most austere, he allowed himself to indulge his taste for profane pomps. The second day of the festival he entered the theatre very early in the morning, clothed in a tunic of silver fabric, of marvellous brilliancy. The effect of this tunic, glittering in the rays of the rising sun, was extraordinary. The Phoenicians who surrounded the king lavished upon him adulations borrowed from Paganism. "It is a god," they cried, "and not a man." The king did not testify his indignation, and did not blame this expression. He died five days afterwards; and Jews and Christians believed that he was struck dead for not having repelled with horror a blasphemous flattery. Christian tradition represents that he died of a vermicular malady, the punishment reserved for the enemies of God. The symptoms related by Josephus would lead rather to the belief that he was poisoned; and what is said in the Acts of the equivocal conduct of the Phoenicians, and of the care they took to gain over Blastus, valet of the king, would strengthen this hypothesis.

The death of Herod Agrippa I. led to the end of all independence for Jerusalem. The administration by procurators was resumed, and this régime lasted until the great revolt. This was fortunate for Christianity; for it is very remarkable that this religion, which was des-tined to sustain subsequently so terrible a struggle against the Roman empire, grew up in the shadow of the Roman rule, under its protection. It was Rome, as we have already several times remarked, which hindered Judaism from giving itself up fully to its intolerant instincts, and stifling the free instincts which were stirred within its bosom. Every diminution of Jewish authority was a benefit to the nascent sect. Cuspius Fadus, the first of this new series of procurators, was another Pilate, full of firmness, or at least of good-will. But Claudius continued to show himself favourable to Jewish pretensions, chiefly at the instigation of the young Herod Agrippa, son of Herod Agrippa I., whom he kept near to his person, and whom he greatly loved. After the short administration of Cuspius Fadus, we find the functions of procurator confided to a Jew, to that Tiberius Alexander, nephew of Philo, and son of the alabarque of the Alexandrian Jews who attained to high position, and played a great part in the political affairs of that century. It is true that the Jews did not like him; and regarded him, not without reason, as an apostate.

To put an end to these incessantly renewed disputes, recourse was had to an expedient based on sound principles. A sort of separation was made between the spiritual and temporal. The political power remained with the procurators; but Herod, king of Chalcis, brother of Agrippa I., was named prefect of the temple, guardian of the pontifical habits, treasurer of the sacred fund, and invested with the right of nominating the high-priests. At his death, in 48, Herod Agrippa II., son of Herod Agrippa I., succeeded his uncle in his offices, which he retained until the great war. Claudius, in all this, manifested the greatest kindness. The high Roman functionaries in Syria, although not so strongly disposed as the emperor to concessions, acted also with great moderation. The procurator, Ventidius Cumanus, carried condescension so far as to have a soldier beheaded in the midst of the Jews, drawn up in line, for having torn a copy of the Pentateuch. But all was in vain; Josephus, with good reason, dates from the administration of Cumanus the disorders which ended only with the destruction of Jerusalem.

Christianity took no part in these troubles. But these troubles, like Christianity itself, were one of the symptoms of the extraordinary fever which devoured the Jewish people, and the Divine work which was being accomplished in its midst. Never had the Jewish faith made such progress. The temple of Jerusalem was one of the sanctuaries of the world, the reputation of which was most widely extended, and in which the offerings were the most liberal. Judaism had become the dominant religion of several portions of Syria. The Asmonean princes had forcibly converted entire populations to it (Idumeans, Itureans, &c.). There were many instances of circumcision having been imposed by force; the ardour for making proselytes was very great. Even the house of Herod aided powerfully the Jewish propaganda. In order to marry princesses of this family, whose wealth was immense, the princes of the little dynasties of Emese, of Pontus, and of Cilicia, vassals of the Romans, became Jews. Arabia and Ethiopia contained also a great number of converts. The royal families of Mesene and of Adiabene, tributaries of the Parthians, were gained over, especially by their women. It was generally admitted that happiness was found in the knowledge and practice of the Law. Even when circumcision was not practised, religion was more or less modified in the direction of Judaism; a sort of monotheism was becoming the general spirit of religion in Syria. At Damascus, a city which was in nowise of Israelitish origin, nearly all the women had adopted the Jewish religion. Behind the Pharisaical Judaism there was thus formed a sort of liberal Judaism containing some alloy, which did not know all the secrets of the sect, brought only its goodwill and kind heart, but which had a much greater future. The situation was, in some respects similar to that of Catholicism of to-day, where we see, on the one hand, narrow and haughty theologians, who, of themselves, would gain no more souls for Catholicism than the Pharisees gained for Judaism; on the other, pious laymen, in many instances heretics, without knowing it, but full of a touching zeal, rich in good works and in poetic sentiments, wholly occupied in dissimulating or in repairing the faults of their doctors.

One of the most extraordinary examples of this pen-chant of religious souls towards Judaism was that given by the royal family of Adiabene, upon the Tiger. This house, Persian by origin and in manners, and in a measure acquainted with Greek culture, became wholly Jewish, and affected extreme devotion; for, as we have said, those proselytes were often more pious than Jews by birth. Izate, the head of the family, embraced Judaism through the preaching of a Jewish merchant named Ananias, who, having occasion to enter the seraglio of Abennerig, King of Mesene, to prosecute his pedlar business, had succeeded in converting all the women, and constituted himself their spiritual preceptor. The women put Izate into communication with him. Helen, his mother, had herself instructed in the true religion by another Jew. Izate, with the zeal of a new convert, desired forthwith to be circumcised. But his mother and Ananias earnestly dissuaded him against it. Ananias proved to him that the keeping of the commandments of God was more important than circumcision, and that one could be a good Jew without submitting to that ceremony. Tolerance such as this existed only in the case of a few of the more enlightened minds. Some time after, a Galilean Jew, named Eleazar, finding the King one day engaged in reading the Pentateuch, proved to him from texts that he could not observe the law without being circumcised. Izate was persuaded by him, and underwent the operation immediately.

The conversion of Izate was followed by that of his brother Monobaze and almost the whole of his family. About the year 44, Helen established herself at Jerusalem, where she had erected for the royal house of Adiabene a palace and a family mausoleum, which still exists. She made herself to be beloved of the Jews by her affability and her alms. It was a source of great edification to see her, like a devout Jewess, frequenting the Temple, consulting the doctors, reading the Law, and instructing her sons in it. In the plague of the year 44, this holy woman was a god-send to the city. She bought a large quantity of wheat in Egypt, and dried figs in Cyprus. Izate, on his part, sent considerable sums to be distributed amongst the poor. The wealth of Adiabene was expended in part at Jerusalem. The son of Izate came there to learn the usages and the language of the Jews. The whole of this family was thus the resource of the city of mendicants. It acquired there a sort of citizenship; several of its members were found there at the time of the siege of Titus; others figure in the Talmudic writings, and are represented as models of piety and disinterestedness.

It is in this way that the royal family of Adiabene belongs to the history of Christianity. Without in fact being Christian, as certain traditions would have it, this family represented, under various aspects, the promises of the Gentiles. In embracing Judaism, it obeyed a sentiment which was to eventuate in Christianizing the entire Pagan world. The true Israelites, according to God, were rather those foreigners animated by so profoundly sincere a religious sentiment than the malevolent and roguish Pharisee, to whom religion was but a pretext for hatred and disdain. These good proselytes, although they were truly saints, were by no means fanatics. They admitted that true religion could be practised under the empire of a code of civil laws the most unduly adverse. They separated completely religion from politics. The distinction between the seditious sectaries, who were savagely to defend Jerusalem, and the pacific devotees who on the first rumour of war were going to flee to the mountains, became more and more manifest.

We see at least that the question of proselytes was put forward in a similar manner, both in Judaism and in Christianity. On both hands the necessity for enlarging the door of entrance was felt. For those who were thus situated, circumcision was a useless or noxious practice; the Mosaic rite was simply a sign of race, of no value except for the children of Abraham. Before becoming the universal religion, Judaism was compelled to reduce itself to a sort of deism, imposing only the duties of natural religion. There was thus a sublime mission to fulfil, and a part of Judaism in the first half of the first century lent itself to it in a very intelligent manner. On one side, Judaism was one of the innumerable forms of natural worship which filled the world, and the sanctity of which came only from what its ancestors had worshipped; on the other, Judaism was the absolute religion made for all and destined to be adopted by all. The frightful outbreak of fanaticism which gained the upper hand in Judea, and which brought about the war of extermination, cut short that future. It was Christianity which undertook the work which the Synagogue had not known how to accomplish. Leaving on one side all questions of ritual, Christianity continued the monotheistic propaganda of Judaism. That which made up the strength of Judaism amongst the women of Damascus; in the harem of Abennerig, with Helen, with so many pious proselytes, composed the force of Christianity in the entire world. In this sense the glory of Christianity is really confounded with that of Judaism. A generation of fanatics deprived this last of its reward and prevented it from gathering the harvest which it had sown.

CHAPTER XV

MOVEMENTS PARALLEL TO CHRISTIANITY OR IMITATED FROM IT--SIMON OF GITTON

Christianity was now really established. In the history of religions it is always the first years which are most difficult to traverse. When once a faith has borne up against the hard trials, which every new institution has to endure, its future is assured. More clever than the other sectaries of the same date, Epenians, Baptists, partizans of John the Gaulonite, which simply came out of the Jewish world, and perished with it, the founders of Christianity, with a singular clearness of sight, cast themselves very early into the great world, and took their place in it. The scantiness of the references to the Christians, which are to be found in Josephus, in the Talmud, and in the Greek and Latin writers, ought not to be surprising. Josephus has reached us through Christian copyists, who have suppressed all that was disagreeable to their faith. It is easy to believe that he spoke at greater length of Jesus and of the Christians than he does in the version which has come down to us. The Talmud has in the same way undergone in the Middle Ages many retrenchments and alterations since its first publication. The Christian censure was exercised with severity upon its text, and a host of unhappy Jews were burned for having been found in possession of a book containing passages which were considered blasphemous. It is not astonishing that the Greek and Latin writers occupied themselves but little with a movement which they could not understand, and which took place in a world which was closed to them, Christianity in their eyes lost itself in the depths of Judaism; it was a family quarrel in the bosom of an abject race; what was the use of troubling about it? The two or three passages in which Tacitus or Suetonius speaks of the Christians prove that, in spite of being outside the circle of everyday affairs, the new sect was already a very considerable fact, since, from one or two glimpses, we see it across the cloud of general inattention, picture itself with sufficient clearness.

The circumstance that Christianity was not an isolated movement has contributed not a little towards the effacement of its outlines in the history of the Jewish world in the first century of our era. Philo, at the moment at which we have arrived, has finished his career--a career consecrated to the love of the good. The sect of Judas, the Gaulonite, still existed. The agitator had for continuers of his idea, his sons James, Simon, and Menahem, Simon and James were crucified by order of the renegade procurator, Tiberius Alexander. Menahem will play an important part in the final catastrophe of the nation. In the year 44 an enthusiast, named Theudas, arose announcing the approaching deliverance, and invited the mob to follow him into the desert, promising, like another Joshua, to make them pass dryshod over Jordan, this passage being, according to his explanation, the true baptism to initiate his believers into the Kingdom of God. More than four hundred souls followed him. (Acts v., 36.) The procurator Cuspius Fadius, sent cavalry against him, dispersed his force, and killed him. Some years earlier all Samaria had been moved by the voice of a fanatic, who pretended to have had a revelation of the site of Garizim, where Moses had hidden the holy instruments of worship. Pilate had repressed this movement with great vigour. Peace was at an end in Jerusalem. After the arrival of the procurator Vontidius Cumanus (48), disturbances were incessant. Excitement was pushed to such a point that life there became impossible; the most insignificant circumstances brought about an explosion. Everywhere was felt a strange fermentation, a sort of mysterious trouble. Imposters multiplied everywhere. The frightful scourge of the zealots (Kenaim), or assassins, began to appear. Scoundrels, armed with daggers, glided into the crowds, struck their victims, and were the first to shriek "Murder." Hardly a day passed without the report of an assassination of this kind. An extraordinary terror prevailed. Josephus represents the crimes of the zealots as sheer wickedness, but it is indubitable that fanaticism mixed itself with them. It was in defence of the Law that these wretches took up the dagger. Whoever neglected to fulfil one of its ordinances, found his sentence pronounced, and immediately executed. They thought in this way to accomplish a work, the most meritorious and agreeable to God.

Dreams like that of Theudas were everywhere renewed. Persons, pretending to be inspired, stirred up the people, and led them out into the desert, under pretence of showing to them, by manifest signs that God was about to deliver them. The Roman authorities exterminated these agitators and their dupes by thousands. A Jew of Egypt, who came to Jerusalem about the year 56, was skilful enough to draw after him 30,000 persons, amongst whom wore 4,000 zealots. From the desert he wished to take them to

Mount Olivet, whence, he said, they might see the walls of Jerusalem fall at the sound of his voice alone. Felix, who was then procurator, marched against him, and dispersed his band. The Egyptian escaped, and was seen no more. But as in an unhealthy body one malady follows another, we very soon afterwards come upon mixed bodies of robbers and magicians, who openly urged the people to rebel against the Romans, threatening those who continued to obey them with death. Under this pretext they killed the rich, pillaged their goods, burned the villages, and filled all Jewry with marks of their fury. A frightful war announced itself. A general spirit of confusion prevailed, and men's minds were in a state not far removed from madness.

It is not impossible that Theudas had a certain after-thought of imitation, as regards Jesus and John the. Baptist. This imitation, at least, is evidently betrayed in Simon of Gitton, if the Christian traditions as to this personage are in any way worthy of credence. We have already met him in connexion with the Apostles apropos of the first mission of Philip to Samaria. It was under the reign of Claudius that he arrived at celebrity. His miracles passed as constant, and everybody in Samaria looked upon him as a supernatural personage.

His miracles, however, were not the only foundation of his reputation. He added to them a doctrine which we can hardly judge of, since the work attributed to him, and entitled the Great Exposition, has reached us only by extracts, and is probably only a very modified expression of his ideas. Simon, during his stay in Alexandria, appears to have drawn from his studies of Greek philosophy, a system of syncretic philosophy, and of allegorical exegesis, resembling that of Philo. The system had its greatness. Sometimes it recalls the Jewish Cabala, sometimes the Pantheistic theories of Indian philosophy; looked at from a certain standpoint it appears to bear the impress of Buddhism and Parseeism. At the head of all things is "He who is, who has been, and who will be"; that is to say, the Samaritan Jahveh, understood, according to the etymological value of his name. The Eternal Being, alone, self-engendered, increasing himself; magnifying himself, finding in himself father, mother, sister, wife, and son. In the breast of that infinite being, every power exists from and to eternity; all things pass into action and reality by the conscience of man, by reason, language, and science. The world explains itself, it may be by a hierarchy of abstract principles, analogous to the Æons of gnosticism and the sephirotic tree of the Cabala, or by an angelic system, which appears to have been borrowed from the beliefs of Persia Sometimes these abstractions are presented as translations of physical and physiological facts. At other times the "Divine powers," considered as separate substances, are realized as successive incarnations, sometimes feminine, sometimes masculine, whose end is the deliverance of the persons concerned from the bondage of matter. The first of these powers is that which is called, by way of especial distinction, "the Great," and which is the intelligence of this world, the universal Providence. It is masculine, and Simon passed as being its incarnation. By its side is the feminine Syzygy, "the Great Thought." Accustomed to clothe its theories with a strange symbolism, and to imagine allegorical interpretations for the ancient, sacred, and profane texts, Simon, or the author of the Great Exposition, gave to that Divine virtue the name of "Helen," signifying thereby that it was the object of universal pursuit, the eternal cause of dispute amongst men, she who avenges herself on her enemies by blinding them, just at the moment when they consent to sing the Palinode; a grotesque theme which, ill-understood or distorted by design, gave rise amongst the Fathers of the Church to the most puerile legends. The knowledge of Greek literature which the author of the Great Exposition possessed, is in any case very remarkable. He maintained that, when properly understood, the Pagan writings sufficed for the knowledge of all things. His large eclecticism embraced all the revelations, and sought to establish all truth in a single order.

At the basis of his system there is much analogy with that of Valentin, and with the doctrines as to the Divine persons which are found in the fourth Gospel, in Philo and on the Targums. The "Metatrône," which the Jews placed by the side of the Divinity, and almost in its breast, has a strong resemblance to the "Great Power." In the theology of the Samaritans may be found a "Great Angel," chief of the others, and of the class of manifestations or "divine virtues," like those which the Jewish Cabala figures on its side. It appears certain then that Simon, of Gitton, was a kind of theosophist of the race of Philo and the Cabalists. It is possible that he approached Christianity for the moment, but he certainly did not definitely embrace it.

Whether he really borrowed something from the disciples of Jesus is very difficult to decide. If the Great Exposition is his in any degree, it must be admitted that in many points he went beyond Christian ideas, and that upon others he adopted them very freely. It would seem that he attempted eclecticism like that which Mahomet practised later on, and that he endeavoured to found his religious character upon the preliminary acceptance of the divine mission of John and of Jesus. He wanted to be in a mystical communion with them. He maintained, it is said, that it was he, Simon, who appeared to the Samaritans as Father, to the Jews the visible crucifixion of the Son, to the Gentiles, by the infusion of the Holy Ghost. He thus prepared the way, it would seem, for the doctrines of the docetes. He said that it was he who had suffered in Judea in the person of Jesus, but that that suffering had only been apparent. His pretension to be the Divinity itself, and to cause himself to be adored as such had probably been exaggerated by the Christians who sought only to render him hateful.

It will be seen besides that the doctrine of the Great Exposition is that of almost all the Gnostic writers; if Simon really professed the doctrines, it was with good reason that the fathers of the Church made him the founder of Gnosticism. We believe that the Great Exposition has only a relative authenticity, and that it really is to the doctrine of Simon--to compare small things with great--what the Fourth Gospel is to the mind of Jesus; that it goes back to the first years of the second century, that is to say, to the period when the theosophic ideas of the Logos definitely gained the ascendency. These ideas, the germ of which we shall find in the Christian Church about the year 60, might however have been known to Simon, whose career we may reason-ably extend to the end of the century.

The idea which we form to ourselves of this enigmatical personage is then that of a kind of plagiarist of Christianity. Counterfeiting appears to have been a constant habit amongst the Samaritans. Just as they had always imitated the Judaism of Jerusalem, their sectaries had also copied Christianity in their ways, their gnoxis, their theosophic speculations, their Cabala. But was Simon a respectable imitator, who only failed of success, or an immoral and profligate conjuror using for his own advantage a doctrine of shreds and patches picked up here and there? This is a question which will probably never be answered. Simon thus maintains in history an utterly false position; he walks upon a light rope where hesitation is impossible; in this order, there is no middle path between a ridiculous fall and the most miraculous success.

We shall again have to occupy ourselves with Simon, and to enquire if the legends as to his stay in Rome are in any way founded on truth. It is certain that the Samarian sect lasted until the third century; that it had churches at Antioch, perhaps even at Rome, that Menanda, and Capharatea, and Cleobius, continued the doctrine of Simon, or rather imitated his part of theurgist with a more or less present remembrance of Jesus and of his apostles. Simon and his disciples were greatly esteemed amongst their co-religionists. Sects of the same time, parallel to Christianity and more or less borrowed from Gnosticism, did not cease to spring up amongst the Samaritans until their quasi destruction by Justinian. The fate of that sort of little religion was to receive the rebound of everything that went on around it, without producing anything at all original.

Amongst the Christians, the memory of Simon of Gitton was an abomination. These illusions, which were so much like their own, irritated them. To have successfully rivalled the apostles was unpardonable. It was asserted that the miracles of Simon and of his disciples were the work of the devil, and they applied to the Samaritan theosophist the title of the "Magician," which the faithful took in very bad part. All the Christian legends of Simon bear the marks of a concentrated wrath. He was credited with the maxims of quietisms, and with the excess which are usually supposed to be its consequence. He was considered to be the father of every error, the first heresiarch. Christians amused themselves by telling laughable stories of him and of his defeats by the apostle Peter. They attributed his approach towards Christianity to the vilest of motives. They were so preoccupied with his name that they fancied they read It in inscriptions which he had not written. The symbolism in which he had enveloped his ideas was interpreted in the most grotesque fashion. The "Helen," whom he identified with the "Highest Intelligence," became a prostitute whom he had bought in the market at Tyre. His very name was hated almost as much as that of Judas, and, taken as synonym of "anti-apostle," became the last insult and as it were a proverbial word to describe a professional impostor, an adversary of the the truth whom it was desirable to indicate with mystery. He was the first enemy of Christianity, or rather the first personage whom Christianity treated as such. It is enough to say that neither pious frauds nor calumnies were spared to defame it. Criticism in such a case will hardly attempt a rehabilitation, the contradictory documents are wanting. All that can be done is to point out the similarity of the traditions, and the determined disparagement which is to be remarked in them.

But criticism, at least, should not forget to mention in connexion with the Samaritan theurgist a coincidence which is perhaps not altogether fortuitous. In a story of the historian Josephus, a Jewish magician named Simon, born in Cyprus, plays the part of pander to Felix. The circumstances of this tale do not fit in with those of Simon of Gitton well enough for him to be made responsible for the acts of a person who could have nothing in common with him, but a name then borne by thousands of men, and a pretension to supernatural powers, which he unhappily shared with a host of his contemporaries.

CHAPTER XVI

GENERAL PROGRESS OF CHRISTIAN MISSIONS

We have seen Barnabas depart from Antioch to carry to the faithful of Jerusalem the alms of their brethren in Syria. We have seen him share in some of the emotions which the persecutions of Herod Agrippa I. caused the Church at Jerusalem. Let us return with him to Antioch where all the creative activity of the sect appears at that moment to have been concentrated.

Barnabas brought with him a zealous collaborator, his cousin John-Mark, the favourite disciple of Peter, and the son of that Mary with whom the first of the apostles loved to dwell. Without doubt in taking with him this new co-operator, he was already thinking of the new enterprise with which he intended to associate him. Perhaps he even foresaw the divisions which that new enterprise would raise up, and was by no means unwilling to mix up with them a man whom he knew to be Peters right hand, that is to say, the right hand of that one of the apostles who had the greatest authority in general matters.

This enterprise was nothing less than a series of great missions, starting from Antioch and having for programme the conversion of the whole world. Like all resolutions taken by the Church, this was attributed to the direct inspiration of the Holy Ghost. A special vocation, a supernatural choice, was believed to have been communicated to the Church of Antioch whilst she was fasting and praying. Perhaps one of the prophets of the Church, Menaham or Lucius, in one of his fits of speaking with tongues, uttered words from which it was concluded that Paul and Barnabas had been selected for this mission. Paul himself was convinced that God had chosen him from his mother's womb for the work to which he was henceforward wholly to devote himself.

The two apostles took as coadjutor, under the name of subordinate, to attend to the material cares of their enterprise, this John-Mark, whom Barnabas had brought with him from Jerusalem. When the preparations were finished there were fastings and prayer; it is said that hands were laid upon the apostles, in sign of a mission conferred by the Church herself; they were commended to the grace of God and they departed. Whither would they go? What world would they evangelize? That is what we have now to inquire.

All the great primitive Christian missions turned towards the West, or in other words, took the Roman Empire for their stage and framework. If we except some small portions of territory tributary to the Arsacides, comprehended between the Tigris and the Euphrates, the Empire of the Parthians received no Christian missions in the first century. The Tigris was on the Eastern side, a boundary which Christianity did not overpass until under the Sapanides. Two great causes, the Mediterranean and the Roman Empire, decided this cardinal fact.

The Mediterranean had been for a thousand years the great route where all civilization and all ideas intermingled. The Romans, having delivered it from piracy, had made it an unequalled means of communication. A numerous fleet of coasters made travelling on the shores of this great lake very easy. The relative security which the routes of the Empire afforded, the guarantees which were found in the public powers, the diffusions of the Jews on all the coasts of the Mediterranean, the use of the Greek language in the Eastern part of that sea, the unity of civilization which the Greeks first, and then the Romans had created there, made the map of the Empire the very map of the countries reserved for Christian missions, and destined to become Christian. The Roman orbis became the Christian orbis, and in this sense it may be said that the founders of the Empire were the founders of the Christian monarchy, or at least, that they sketched its outlines. Every province conquered by the Roman Empire has been a province conquered by Christianity. If we figure to ourselves the apostles in the presence of an Asia Minor, of a Greece, of an Italy divided into a hundred petty republics, of a Spain, an Africa, an Egypt in possession of ancient national institutions, we cannot imagine them as successful, or rather we cannot imagine how the project of them could ever have been conceived. The unity of the Empire was the preliminary condition of every great scheme of religious proselytism setting itself above nationalities. The Empire felt it strongly in the fourth century. It became Christian; it saw that Christianity was the religion which it had made without knowing it, the religion bounded by its frontiers, identified with it, and capable of securing for it a second term of life. The Church on her side made herself altogether Roman, and has remained to our days as a relic of the Empire. Paul might have been told that Claudius was his first coadjutor; Claudius might have been told that this Jew, who set out from Antioch, was about to found the most solid part of the Imperial edifice. Both would no doubt have been infinitely astonished, but the saying would have been true all the same.

Of all the countries outside Judea, the first in which Christianity established itself was naturally Syria. The neighbourhood of Palestine and the great number of Jews established in that country rendered such a thing inevitable. Cyprus, Asia Minor, Macedonia, Greece, and Italy, were visited by the apostolic messengers after some years. The south of Gaul, Spain, the coast of Africa, though they may have been evangelized sufficiently early, may be considered as forming a more recent course in the substructure of Christianity.

It was the same in Egypt. Egypt plays scarcely any part in apostolic history. Christian missionaries appear to have systematically turned their backs upon it. This country, which from the beginning of the third century became the scene of such important events in the history of religion, was at first greatly behind hand in its Christianity. Apollos is the only Christian doctor produced by the school of Alexandria, and even he learned Christianity in his travels. The cause of this remarkable phenomenon must be sought in the little communication which then existed between the Jews of Egypt and those of Palestine, and above all, in the fact that Jewish Egypt had in some sort its separate religious development. Egypt had Philo and the Therapeutics; that was its Christianity which deterred it from lending an attentive ear to the other. Pagan Egypt possessed religious institutions much more definite than those of Græco-Roman Paganism the Egyptian religion was still in all its strength; it was almost at this very time that the great temples of Enoch and of Ombos were built, and that the hope of having in the little Cæsarion a last king Ptolemy, a national Messiah, raised from the earth those sanctuaries of Dendereh, of Hermonthis, comparable to the finest Pharaohnic work. Christianity seated itself everywhere on the ruins of national sentiment and local religions. The spiritual degradation of Egypt besides caused there a variety of aspirations which elsewhere opened an easy way to Christianity.

A rapid flash, coming out of Syria, illuminating almost simultaneously the three great peninsulas of Asia Minor, Greece, and Italy, and soon followed by a second reflection which embraced almost all the coasts of the Mediterranean, such was the first apparition of Christianity. The journey of the apostolic ship is almost always the same. Christian preaching appears to follow almost invariably in the wake of the Jewish emigration. As an infection which, taking its point of departure from the bottom of the Mediterranean, appears at the same moment at a certain number of points on the littoral by a secret correspondence, so Christianity had its ports of arrival as it were settled beforehand. These ports were almost all marked by Jewish colonies. A synagogue preceded in general the establishment of the Church. One might say a train of powder, or better still a sort of electric chain along which the new idea ran in an almost instantaneous fashion.

For five hundred years, in effect, Judaism, until then confined to the East and to Egypt, had taken its flight towards the West. Cyrene, Cyprus, Asia Minor, certain cities of Macedonia and of Greece and Italy, had important Jewries. The Jews gave the first example of that species of patriotism, that the Parsees, the Armenians, and up to a certain point the modern Greeks were to exhibit later: a patriotism which was extremely energetic although not attached to a definite soil; a patriotism of merchants scattered everywhere; recognizing one another as brothers everywhere; a patriotism aiming at the formation not of great compact states but of little autonomous communities in the bosoms of other states. Strongly associated together, the Jews of the dispersion constituted in the cities, congregations almost independent having their own magistrates and their own council. In certain cities they had an ethnarch or alabarch, invested with almost sovereign rights. They inhabited separate districts, withdrawn from the ordinary jurisdiction, much despised by the rest of the world, but very happy in themselves. They were rather poor than rich. The time of the great Jewish fortunes had not yet come; they began in Spain under the Visigoths. The monopoly of finance by the Jews was the effect of the administrative incapacity of the barbarians, of the hatred which the Church conceived for monetary science, and its superficial ideas on the subject of usury. Under the Roman Empire there was nothing of this kind. Now when the Jew is not rich his pour, easy middleclass life is not to his taste. In any case he well knows how to support poverty. What he knows even better is how to ally religious preoccupation of the most exalted kind with the rarest commercial ability. Theological eccentricites by no means exclude good sense in business. In England, in America, in Russia, the most eccentric sectaries (Irvingites, Latter-day Saints, Raskolniks) are exceedingly good merchants.

It has always been the peculiarity of the Jewish life, piously practiced, to produce great gaiety and cordiality. There was love in that little world; they love a past, and the same past; the religious ceremonies surrounded life very gently. Something analogous to these communities exist to this day in every great Turkish city; for example Greek, Armenian, Jewish, Smyrniots, communities, close brotherhoods in which every member knows every other, live together and--intrigue together. In these little republics, religious questions always prevail over questions of politics, or rather make up for the want of them. A heresy is there an affair of the State; a schism is always a personal question at bottom. The Romans, with but few exceptions, never penetrated these reserved quarters. The synagogues promulgated their decrees, decreed honours, and acted like living municipalities. The influence of the corporations was very great. At Alexandria it was of the first order and governed the whole internal history of the city. At Rome the Jews were numerous and formed an element which was not to be despised. Cicero represents having dared to resist them as an act of courage. Cæsar favoured them, and found them faithful. Tiberius, in order to restrain them, resorted to the severest measures. Caligula, whose reign was a mournful one for them in the East, gave them their liberty of association in Rome. Claudius, who favoured them in Judea, found himself obliged to drive them out of the city. They were to be met with everywhere, and it was openly said of them, as of the Greeks, that though conquered they had imposed their laws upon their conquerors.

The disposition of the native populations towards these strangers varied greatly. On the one hand the sentiment of revulsion and of antipathy, that the Jews by their spirit of jealous isolation, their rancorous temper and unsociable habits, produced around them everywhere where they were numerous and organised, manifested itself most strongly. When they were free, they were in reality privileged; since they enjoyed the advantages of society without bearing its cost. Impostors profited by the movement of curiosity which their worship excited, and under the pretence of exposing its secrets delivered themselves to friends of every kind. Violent and half-burlesque pamphlets like that of Apion, pamphlets from which profane writers have too often drawn their inspiration, were circulated and served as food for the wrath of the Pagan public. The Jews seem to have been generally niggardly and given to complaining. They were believed to be a secret society, bearing no good will to the rest of the world, whose members advanced themselves at any cost to the injury of others. Their strange customs, their aversion to certain meats, their dirtiness, their want of distinction, the fetid odour which they exhaled, their religious scruples, their minuteness in the observance of the Sabbath, were found ridiculous. Placed under the ban of society, the Jews by a natural consequence, took no pains to figure as gentle people. They were met everywhere travelling in clothes shining with filth, an awkward air, a fatigued demeanour, a pale complexion, large diseased eyes, a sanctimonious expression, shutting themselves apart with their wives, their children, their bundles of bedding, and the basket which contained all their goods. In the cities they carried on the meanest trades; they were beggars, rag-pickers, dealers in second-hand goods, sellers of tinder boxes. Their law and their history were unjustly depreciated. At one time they were found to be superstitious and cruel; at another, atheists and despisers of the gods. Their aversion to images was looked upon as sheer impiety. Circumcision especially furnished the theme for interminable raillery.

But those superficial judgments were not those of all. The Jews had as many friends as detractors. Their gravity, their good morals, the simplicity of their worship, charmed a crowd of people. Something superior was felt in them. A vast monotheistic and Mosaic propaganda was organised; a sort of singular whirlwind formed itself around this singular little people. The poor Jewish pedlar of the Transtevere, going out in the morning with his flat basket of haberdashery, often returned in the evening rich with the alms of a pious brother. Women were especially attracted by these missionaries in tatters. Juvenal reckons this love for the Jewish religion amongst the vices with which he reproaches the women of his time. Those who were converted boasted of the treasure which they had found, and the happiness which they enjoyed. Only the Greek and the Roman spirit resisted energetically; contempt and hatred of the Jews are the sign of all cultivated minds: Cicero, Horace, Seneca, Juvenal, Tacitus, Quintilian, Suetonius. On the contrary that enormous mass of mixed populations which the empire had subjugated, populations to which the Roman spirit and the Greek wisdom were foreign or indifferent, attached themselves in crowds to a society in which they found touching examples of concord, of charity, of mutual help, of clannish attachment, of a taste for work, of a proud poverty. Mendicity, which was at a late date an exclusively Christian business, was then a Jewish trade. The beggar by trade, "born to it," presented himself to the poets of the time as a Jew.

The exemption from certain civil charges, particularly the military, helped also to cause the fate of the Jews to be regarded as enviable. The State then demanded many sacrifices and gave little moral satisfaction. Everything was icily cold as on a flat plain without shelter. Life, so sad in the midst of Paganism regained its charm and its value in the warm atmosphere of synagogue and church. It was not liberty which was to be found there. The brethren spied much upon each other, everyone worrying himself about the affairs of everyone else. But although the interior life of these little communities was greatly agitated, they were happy enough; no one quitted them; there were no apostasies. The poor were content in them; they regarded the rich without envy, with the tranquility of a good conscience. The really democratic sentiment of the folly of the world, of the vanity of riches and of earthly grandeur finely expressed itself there. Little was known about the Pagan world and it was judged with an outrageous severity; Roman civilization was regarded as a mass of impurities and of odious vices, just as the honest workman of our own days, saturated with socialistic declamations, pictures the "aristocrats" to himself in the darkest colours. But there was then life, gaiety and interest just as there is to-day in the poorest synagogues of Poland and Galicia. The want of delicacy and of elegance in the habits of the people was atoned for by the family spirit and patriarchal good feeling. In high society, on the contrary, egotism and isolation of soul had borne their last fruits.

The word of Zachariah was verified: that men "shall take hold of the skirt of him that is a Jew, saying we will go with you, for we perceive that God is with you." There was no great town where the Sabbath fasts and other ceremonies of Judaism were not observed. Josephus dares to provoke those who doubted it, to consider their country and even their own house to see if there were not confirmation of what he said. The presence in Rome and near the Emperor of many members of the family of the Herods, who practised their worship ostentatiously in the face of all, contributed much to this publicity. The Sabbath besides imposed itself by a sort of necessity in the quarters where there were Jews. Their obstinate determination not to open their shops on that day forced their neighbours to modify their habits. It is thus that at Salonica one might say that the Sabbath is still observed, the Jewish population there being rich enough and numerous enough to make the law and to order the day of rest by closing its places of business. Almost the equal of the Jew, often in company with him, the Syrian was an active instrument in the conquest of the West by the East. They were confounded occasionally, and Cicero thought he had found the common feature which united them, when he called them "the nations born for servitude." It was by that, that their future was assured, for the future was then for the slaves. A not less essential characteristic of the Syrian was his facility, his suppleness, the superficial clearness of his mind. The Syrian nature is like a fugitive image in the clouds of Heaven. From time to time we see certain lines traced there with grace, but those lines never form a complete design. In the shade, by the undecided light of a lamp, the Syrian woman under her veil, with her vague eyes and her infinite softness, produces some instants of illusion. But when we wish to analyse that beauty it vanishes; it will not bear examination. All that besides lasts but three or four years. That which is charming in the Syrian race is the child of five or six years of age; the universe of Greece where the child is nothing, the young man inferior to the mature man, the mature man to the old. Syrian intelligence attracts by an air of promptitude and lightness, but it wants firmness and solidity; something like the golden wine of the Lebanon which is very pleasant at first but of which one tires very soon. The true gifts of God have in them something at once fine and strong, something intoxicating, yet lasting. Greece is more appreciated to-day than she has ever been and she will be appreciated more and more.

Many of the Syrian emigrants whom the desire of making their fortunes had drawn westwards, were more or less attached to Judaism. Those who were not, remained faithful to the worship of their villages; that is to say to the memory of some temple dedicated to a local "Jupiter," who was usually simply the supreme being, differentiated by a particular title. It was at bottom a species of monotheism, which these Syrians brought under cover of their strange gods. Compared at least with the profoundly distinct divine personalities, which Greek and Roman polytheism offered, the gods whom they worshipped, for the most part synonyms of the Sun, were almost the brothers of the One God. Like long enervating chants these Syrian rites, might appear less dry than the Latin worship, less empty than the Greek. The Syrian women found in them something at once voluptuous and exalted. These women were at all times eccentric beings, disputing between the devil and God, floating between saintliness and demoniacal possession. The saint of serious virtues, of heroic renunciations, of steadfast resolutions, belongs to other races, and other climates: the saint of strong imagination, absolute enthusiasm, of ready love, is the saint of Syria. The witch of our middle ages is the slave of Satan by vulgarity or by sin; the "possessed" of Syria, is the mad-woman of the ideal world, the woman whose sentiment has been wounded, who avenges herself by frenzy or shuts herself up in silence, who only needs a gentle word or a benignant look to cure her. Transported to the Western World, these Syrians acquired influence, sometimes by the evil arts of woman, more often by a certain moral superiority and a real capacity. Fifty years later this will be specially seen, when the most important persons in Rome married Syrian women, who immediately acquired a great ascendency in affairs. The Mussulman woman of our days, a clamorous, Megæra, stupidly fanatical, scarcely existing save for evil, almost incapable of virtue, ought not to make us forget the Julia Domna, the Julia Mæsa, the Julia Maæmsa, the Julia Soemia, who upheld in Rome in the matter of religion mystical instincts, and a tolerance, hitherto unknown. What is very remark-able, also, is that the Syrian dynasty, conducted by fate, showed itself favourable to Christianity, that Mamacus, and later, the Emperor Philippus, the Arabian, passed for Christians. Christianity in the third and fourth centuries was especially the religion of Syria. After Palestine, Syria had the greatest share in its foundation.

It was especially at Rome that the Syrian in the first century exercised his penetrating activity. Charged with almost all the minor trades, guide, messenger; letterbearer, the Syrus entered everywhere, introducing with himself the language and the manners of his country. He had neither the pride nor the philosophical hauteur of the European. Still less their bodily strength: weak of body, pale, often nervous, not knowing how to eat or to sleep at regular hours after the fashion of our heavy and solid races, eating little meat, living upon onions and pumpkins, sleeping but little and lightly, the Syrian died young, and was habitually ill. What were peculiar to him, were his humility, his gentleness, his affability, and a certain goodness; no solidity of mind, but an infinite charm; little good sense, except in matters of business, but an astonishing ardour, and a seductiveness altogether feminine. The Syrian, having never had any political life, has an altogether special aptitude for religious movements. This poor

Maronite, humble, ragged as he is, has made the greatest of revolutions. His ancestor, the Syrus of Rome, was the most zealous bearer of the good news to all the afflicted. Every year brought to Greece, to Italy, to Gaul, colonies of these Syrians, urged by the natural taste which they had for small business. They were recognized on the ships by their numerous families, by their troops of pretty children almost of the same age, who followed them: the mother, with the childish air of a little girl of fourteen, holding herself by the side of her husband, submissive, gently smiling, scarcely bigger than her elder sons. The heads in these little groups are not strikingly marked; there is certainly no Archimedes, Plato or Phidias amongst them. But the Syrian merchant arrived in Rome, will be a man, good and pitiful, charitable to his fellow countrymen, loving the poor. He will talk with the slaves, revealing to them an asylum, where those unhappy wretches, reduced by Roman harshness to the most desolating solitude may find a little consolation. The Greek and Latin races of masters did not know how to profit by a humble position. The slave of these races passed his life in rebellion, and the desire of evil. The ideal slave of antiquity has all the defects; he is gluttonous, a liar, malicious, the natural enemy of his master. In this way he proved his nobility in a sort of way; he protested against an unnatural position. The good Syrian did not protest; he accepted his ignominy and sought to profit by it as much as possible. He conciliated the good-will of his master, dared to speak to him; knew how to please his mistress. This great agent of democracy went thus unpicking, stitch by stitch, the knot of antique civilization. The old societies founded upon disdain, upon the inequality of races, upon military courage, were lost. Weakness and humility were now to become an advantage for the perfecting of virtue. Roman aristocracy and Greek wisdom, will keep up the struggle for three centuries. Tacitus will find it good that thousands of these unfortunates should be transported: Si interissent, vile damnum. The Roman aristocracy will grow angry, will find it bad that such scum should have their gods, their institutions. But the victory is written beforehand. The Syrian, the poor man who loves his kind, who shares with them, who associates with them, will win the day. The Roman aristocracy will perish for want of mercy.

To explain the revolution which is about to be accomplished, we must take into account the political, social, moral, intellectual, and religious state of the countries, where Jewish proselytism had opened the soil for Christian preaching to fertilize. That study will show, I hope, convincingly that the conversion of the world to Jewish and Christian ideas was inevitable, and will leave room for astonishment, only upon one point, which is, that conversion should be effected so slowly and so late.

CHAPTER XVII

STATE OF THE WORLD AT THE MIDDLE OF THE FIRST CENTURY

The political state of the world was of the saddest kind. All authority was concentrated at Rome and in the legions. There occurred the most shameful and degrading scenes. The Roman aristocracy, which had conquered the world, and which, in short, had alone governed under the Cæsars, delivered itself up to the most frightful Saturnalia of grime which the world has ever seen. Cæsar and Augustus, in establishing the aristocracy, had seen with perfect accuracy the necessities of their times. The world was so low in the political sense that no other government was possible. Since Rome had conquered provinces innumerable, the ancient constitution, founded on the privileges of patrician families, a species of obstinate and malevolent Tories, could not subsist. But Augustus had failed in all the duties of true policy in that he left the future to chance. Without regular hereditary succession, without fixed rules of adoption, without electoral laws, without constitutional limitations, Cæsarism was like a colossal weight on the deck of a ship without ballast. The most terrible shocks were inevitable. Thrice in a century, under Caligula, under Nero, and under Domitian, the greatest power which had ever existed fell into the hands of execrable or extravagant men. Hence, horrors, which have scarcely been exceeded by the monsters of the Mongal dynasties. In that fatal series of sovereigns we are reduced almost to excusing a Tiberius, who was absolutely wicked only towards the close of his life! a Claudius, who was simply eccentric, awkward and surrounded by evil advisers. Rome became a school of vice and cruelty. It must be added that the evil came especially from the East, from those flatterers of low rank, from these infamous men whom Egypt and Syria sent to Rome, where profiting by the oppression of the true Romans, they felt themselves all powerful with the scoundrels who governed them. The most shocking ignominies of the Empire, such as the apotheosis of the Emperor, his deification, when alive, came from the East, and especially from Egypt which was then one of the most corrupt countries in the universe.

The true Roman spirit, in effect, still survived. Human nobility was far from being extinct. A great tradition of pride and of virtue was kept up in some families, which came to power with Nerva, and made the splendour of the century of the Antonines of which Tacitus has been the eloquent interpreter. A time, which was that of minds so profoundly honest as Quintilian, Pliny the younger and Tacitus, is not a time of which we need despair. The disturbance of the surface did not affect the great basis of honesty and of seriousness which underlay good society in Rome; some families still afforded models of valour, of devotion to duty, of concord, of solid virtue. There were in the noble houses admirable wives, admirable sisters. Was there ever a more touching fate than that of the young and chaste Octavia, daughter of Claudius, and wife of Nero, pure amidst so many infamies, killed at twenty-two years of age, before she had had time to enjoy her life? The women described in the inscriptions as Castissimæ, univiræ are not rare. Wives accompanied their husbands in exile; others shared their noble deaths. The old Roman simplicity was not lost; the education of children was grave and careful. The noblest women laboured with their hands at woolwork; the cares of the toilette were almost unknown in good families.

The excellent statesmen who sprang up under Trajan were not improvised. They had served under preceding reigns; only they had had little influence, cast into the shade as they were by the freedmen and the basest favourites of the Emperor. Men of the highest character thus occupied exalted positions under Nero. The skeleton was good, the accession of the bad Emperors to power, disastrous though it was, did not suffice to change the general course of affairs and the principles of the State. The Empire, far from being in decadence, was in all the force of the most robust youth. The decadence was coming, but that would be two centuries later, and, strange to say, under the least evil of the sovereigns. Looked at from the political point of view, the situation was analogous to that of France, which, for want of an invariable rule since the Revolution as to the succession of powers, has gone through the most perilous adventures, without its internal organisation and national force suffering too much. From the moral point of view we may compare the time of which we speak with the eighteenth century, an epoch which we might fancy to be altogether corrupt, if we judged by the memories, the manuscript literature, the collection of anecdotes of the times, yet, in which houses maintained a great severity of morals.

Philosophy had allied itself with the honest Roman families, and resisted nobly. The Stoic school produced the great characters of Cremastius Cordus, of Thraseas, of Arria, of Helvidius Priscus, of Annæus Cornelius, of Musonius Rufus--admirable masters of aristocratic virtue. The stiffness and the exaggerations of this school, arose from the horrible cruelty of the government of the Cæsars. The perpetual thought of the good man was how he might best endure tortures and prepare for death. Lucan, with bad taste, Persius, with greater talents, expressed the highest sentiments of a great soul. Seneca the philosopher, Pliny the elder, Papirius Fabianus, maintained an elevated tradition of science and philosophy. Everyone did not yield, there were still wise men. But, too often, they had no other resource than death. The ignoble parts of humanity were at times in the ascendent. The spirit of vertigo and cruelty then overflowed and turned Rome into a veritable hell.

This government, so frightfully unequal at Rome, was much better in the provinces. Few of the disorders which shocked the capital were felt there. In spite of its defects the Roman administration was much better than the royalties and republics which the conquest had suppressed. The time of the sovereign municipalities had gone by for centuries. These little states had destroyed themselves by their egotism, their jealous spirit, their ignorance, or their little care for private liberties. The ancient Greek life, all struggles, all exterior, satisfied no one. It had been charming in its day, but this brilliant Olympus of a democracy of demi-gods having lost its freshness, had become something dry, cold, insignificant, vain, superficial, for want of goodness and of solid honesty. This, it was, which constituted the legitimacy of the Macedonian domination, then of the Roman administration. The Empire did not yet know the excess of centralization. Until the time of Diocletian, it left much liberty to the provinces and cities. Kingdoms, almost independent, existed in Palestine, in Syria, in Asia Minor, in little Armenia, in Thrace under the protection of Rome. These kingdoms became dangers only in the days of Caligula, because the rules of the great and profound political policy of Augustus were neglected. The free cities, and they were numerous, governed themselves according to their own laws; they had the legislative power and all the magistracy of an autonomous state, until the third century, municipal decrees began with the formula, "The senate and the people . . ." The theatres served, not only for the pleasures of the stage, they were the centres of opinion and of movement. The majority of the towns were under various names, little republics. The municipal spirit was very strong in them; they had not lost the right of declaring war--a melancholy right which had turned the world into a field of carnage. "The benefits conferred by the Roman people on the human race," were the theme of declamations which were sometimes adulatory, but the sincerity of which cannot always be denied with justice. The worship of the "Roman peace," the idea of a great democracy organised under the protection of Rome was at the bottom of all thoughts. A Greek orator exhibited vast erudition in proving that the glory of Rome ought to be gathered amongst all the branches of the Hellenic race as a sort of common patrimony. In what concerned Syria, Asia Minor, Egypt, it may be said that the Roman conquest destroyed no liberty. These countries had long been dead to the political life which they had never had.

In short, notwithstanding the exactions of the governors, and the violence, inseparable from an absolute government the world in many respects had never yet been so happy. An administration coming from a distant centre was so great an advantage that even the plunderings of the Prætors in the last days of the Republic had not been sufficient to make it odious. The Julian law, besides, had greatly narrowed the field of abuse and of collusions. The follies or the cruelties of the Emperor, except under Nero, affected only the Roman aristocracy and the immediate surroundings of the Prince. There never was a time when a man who did not meddle in politics could live more comfortably. The republics of antiquity, in which everyone was forced to occupy himself with the quarrels of parties, were exceedingly uncomfortable places of abode. People were incessantly upset or proscribed. Now the time seemed expressly fitted for large proselytisms above the quarrels of the little towns and the rivalries of dynasties. Such attempts against liberty as there were, arose out of what was still left of independence in provinces or communities much more than from the Roman administration. We have had, and we shall still have, numerous instances of this kind of thing to remark.

In those of the conquered countries in which political necessities had not existed for centuries, and where the people were deprived only of the right to tear each other to pieces by continual wars, the Empire was a period of prosperity and of well-being, such as had never been known, we may even add without paradox, of liberty, On the one hand, freedom of trade and of industry, of which the Greek Republics had no idea, became possible. On the other, liberty of thought could only gain by the new system. That liberty is always stronger when it has to deal with a king or a prince, than when it has to negotiate with a narrow and jealous citizen. The ancient republics did not possess it. The Greeks did without it in great things, thanks to the incomparable strength of their genius, but it ought not to be forgotten that Athens had her inquisition. The inquisition was the archon king; the holy office was the Royal Porch, whither were taken accusations of "impiety." Accusations of that kind were very numerous; it is concerning cases of this description that most of the great Attic orations were delivered. Not merely philosophical crimes, such as denying God or providence, but the slightest blow struck at the municipal worship, the preaching of foreign religions, the most childish infractions of the scrupulous legislation of the mysteries, were crimes which might be punished with death. The gods whom Aristophanes mocked at on the stage, killed sometimes. They killed Socrates, they wanted to kill

Alcibiades. Anaxagoras, Protagoras, Theodorus the Atheist, Diagoras of Melos, Prodicus of Ceos, Stilpo, Aristotle, Theophrastus, Aspasia, Euripides, were more or less seriously disquieted. Liberty of thought was, in short, the fruit of the royalties which sprang out of the Macedonian conquest. It was the Attali, the Ptolemies, who first gave to thinkers the facilities that none of the old republics had ever offered to them. The Roman Empire continued the same tradition. There was, under the empire, more than one arbitrary act against the philosophers, but they arose always, through their interfering with politics. We may seek in vain in the list of Roman laws before Constantine for a text against the liberty of thought, in the history of the emperors for a process against abstract doctrine. Not one scholar was disturbed. Men who would have been burned in the middle ages, such as Galen, Lucian, Plotinus, lived on in peace, protected by the law. The empire inaugurated a period of liberty, inasmuch as it extinguished the absolute sovereignty of the family, of the city, of the tribe, and replaced or tempered these sovereignties by that of the state. Now an absolute power becomes more vexatious in proportion to the narrowness of the limits within which it is exercised. The ancient republics, feudality, tyrannized over the individual much more than the State did. We must admit that the Roman Empire at certain periods persecuted Christianity cruelly, but, at least, it did not stop it. Now the republics would have rendered it impossible; Judaism, if it had not submitted to the pressure of Roman authority, would have been sufficient to stifle it. The Pharisees were prevented from crushing out Christianity only by the Roman magistrates.

Large ideas of universal brotherhood springing for the most part out of stoicism, a sort of general sentiment of humanity, were the fruits of the less narrow system and of the less exclusive education to which the individual was subjected. There were dreams of a new era and of new worlds. The public wealth was great, and, notwithstanding the imperfection of the economic doctrines of the times, wealth was widely spread. Morals were not what they have often been imagined to be. At Rome, it is true, all the vices were displayed with a revolting cynicism; the spectacles, especially, had introduced a frightful corruption. Certain countries, like Egypt, have thus sunk into the lowest depths. But there was, in most of the provinces, a middle class, where goodness, conjugal faith, the domestic virtues, probity, were sufficiently spread out. Is there anywhere an idea of family life in a world of honest citizens of small towns, more charming than that which Plutarch has left us? What bonhomie! What gentleness of manners! What chaste and amiable simplicity! Chæronea was evidently not the only place where life was so pure and so innocent.

Customs even outside Rome were still to a certain ex-tent cruel, it may be through the memory of antique manners, everywhere rather sanguinary, it may be through the special influence of Roman hardness. But there was progress even in this respect. What soft and pure sentiment, what impression of tender melancholy had not found its tenderest expression by the pen of Virgil or Tibullus? The world grew more yielding, lost its antique rigour, acquired gentleness and susceptibility. Maxims of humanity grew common; equality, the abstract idea of the rights of man, were loudly preached by stoicism. Woman, thanks to the dowry system of the Roman law, became more and more her own mistress; precepts on the manner of treating slaves improved; Seneca ate with his. The slave was no longer of necessity that grotesque and malicious being, whom Latin comedy introduced to provoke outbursts of laughter, and whom Cato recommended to be treated as a beast of burden. The times have now greatly changed. The slave is morally the equal of his master; it is admitted that he is capable of virtue, of fidelity, of devotion, and he has given proofs that he is so. Prejudices as to nobility of birth are dying out. Many very humane and very just laws are enacted even under the worst of the Emperors. Tiberius was an able financier; he founded upon an excellent basis an establishment of the nature of a land-bank. Nero brought to the system of taxation, until then iniquitous and barbarous, improvements which put our own times to the blush. The progress of legislation was considerable, though the punishment of death was stupidly frequent. Love of the poor, sympathy for all, alms-giving, became virtues.

The theatre was one of the most insupportable scandals to honest people, and was one of the first causes of the antipathy of Jews and Judaizers of every class against the profane civilization of the time. These gigantic circles appeared to them the sewer in which all the vices festered. Whilst the front ranks applauded, repulsion and horror alone were produced on the upper benches. The spectacles of gladiators were established in the provinces only with difficulty. The Greek countries at least objected to them, and clung more often to their ancient Greek exercises. The sanguinary games preserved always in the East a very pronounced mark of their Roman origin. The Athenians in emulation of the Corinthians having, one day deliberated as to imitating these barbarous games, a philosopher is said to have risen and moved that before this was done, the altar of Pity should be overthrown. The horror of the theatre, of the stadium, of the gymnasium, that is to say, of the public places, and of what constituted essentially a Greek or a Roman city, was thus one of the deepest sentiments of the Christian, and one of those which produced the greatest results. Ancient civilization was a public civilization; everything was done in the open air, before the assembled citizens. It was the reverse of our societies, where life is altogether private and closed within the compass of the house. The theatre was the heir of the agora and of the forum. The anathema uttered against the theatre rebounded upon all society. A profound rivalry was established between the Church on the one hand, the public games on the other. The slave, driven from the games, betook himself to the Church. I never sit down in these mournful arenas, which are always the best preserved ruins of an ancient city, without seeing there in the spirit the struggle of the two worlds--here the honest poor man, already half a Christian, sitting in the last rank, veiling his face, and going out indignant--there a philosopher rising suddenly and reproaching the crowd with its baseness. These examples were rare in the first century, but the protest began to make itself heard. The theatre began to fall into evil repute.

Legislation and the administrative rules of the Empire were still a veritable chaos. The central despotism, the municipal and provincial franchises, the caprice of the governors, the violences of the independent communities clashed in the strangest manner. But religious liberty gained by these conflicts. The splendid unitary administration of Trajan will be more fatal to the rising worship than the irregular state, full of the unforeseen, without rigorous police of the time of the Cæsars.

The institutions of public assistance, founded on the principle that the State has paternal duties towards its members, developed themselves extensively only after the period of Nerva and Trajan. Some traces of them are, however, found in the first century. There were already charities for children, distributions of food to the poor, an assize of bread, with indemnities to the corn merchants, precautions about provisions, premiums and assurances for ship owners, bread bonds, which permitted corn to be bought at a reduced price. All the emperors, without exception, showed the greatest solicitude about these questions, minor ones, if you like, but on certain occasions of primary importance. In the earliest ages it is possible that the world had no need of charity. The world was young and valiant, the hospital was useless. The good and simple Homeric moral, according to which the host and the beggar alike come from Jupiter, is the moral of robust and cheerful youth. Greece, in her classic age, enunciated the most exquisite maxims of pity, of benevolence, of humanity, without mixing up with them any after-thought of social inquietude, or of melancholy. Man, at this time, was still healthy and happy; he could not take evil into account. In connection with institutions of mutual succour, the Greeks had besides, a great priority over the Romans. Never did a liberal or benevolent disposition spring from that cruel nobility, who exercised during the period of the Republic, so oppressive a power. At the time of which we speak, the colossal fortunes of the aristocracy, luxury, the great agglomerations of men at certain points, and above all, the hard-heartedness peculiar to the Romans, their aversion to pity had given birth to pauperism. The civilities of certain Emperors to the Roman canaille had only served to aggravate the evil. The sportula, the tesseræ frumentariæ encouraged vice and idleness, but brought no remedy to misery. Here, as in many other matters, the East had a great superiority over the Western world. The Jews possessed real charitable institutions. The temples of Egypt appear sometimes to have had a poor box. The college of recluses, male and female, in the Serapeum, at Memphis, was also in a way, a charitable establishment. The terrible crisis, through which humanity passed in the capital of the Empire, was but little felt in distant countries, where life remained more simple. The reproach of having poisoned the earth, the comparison of Rome with a courtezan, who has poured forth upon the world the dregs of her immorality, was just in many ways. The provinces were better than Rome, or rather the impure elements from all parts, which were collected at Rome, as in a sewer, had formed there a centre of infection where the old Roman virtues were stifled, and where the good seed from elsewhere developed itself but slowly.

The intellectual state of various parts of the Empire was not very satisfactory. In this respect there was a real falling off. The higher culture of the mind is not as independent of political circumstances as is private morality, though the progress of the two may be on parallel lines. Marcus Aurelius was certainly a more honest man than all the old Greek philosophers, yet his positive notions of the realities of the universe are inferior to those of Aristotle or of Epicurus; for he believed at times in the gods as finished and distinct personages, in dreams and in omens. The world at the Roman period made progress in morality, and suffered a scientific decline. From Tiberius to Nerva, the decline is altogether sensible. The Greek genius, with an originality, a force, a richness, which have never been equalled, had created in the course of centuries, the national encyclopædia, the normal discipline of the mind. This marvellous movement dating from Thales, and from the first schools of Ionia (six hundred years before Jesus Christ) had almost stopped about the year 120 B.C. The last survivors of these five centuries of genius, Apollonius of Perga, Eratosthenes, Aristarchus, Hero, Archimedes, Hipparchus, Chrysippus, Carneades, Panetius, had died without leaving successors. I see only Posidonius and some astronomers who continued still the old traditions of Alexandria, of Rhodes, of Pergamus. Greece, so able in creating, had not known how to extract from her science, or her philosophy, a popular teaching, a remedy against superstition. Whilst possessing in their bosom admirable scientific institutions, Egypt, Asia Minor, Greece itself, were given over to the most foolish beliefs. Now, when science cannot control superstition, superstition chokes science. Between these two opposed forces, the duel is to the death.

Italy, in adopting Greek science, had learned for a moment to animate it with a new sentiment. Lucretius had furnished the model of the great philosophical poem, at once hymn and blasphemy, inspiring in turn, serenity and despair, penetrated with that profound sentiment of human destiny, which was always wanting to the Greeks. They, like true children, as they were, took life in so gay a fashion, that they never dreamed of cursing the gods, or of finding nature unjust or perfidious towards man. Graver thoughts arose amongst the Latin philosophers. But Rome knew no better than Greece how to make science the basis of popular education. Whilst Cicero gave with an exquisite tact, a finished form to the ideas which he borrowed from the Greeks; whilst Lucretius wrote his astonishing poem; whilst Horace avowed to Augustus, who was in no way moved by it, his frank incredulity; whilst Ovid, one of the most charming poets of the time, treated the most respectable fables like an elegant literature; whilst the great Stoics drew practical consequences from the Greek philosophy, the maddest chimeras found believers, the faith in the marvellous was unbounded. Never was the world more occupied with prophecies and prodigies. The fine eclectic deism of Cicero, continued and perfected still more by Seneca, remained the belief of a small number of lofty minds exercising no influence whatever upon their age.

The Empire until the time of Vespasian had nothing which could be called public instruction. What there was of this kind at a later date was confined almost exclusively to the insipid exercises of the grammarians; the general decadence was rather pressed on than delayed. The last days of the republican government, and the reign of Augustus, were witnesses to one of the finest literary movements that ever took place. But after the death of the great Emperor the decadence is rapid, or, more correctly, altogether sudden. The intelligent and cultivated society of Cicero, Atticus, Cæar, Mæcenas, Agrippa, Pollio, had disappeared like a dream. Without doubt there were still enlightened men, men abreast of the science of their time, occupying high social positions, such as Seneca and the literary society of which he was the centre, Lucilius, Gallio, Pliny. The body of Roman law, which is philosophy itself in the form of a code, the putting in practice of Greek rationalism, continued its majestic growth. The great Roman families had preserved a bottom of elevated religion, and a great horror of superstition. The geographers, Strabo and Pomponius Mela, the doctor and encyclopædist, Celsus, the botanist, Dioscorides, the jurisconsult Sempronius Proculus, were very able men. But they were the exceptions. Except for some thousands of enlightened men, the world was plunged into the most complete ignorance of the laws of nature. Credulity was a general disease. Literary culture was reduced to hollow rhetoric, which taught nothing. The essentially moral and practical direction which philosophy has taken banished grand speculations. Human knowledge, if we except geography, made no progress. The instructed and well-read amateur replaced the creative scholar. The supreme defect of the Romans here made its fatal influence felt. This people so great for empire were second-rate in mind. The best educated Romans, Lucretius, Vitruvius, Celsus, Pliny, Seneca, were in positive knowledge the pupils of the Greeks. Too often even it was the most mediocre Greek science that they copied indifferently. The city of Rome had never had a great scientific school. Charlatanism reigned there almost without control. In short, the Latin literature which certainly had admirable parts, flourished but a short time and did not go out of the Western world.

Greece happily remained faithful to her genius. The prodigious blaze of the Roman power had dazzled her, crushed her down, but had not destroyed her. In fifty years she will have reconquered the world, she will again be the mistress of all who think, she will sit on the throne with the Antonines. But now Greece herself is in one of her hours of lassitude. Genius is rare there; original science inferior to what it had been in the six preceding centuries and to what it will be in the pet, The school of Alexandria, decaying for nearly two centuries but which however in the time of Cæsar still possessed Sosigenes, is now mute.

From the death of Augustus to the accession of Trajan must be reckoned as a period of momentary abasement of the human mind. The antique world was far from having said its last word; but the cruel trial through which it had passed, had robbed it of voice and heart. Better days are dawning, and the mind relieved from the desolating rule of the Cæsars will appear to revive. Epictetus, Plutarch, Dionysius, the golden-mouthed, Chrysostom, Tacitus, Quintilian, Pliny, the younger, Juvenal, Rufus of Ephesus, Aretæus, Galen, Ptolemy, Hypsicles, Theon, Lucian, will recall the best days of Greece, not of that inimitable Greece which existed but once for the despair and the charm of those who love the beautiful, but a Greece rich and flourishing yet, which whilst confounding her gifts with those of the Roman spirit will produce new fruits full of originality.

The general taste was very bad. There are no great Greek writers. The Latin authors whom we know, with the exception of the satirist Persius, are mediocre and without genius. Declamation spoiled everything. The principle by which the public judged the works of the mind was pretty much the same as in our own day. They only looked for the brilliant strokes. The word was no longer the simple vesture of the thought, drawing all its elegance from its perfect proportion to the idea it expressed. Words were cultivated for their own sake. The object of an author in writing was to show his talent. The excellence of a recitation or public lecture was measured by the number of applauded words with which it was sown. The great principle that in matters of art everything ought to serve for ornament, but that all that is put in expressly as ornament is bad, this principle, I say, was profoundly forgotten. The time was if you will, very literary. They only spoke of eloquence, of good style, and at bottom almost all the world wrote ill; there was not a single orator, for the good orator, and the good writer are men who make a trade of neither one nor the other. At the theatre the principal actor absorbed attention; plays were suppressed that showy pieces might be recited--the cantica. The spirit of literature was a silly dilettantism which seized even upon the Emperors, a foolish vanity which led everybody to try to prove that he had wit. Hence an extreme insipidity, interminable "Theseids," dramas written to be read in society, a whole poetic banality which can only be compared to the classic tragedies and epics of sixty years ago.

Stoicism itself could not escape this defect, or at least did not know before Epictetus and Marcus Aurelius, how to find a graceful form to envelope its doctrines. The tragedies of Seneca are really extraordinary monuments where the loftiest sentiments are expressed in the tone of a literary charlatanism, wholly fatiguing and indicative at once of moral progress and an irredeemable decadence of taste. The same maybe said of Lucan. The tension of soul, the natural effect of the eminently tragic character of the situation gave birth to an inflated style, where the only care was to shine by fine sentences. Something of the same kind happened amongst us under the Revolution; the severest crisis that had ever been known produced scarcely anything but a literature of rhetoricians, full of declamation. We must not stop at that. The new thoughts were sometimes expressed with a great deal of pretension. The style of Seneca is sober, simple, and pure compared with that of S. Augustine. But we forgive S. Augustine his, detestable though it often is, and his insipid concetti, for the sake of his fine sentiments.

In any case that education, noble and distinguished as it was in many ways, never reached the people. That would have been a comparatively slight inconvenience, if the people had had at least a religious training analogous in some sort to that which the most disinherited portions of our societies receive in the Church. But religion in all parts of the Empire was at the lowest ebb. Rome with good reason had left the ancient worships undisturbed, cutting away only those things which were inhuman, seditious, or injurious to others. She had extended over all a sort of official varnish which made them all very much alike, and after a fashion melted them down together. Unfortunately these old worships, of very diverse origin, had one feature in common; it was equally impossible to arrive at theological instruction; at an applied morality; at an edifying preaching; at a pastoral ministry really fruitful for the people. The Pagan temple was in no way what the synagogue and the church were in their palmy days. I mean that common house, school, hostelry, hospital, shelter, where the poor may find an asylum. It was a cold cella, where one scarcely entered, and where one learned nothing. The Roman worship was perhaps the least bad of those which were still practised. Purity of heart and of body were there considered as making part of real religion. By its gravity, its decency, its austerity, this worship, but for some farces like those of our carnival, was superior to the bizarre and often ridiculous ceremonies which persons afflicted with Oriental notions secretly introduced. The affectation which led the Roman patricians to distinguish "religion" --that is to say their own worship, from "superstition," that is to say foreign modes of worship, appears to us sufficiently puerile. All Pagan worship was essentially superstitious. The peasant who in our days puts a halfpenny into the box of some miracle-chapel, who invokes such a saint for his oxen or his horses, who drinks a certain water for certain diseases, is in those matters distinctly Pagan. Almost all our superstitions are the relics of a religion anterior to Christianity, which the latter has not been able entirely to root out. If one desired to find in our days the image of Paganism, it is in some secluded village at the bottom of the most backward country, that it is to be looked for.

Having for guardians only a vacillating popular tradition and interested sacristan, the worship could not but fall back into adulation. Augustus, although with hesitation, suffered himself to be worshipped in the provinces while yet alive. Tiberius allowed that ignoble meeting of the Asiatic townsmen, who disputed the honour of erecting a temple to him, to be held under his eyes. The extravagant impieties of Caligula produced no re-action; outside Judaism there was not a single priest to resist such follies. Sprung for the most part from a primitive worship of natural forces, ten times transformed by mixtures of all kinds, and by the imagination of the people, Pagan worship was limited by its past. It was impossible to extract from them what they did not contain--deism, edification. The Fathers of the Church make us smile when they talk of the misdeeds of Saturn as of those of the father of a family, and Jupiter as a husband. And surely it was much more ridiculous still to erect Jupiter (that is to say the atmosphere) into a moral god who commands, forbids, rewards, punishes. In a world which aspired to possess a catechism, which can be done with a worship like that of Venus, which arose out of an old social necessity of the first Phoenecian navigators in the Mediterranean, but became with time an outrage to those who looked up to it more and more as the essence of religion?

In all quarters, in short, the need of a monotheistic religion, having the morality of the divine prescriptions for its basis, was felt more and more. There thus came a time when natural religion, reduced to pure childishness, to the grimaces of sorcerers, would not suffice for society where humanity wanted a moral and philosophical religion. Buddhism, Zoroasterism answered to that need in India, in

Persia. Orpheism and the Mysteries had attempted the same thing in the Greek world, with-out succeeding in a durable manner. At this epoch the problem presented itself to the whole of the world with a sort of solemn unanimity and imperious grandeur.

Greece, it is true, formed an exception in this respect. Hellenism was much less used than other religions of the empire. Plutarch in his little Boeotian town lived by Hellenism, tranquil, happy, contented as a child with the calmest religious conscience. With him, not a trace of crisis, of rending, of disquiet, of imminent revolution. But it was only the Greek spirit which was capable of so infantine a serenity. Always satisfied with herself, proud of her past and of that brilliant mythology of which she possessed all the holy places, Greece did not share all the internal torments, which worried the rest of the world. Only she did not call for Christianity; only she wished to pass it by; only she thought to do better. She held to that eternal youth, to that patriotism, to that gaiety which have always characterised the veritable Hellene, and which to-day cause the Greek to be a stranger to the profound cares which eat us up. Hellenism thus found itself in a position to attempt a renaissance which no other of the religions of the empire would have been able to attempt. In the second, third, and fourth centuries of our era, Hellenism will constitute itself an organised religion by a sort of fusion of the Greek mythology and philosophy, and with its wonder-working philosophers, its ancient sages promoted to the rank of prophets, its legends of Pythagoras and of Apollonius, will enter into a rivalry with Christianity, which, though it remained powerless, was none the less the most dangerous obstacle which the religion of Jesus found in its path.

That attempt was not made so early as the time of the Cæsars. The first philosophers who attempted a species of alliance between philosophy and Paganism--Euphrates of Tyre, Apollonius of Tyana, and Plutarch, are of the end of the century. Euphrates of Tyre is but little known to us. Legend has so covered up the warp and woof of the real biography of Apollonius that it is difficult to say, whether he is to be reckoned amongst the sages, amongst the founders of religions, or amongst the charlatans. Plutarch is less a thinker, an innovator than a man of moderate mind who wishes to make all the world agree by rendering philosophy timid and religion half reasonable. There is nothing in him of Porphyry or of Julian. The attempts at allegorical exegesis by the Stoics are very weak. The mysteries like those of Bacchus, where the immortality of the soul was taught by graceful symbols, were limited to certain countries and had no extended influence. The unbelief in the official religion was general in the enlightened class. The politicians who most affected to sustain the worship of the State made a jest of it with much wit. They openly put forward the immoral system that religious fables are good only for the people and ought to be maintained for them. The precaution was wholly useless, for the faith of the people was itself profoundly shattered.

After the accession of Tiberius, it is true, a religious reaction made itself felt. It appears that the world was frightened by the avowed incredulity of the times of Cæsar and Augustus; the unlucky attempt of Julian was anticipated; all the superstitions found themselves revivified for reasons of State. Valerius Maximus gives us the first example of a writer of the lower class, making himself the auxiliary of the theologians at bay; of a venal or prostituted pen put at the service of religion. But it is the foreign religions which profit most by this return. The serious reaction in favour of the Græco-Roman cult will only be produced in the second century. Now the classes which have been seized with religious disquiet turn towards the religions, come from the East. Isis and Serapis find more favour than ever. Importers of every species, miracle-mongers, magicians, profit by the demand, and as usually happens at periods when and in countries where the religion of the State is weak, increased on every side, recalling the real or fictitious types of Apollonius of Tyana, Alexander of Abonoticus, of Peregrinus, of Simon of Gitton. These very errors and chimeras were as a prayer of the travailing earth, like the unfruitful efforts of a world seeking its rule and arriving sometimes in its convulsive efforts at monstrous creations destined to oblivion.

To sum up:--the middle of the first century is one of the worst epochs of ancient history. Greek and Roman society show themselves in decadence after what has gone before, and much behind hand with respect to what is to follow But the grandeur of the crisis revealed clearly some strange and sacred formation. Life appeared to have lost its motive: suicides were multiplied. Never had a century presented such a struggle between good and evil. The evil was a powerful despotism, which put the world into the hands of men, who were either criminals or lunatics; it was the corruption of morals, the result of introducing into Rome the vices of the East; it was the absence of a good religion, and of a serious public instruction. The good was on one side, philosophy fighting with uncovered breast, against the tyrants, defying the monsters, three or four times proscribed in in half a century (under Nero, Vespasian and Domitian) it was on another side the efforts after popular virtue these legitimate aspirations after a better religious state, this tendency towards confraternities, towards mono-theistic worship; this rehabilitation of the poor, which was principally produced under cover of Judaism, or Christianity. These two great protestations were far from being in agreement. The philosophical party and the Christian party did not know each other, and they had so little idea of the community of their efforts, that the philosophical party, having come to power by the advent of Nerva, was far from being favourable to Christianity Truth to tell, the design of the Christian was much more radical. The stoic masters of the Empire, reformed it and presided over it during the hundred best years in the history of humanity The Christian Masters of the Empire, after Constantine, succeeded in ruining it. The heroism of some ought not to make us forget that of others. Christianity, so unjust to Pagan virtues, took up the task of depreciating those who had fought against the same enemies that it had. There was in the resistance of philosophy as much grandeur as in that of Christianity, but the rewards have been unequal. The martyr who turned away from the feet of the idols has his legend: why should not Annæus Cornutus, who declared before Nero, that his books would never be worth those of Chrysippus; why should not Helvidius Priscus, who told Vespasian to his face, It is for you to kill, and for me to die"; why should not Demetrius, the cynic, who answered the angry Nero "You threaten me with death but nature threatens you,"--why should not these men have their place amongst the popular heroes whom all men love and salute? Does humanity dispose of so many forces against vice and baseness, that every school of virtue should be allowed to reject the aid of others, and to maintain that it only has the right to be courageous, proud, resigned?

CHAPTER XVIII

RELIGIOUS LEGISLATION AT THIS PERIOD

The Empire in the first century, even whilst showing itself hostile to the religious innovations which came from the East, did not offer a constant resistance to them. The principle of the religion of the State was but moderately maintained. Under the Republic at various intervals, foreign religions had been forbidden, in particular the worship of Sabazius, of Isis, of Serapis. The people were impelled towards these religions by an irresistible force. When the demolition of the temple of Isis and Serapis, was decreed at Rome, in the year 535, not a workman was found who would put a hand to the work, and the Consul himself was obliged to break in the door with the blows of an axe It is clear that the Latin rite was not sufficient for the mob. Not unreasonably it has been supposed, that it was to gratify the popular instinct that Cæsar re-established the worship of Isis and Serapis.

With the profound and liberal intention characteristic of him, this great man showed himself favourable to a complete liberty of conscience. Augustus was more attached to the national religion. He had antipathy for the Oriental religions; he forbade even the propagation of Egyptian ceremonies in Italy; but he wished that every religion, that of the Jews especially, should be supreme at home. He exempted the Jews from every-thing that might distress their consciences, especially from secular work on the Sabbath. Some persons of his court were less tolerant, and would willingly have made him a persecutor for the benefit of the Latin religion. He does not appear to have yielded to these wretched counsels. Josephus, who is suspected of exaggeration in this matter, will even have it that he made gifts of sacred vessels to the temple at Jerusalem.

It was Tiberius who first laid down the principle of the religion of the State, with clearness, and took serious precautions against the Jewish and Oriental propaganda. It must be remembered that the Emperor was "Grand Pontiff," that in protecting the old Roman religion he did but execute a duty laid upon him. Caligula withdrew the edicts of Tiberius, but his madness prevented anything further from being done. Claudius appears to have imitated the policy of Augustus. At Rome he strengthened the Latin religion, showed himself interested in the progress made by foreign religion, displayed harshness to the Jews, and pursued the confraternities with fury. In Judea, on the contrary, he showed himself well disposed towards the natives. The favour which the Agrippas displayed at Rome under these two last reigns, assured to their co-religionists a powerful protection, except in those cases when the police of Rome required measures of safety.

Nero concerned himself but little with religion. His odious treatment of the Christians came from native ferocity and not from legislative disposition. The examples of persecution which were quoted in Roman society at this time sprang rather from family than public authority. Such things still happened only in the noble houses of Rome, which preserved the old traditions. The provinces were perfectly free to follow their own religions on the single condition that they did not insult the religions of other countries. The provincials of Rome had the same right, provided they made no scandal. The only two religions against which the Empire made war in the first century, Druidism and Judaism, were fortresses where nationalities defended themselves. All the world was convinced that the profession of Judaism implied contempt for the civil law, and indifference to the prosperity of the State. When Judaism was content to be a simple personal religion, it was not persecuted. The severities against the worship of Serapis, arose perhaps from the mono-theistic character which it presented, and which already caused it to be confounded with the Jewish and the Christian religion.

No fixed law then forbade in the time of the apostles the profession of monotheistic religion. These religions, until the accession of the Syrian Emperors, were always watched, but it was not until the time of Trajan that the Empire began to prosecute them systematically as hostile to others, as intolerant, and as implying the negation of the State. In short, the only thing against which the Roman Empire declared war in the matter of religion was theocracy. Its principle was that of the lay state; it did not admit that a religion had civil or political consequence in any degree; above all it did not allow of any association within the State for objects outside of it. This last point is essential, seeing that it really was at the root of all the persecutions. The law upon confraternities, much more than religious intolerance, was the fatal cause of the violences which dishonoured the reigns of the best sovereigns.

The Greek countries, associated as they were with all things good and delicate, had had the priority over the Romans. The Greek Eranes or Thiases of Athens, Rhodes, of the inlands of the Archipelago, had been excellent societies for mutual help, credit, assurance in case of fire, piety, honest pleasures. Every Erane had its decisions engraved upon the arches (stelos), its archives, its common chest, fed by voluntary gifts and assessments. The Eranites or Thiastes celebrated together certain festivals and met for banquets, where cordiality reigned. A member, embarrassed for money, might borrow from the chest on condition of repayment. Women formed part of these Eranes, and had their separate President (proëranistria). The meetings were absolutely secret; a rigid order was maintained in them; they took place, it would seem, in closed gardens, surrounded by porches or small buildings, in the midst of which rose the altar of sacrifice. Finally, every congregation had a body of dignitaries, drawn by lot for a year (Clerotes), according to the custom of ancient Greek democracies, from whom the Christian "clergy" may have taken their name. The president alone was elected. These officers caused the new members to submit to a species of examination, and were bound to certify that he was "holy, pious and good." There was in these little confraternities, during the two or three centuries which preceded our era, a movement almost as varied as that which in the middle ages produced so many religious orders and subdivisions of these orders. In the single island of Rhodes there were computed to be as many as nineteen, many of which bore the names of their founders or their reformers. Some of these Thiastes, especially those of Bacchus, held elevated doctrines, and sought to give some consolation to men of good will. If there still remained in the Greek world a little love, pity, religious morality, it was due to the liberty of such private religions. These religions were in a sort of way associated with the official religion, the abandonment of which became every day more and more marked.

At Rome association of the same kind encountered greater difficulties and not less favour amongst the proscribed classes. The principles of the Roman policy concerning confraternities had been promulgated for the first time under the Republic (186 B.C.) apropos of the Bacchanals. The Romans by their natural taste were greatly inclined to associations, especially to religious associations; but permanent congregations of this kind displeased the patricians, guardians of public powers, who, in their narrow and dry conception of life, admitted only the Family of the State as the social group. The most minute precautions were taken; a preliminary authorization was made a necessity, the number of members was limited; it was forbidden to have a permanent magister sacrorum, and to create a common fund by means of subscriptions. The same solicitude was manifested on various occasions in the history of the empire. The laws contained texts for repressions of every kind. But it was for the authorities to say, if they should or should not be used. The proscribed religions often appeared a very few years after their proscription. The foreign emigration, besides, especially that of the Syrians, perpetually renewed the funds from which the beliefs were nourished, which it was vainly sought to extirpate.

It is remarkable to note, to how great a degree a subject in appearance so wholly secondary occupied the strongest heads. One of the principal cares of Cæsar and of Augustus was to prevent the formation of new societies and to destroy those which had already been established. It appears that a decree was issued under Augustus, in which an attempt was made to define with clearness the limits of the law of union and association. These limits were extremely narrow. The societies were to be exclusively burial clubs. They were not permitted to meet more often than once a month; they might occupy themselves only with the funerals of deceased members; under no pretext might they extend their powers. The Emperor strove after the impossible. He wished out of his exaggerated idea of the state to isolate the individual, to destroy every moral tie between man, to repress a legitimate desire of the poor, that of crowding together in a small space to keep each other warm. In ancient Greece the city was very tyrannical, but it gave in exchange for its vexations so much pleasure, so much light, so much glory, that no one dreamed of complaining. Men would have died for her with joy; her most unjust caprices were submitted to without murmuring. The Roman Empire was too large for patriotism. It offered to all immense material advantages; it gave nothing to love. The insupportable sadness inseparable from such a life appeared worse than death.

Thus, notwithstanding all the efforts of the politicians, the confraternities developed themselves enormously. They were exactly analogous to our middle age confraternities with their patron saints and their corporation meals. The great families were careful of their name, of their country, of their tradition; the humble, the small, had only their collegium. There they found all their pleasures. All the texts show us collegia or coetus, as formed of slaves, of veterans, of small people (tenuiores). Equality reigned there among the freemen, emancipated slaves and servile persons. The women in them were numerous. At the risk of a thousand cavils, sometimes of the most severe punishments, men became members of these collegia, where they lived in the bonds of an agreeable confraternity, where they found mutual help, where they contracted relations which lasted after death. The place of meeting, or schola collegii, had usually a tetrastyle (a four sided porch), where was put up the rules of the college, by the side of the altar of the tutelary deity and a triclinium for meals. The meals were, in fact, impatiently expected; they took place on the feast days of the patron (God), and on the anniversaries of certain brethren who had founded benefactions. Every one carried thither his little basket (sportula); one of the brethren in turn furnished the accessories of the feast, the beds, the plate, bread, wine, sardines and hot water. The slave, who had been enfranchised gave his comrades an amphora of good wine. A gentle joy animated the festival; it was expressly stipulated that there should be no discussion of the business of the college, so that nothing should trouble the quarter of an hour of joy and rest which these poor people reserved to themselves. Every act of turbulence and every ill-natured word was punished with a fine.

To all appearance, these colleges were only burial societies, to use the modern phrase. But that alone would not have sufficed to give them a moral character. In the Roman period, as in our time, and at all periods when religion is weakened, the piety of the tombs was almost the only one which the people retained. They liked to believe that they would not be thrown into the horrible common trench, that the college would provide for their funerals, that the brethren would come on foot to the funeral pile to receive a little honorarium of twenty centimes. Slaves especially wished to hope that if their masters caused their bodies to be thrown into the sewers, there would be some friends to make for them "imaginary funerals." The poor man put his half-penny per month into the common fund, to provide for himself, after his death, a little urn in a Columbarium, with a slab of marble, on which his name might be engraved. Sepulture amongst the Romans being intimately bound up with the sacra gentilitia, or family rites, had an extreme importance. The persons, intending to be buried together, contracted a species of intimate brotherhood and relationship.

It thus came about that Christianity presented itself for a long time in Rome as a kind of funeral collegium, and that the first Christian sanctuaries were the tombs of the martyrs. If Christianity had been that one, however, it would not have provoked so many severities; but it was besides quite another thing; it had common treasuries; it boasted of being a complete city; it believed itself assured of the future. When, on a Saturday evening, one enters the limits of a Greek Church in Turkey, for example that of S. Photinus in Smyrna, he is struck with the strength of these associated religions, in the midst of a persecuting and malevolent society. This irregular accumulation of buildings (church, presbytery, schools, prison), those faithful ones coming and going in their enclosed city, those lately opened tombs, on each of which a lamp is burning, the corpse-like odour, the impression of damp mustiness, the murmur of prayers, the appeals for charity, from a soft and warm atmosphere, that a stranger at times must find sufficiently sickening, but that is to the initiated eminently grateful.

These societies, once provided with a special authorization, had in Rome all the rights of civil persons; but such an authorization was granted only with infinite reserves, as soon as the societies had funds in hand, and other matters than funerals might occupy them. The pretext of religion, or of the accomplishment of vows in common is foreseen, and formally pointed out as being amongst the circumstances, which give to a meeting the character of au offence; and this offence was no other than that of treason, at least for the person who hail called the assembly together. Claudius went so far as to close the inns where the confraternities met, and even to interdict the little eating-houses, where these poor people could get soup and hot water cheaply. Trajan and the best Emperors defied all the associations. The extreme humility of the persons was an essential condition that the right of religious meeting should be accorded, and even then, only with many restrictions. The legists, who put together the Roman law, eminent though they were as jurisconsults, afforded a measure of their ignorance of human nature by pursuing in every way, even by threats of capital punishment, in restraining by every kind of odious and puerile precaution, an eternal need of the soul. Like the authors of our Civil Code, they figured life to themselves with a mortal coldness. If life consisted in amusing oneself by superior orders, in eating a morsel of bread, in tasting pleasure in one's rank and under the eye of a chief, everything would be well imagined. But the punishment of societies which abandoned that false and limited direction, is first weariness, then the violent triumph of religious parties. Never will man consent to breathe that glacial air; he wants the little enclosure, the confraternity in which men live and die together. Our great abstract societies are not sufficient to answer to all the instincts of sociability which are in man. Let him put his heart into anything, seek consolation where it may be found, create brethren for himself, contract ties of the heart. Let not the cold hand of the State interfere in this kingdom of the soul, which is the kingdom of liberty. Life and joy will not re-enter the world until our defiance of the collegia, that sad inheritance from the Roman law, shall have disappeared. Association outside the State, without destroying the State, is the capital question of the future. The future law as to associations will decide if modern society shall or shall not share the fate of ancient society. One example may suffice: the Roman Empire had bound up its destiny with the law upon the coetus illiciti, the illicita collegia. Christians and barbarians accomplishing in this the work of the human conscience, have broken the law; the empire to which that law was attached has foundered with it.

The Greek and Roman world; the lay world; the profane world, which did not know what a priest is, which had neither divine law nor revealed book, touched here upon problems which it could not solve. We may add that if there had been priests, a severe theology, a strongly organized religion, it would not have created the lay State, inaugurated the idea of a rational society, of a society founded upon simple human necessities, and upon the natural relations of individuals. The religious inferiority of the Greeks and Romans was the consequence of their political and intellectual superiority. The religious superiority of the Jewish people, on the contrary, was the cause of their political and philosophical inferiority. Judaism and primitive Christianity embodied the negation, or rather the subjection of the civil State. Like Islamism, they established society upon religion. When human affairs are taken up in this way, great universal proselytisms are founded, apostles run about from one end of the world to another converting it; but political institutions, national independence, a dynasty, a code, a people--none of these are founded.

CHAPTER XIX

THE FUTURE OF MISSIONS

Such was the world which Christian missionaries undertook to convert. It appears to me, however, that we may here see that such an enterprise was not a madness, and that no miracle was required to insure its success. The world was troubled with moral necessities, to which the new religion answered admirably. Manners were growing softer; a purer worship was required; the notion of the rights of man, the ideas of social ameliorations were everywhere gaining ground. On the other hand there was extreme credulity; the number of educated persons inconsiderable. Let ardent apostles, Jews, that is to say, monotheists, disciples of Jesus, that is to say, men penetrated with the sweetest moral teaching that the ears of man have yet heard, present themselves to such a world, and they will assuredly be listened to. The dreams, which mingle with their teaching, will not be an obstacle to their success; the number of those who do not believe in the supernatural, in miracles, is very small If they are humble and poor, so much the better. Humanity, at its present point, can be saved only by an effort coming from the people. The ancient Pagan religions cannot be reformed; the Roman State is what the State always will be, harsh, dry, just, and hard. In this world, which is perishing for want of love, the future belongs to him, who will touch the living source of popular piety. Greek liberalism, the old Roman gravity, are altogether impotent for that.

The foundation of Christianity, from this point of view, is the greatest work that the men of the people have ever achieved. Very quickly, without doubt, men and women of the high Roman nobility joined themselves to the Church. At the end of the first century, Flavius Clemens and Flavia Domitilla, show us Christianity penetrating almost into the palace of the Cæsars. In the time of the first Antonines, there are rich people in the community. Towards the end of the second century, it embraces some of the most considerable persons in the Empire. But in the beginning all, or almost all, were humble. In the most ancient churches, nobles and powerful men were no more to be found than in Galilee about Jesus. Now, in these great creations, it is the first hour which is decisive. The glory of religions belongs wholly to their founders. Religion is, in fact, a matter of faith. To believe is something vulgar; the great thing to do is to inspire faith.

When we attempt to delineate these marvellous beginnings, we usually represent things on the model of our own times, and are thus brought to grave errors. The man of the people in the first century of our era, especially in Greek and Oriental countries, in no way resembled what he is to-day. Education did not then mark out between the classes a barrier as strong as now. These races of the Mediterranean, if we except the population of Latium, which had disappeared, or had lost all their importance since the Roman Empire, in conquering the world, had become the heritage of the conquered peoples--these races, I say, were less solid than ours, but lighter, more lively, more spiritual, more idealistic. The heavy materialism of our disinherited classes, that something mournful and burnt out, the effect of our climate, and the fatal legacy of the middle ages, which gives to our poor so wretched a countenance, was not the defect of the poor of those earlier days. Though very ignorant and very credulous, they were scarcely more so than rich and powerful men. We ought therefore not to represent the establishment of Christianity as analogous in any way to a movement amongst ourselves, starting from the lower classes (a thing in our eyes impossible) by obtaining the assent of educated men. The founders of Christianity were men of the people, in the sense that they were dressed in a common fashion, that they lived simply, that they spoke ill, or rather sought in speaking only to express their ideas with vivacity. But they were inferior in intelligence to only a very small number of men, the survivors who were becoming every day more rare, from the great world of Cæsar and of Augustus. Compared with the elite of the philosophers, who formed the bond between the century of Augustus and that of the Antonines the first Christians were feeble. Compared with the mass of the subjects of the Empire, they were enlightened. Sometimes they were treated as freethinkers; the cry of the populace against them was, "Death to the atheists!" And this is not surprising. The world was making frightful progress in superstition. The two first capitals of the Christianity of the Gentiles, Antioch and Ephesus, were the two cities of the Empire, the most addicted to supernatural beliefs. The second and third centuries pushed even to insanity, credulity, and the thirst for the marvellous.

Christianity was born outside the official world, but not precisely below it. It is in appearance, and according to earthly prejudices that the disciples of Jesus were unimportant persons. The worldly man loves what is proud and strong; he speaks without affability to the humble man; honour as he understands it, consists in not allowing himself to be insulted; he despises those who avow themselves weak, who suffer everything, yield to everything, who give up their coat to him who would take their cloak, who turn their cheeks to the smiters. There lies his error, for the weak, whom he despises, are usually superior to him; the highest virtue is amongst those who obey (servants, work-people, soldiers, sailors, etc.)--higher than amongst those who command and enjoy. And that is almost in order, since to command and to enjoy, far from aiding virtue, make virtue difficult.

Jesus marvellously comprehended that the people carry in their bosoms the great reserve of devotion and of resignation which will save the world. This is why he proclaimed the blessedness of the poor, judging that they find it more easy than other people to be good. The primitive Christians were essentially poor. "Poor" (Ebionim) was their name. Even when the Christian was rich, in the second and third centuries, he was in spirit a tenuior; he escaped, thanks to the law of the Collegia tenuiorum. Christians were certainly not all slaves and people of low condition; but the social equivalent of a Christian was a slave; what was said of a slave was said of a Christian also. On both sides they honoured the same virtues, goodness, humility, resignation, sweetness. The judgment of Pagan authors is unanimous on that point. All, without exception, recognize in the Christian, the features of the servile character; indifference to great affairs, a sad and contrite air, morose judgments upon the age, aversion to games, theatres, gymnasia, baths.

In a word, the Pagans were the world; Christians were not of the world. They were a little flock apart, hated by the world, finding the world evil, seeking "to keep themselves unspotted from the world." The ideal of Christianity will be the reverse of that of the worldly man. The perfect Christian will love abjection; he will have the virtues of the poor and the simple, of him who does not seek to exalt himself. But he will also have the defect of his virtues; he will declare many things to be vain and frivolous, which are not so at all; he will depreciate the universe; he will be the enemy of the admirer of beauty. A system where the Venus of Milo is but an idol is a system, partial, it not false for beauty, is almost as valuable as the good and the true. A decadence of art is in any case inevitable with such ideas. The Christian will not care to build well, nor to sculpture well, nor to design well; he is too idealistic. He will care little for knowledge; curiosity seems a vain thing to him. Confounding the great voluptuousness of the soul, which is one of the methods of reaching the infinite, with vulgar pleasure, he will for-bid himself to enjoy it. He is too virtuous.

Another law shows itself as dominating this history. The establishment of Christianity corresponds to the suppression of political life in the world of the Mediterranean. Christianity was born and expanded itself at a period when there was no such thing as patriotism. If anything is wholly wanting to the founders of the Church it is that quality. They are not Cosmopolitan; for, the whole planet is for them, but a place of exile, they are idealistic in the most absolute sense. Our country is composed of body and soul. The soul: its memories, images, legends, misfortunes, hopes, common regrets; the body: the soil, race, language, mountains, rivers, characteristic products. Now, never were people more detached from all that than the primitive Christians. They did not hold to Judea; at the end of a few years they had forgotten Galilee; the glory of Greece and Rome was indifferent to them. The countries where Christianity first established itself, Syria, Cyprus, Asia Minor, no longer remembered the time when they had been free; Greece and Rome had still a great national sentiment. But in Rome patriotism was confined to the army and to some families; in Greece, Christianity fructified only in Corinth, a city, which since its destruction by Mummius and its reconstruction by Cæsar, was a collection of people of all sorts. The true Greek countries then, as now, very jealous, much absorbed by the memory of their past, paid little attention to the new preaching; they were always indifferently Christian. On the contrary, those soft, gay, voluptuous countries of Asia, countries of pleasure, of free manners, of easy indifference, habituated to take life and government from others, had nothing to abdicate in the matter of pride and of traditions. The ancient metropolitan cities of Christianity, Antioch, Ephesus, Thessalonica, Corinth, Rome, were common cities, if I may dare to say so, cities after the fashion of modern Alexandria, into which poured men of all races, and in which the marriage between man and the soil, which constitutes a nation, was absolutely broken through.

The importance given to social questions is always in an inverse ratio to political pre-occupations. Socialism rises when patriotism grows weak. Christianity was the explosion of social and religious ideas for which the world had been waiting, since Augustus put an end to political conflicts. As with Islamism, Christianity being a universal religion, will be at bottom the enemy of nationalities. It will require many centuries and many schisms before the idea takes root of forming national churches with a religion, which was at first the negation of all earthly countries, which was born at a period when there were no cities and citizens in the world, and when the old rough and strong republics of Italy and of Greece would surely have been expelled from the State as a mortal poison.

And this was one of the causes of the greatness of the new religion. Humanity is a varying, changeable thing at the mercy of contradictory desires. Great is the country; its saints are the heroes of

Marathon, of Thermopylæ, of Valmy, and of Fleurus. Country, however, is not everything here below. One is man and Son of God before being Frenchman or German. The Kingdom of God, eternal dream which will never be torn from the heart of man, is a protest against a too exclusive patriotism. The thought of an organization of humanity in view of its greatest happiness and its moral amelioration is Christian and legitimate. The State knows but one thing--how to organise egotism. That is not indifferent, for egotism is the most powerful and the most assailable of human motives. But that is not sufficient. Governments which have started with the belief that man is swayed only by his instincts of cupidity, are deceived. Devotion is as natural as egotism to the man of a noble race, and the organization of devotion, is religion. Let no one hope then to get away from religion or from religious associations. Every step in the progress of modern society has made the need for them more imperious.

It is in this way that these accounts of strange events may be for us full of both teaching and of example. There is no need for delay over certain details which the difference of time renders strange and eccentric. When it is a question of popular beliefs there is always an immense disproportion between the grandeur of the idealism, which faith pursues, and the triviality of the material circumstances, which we are called upon to accept. Hence the particularity, with which in religious history shocking details and acts like those of madness may be mixed up with everything that is really sublime. The monk who invented the holy ampulla was one of the founders of the kingdom of France. Who would efface from the life of Jesus the episode of the demoniac in the country of the Gergesenes? Never has man in cold blood done the things that were done by Francis of Assisi, Joan of Arc, Peter the Hermit, Ignatius Loyola. Nothing is of more relative application than the word "madness" as applied to the past of the human mind. If we carried out the ideas which are current in our own times there is not a prophet, not an apostle, not a saint, who would not be locked up. The human conscience is very unstable at times when reflection has not advanced; in these conditions of the soul it is by insensible transitions that good becomes evil, that the beautiful borders upon the ugly, and that the ugly becomes the beautiful. There is no possible justice towards the past if so much is not admitted. A single divine breath penetrates all history, and makes an admirable whole of it; but the variety of the combinations which the human faculties may produce is infinite. The apostles differ less from us than the founders of Buddhism, who were, however, nearer to us by language. and perhaps by race. Our age has seen religious movements quite as extraordinary as those of old times, movements which have excited quite as much enthusiasm, which have had already--proportion being kept in view--more martyrs, and the future of which is still uncertain.

I do not speak of the Mormons, a sect which is in some respects so silly and so abject that it is hard to speak of it seriously. It is, however, instructive to see in the middle of the nineteenth century, thousands of men living by miracle, believing with a blind faith in the marvels, which, they say, they have seen and handled. There is already a whole literature on the agreement between Mormonism and science; what is better, that religion, founded as it is upon the most silly impostures, has been able to accomplish miracles of patience and self-abnegation? In five hundred years learned men will prove its divine origin by the miracles of its establishment. Babism, in Persia was a phenomenon otherwise considerable. A gentle and unpretentious man, a sort of modest and pious Spinoza, has found himself almost against his own will raised to the rank of miracle worker, of incarnation of the divine, and has become the leader of a numerous, ardent and fanatical sect, which has very nearly brought about a revolution comparable to that of Islam. Thousands of martyrs have run to him with joy before death. A day unequalled perhaps in the history of the world was that of the day of the great butchery which was made of the babis of Teheran. "On that day were seen in the streets and bazaars of Teheran," says a writer of undoubted authority, "a spectacle which it would seem as if the population were likely never to forget. When the conversation even yesterday turned upon that matter, you may judge of the admiration mixed with horror, which the crowd felt and which years have not diminished. We saw advancing amongst the executioners women and children, their flesh gashed all over their bodies, with lighted and flaming wicks fixed in their wounds. The victims were hauled along with cords and forced to walk by strokes of the whip. Children and women advanced singing a verse which said:--Of a truth we come from God and return to Him.' Their voices rose loudly above the profound silence of the crowd. When one of the victims fell and was forced to rise by blows from the whip or thrusts of the bayonet, though the loss of blood, which ran over all his limbs, left him yet a little strength, he began to dance and to cry with an increase of enthusiasm, Of a truth we come from God and we return to Him.' Some of the children died during the journey. The executioners cast their corpses under the feet of their fathers and their sisters, who walked proudly over them and did not glance twice at them. When they arrived at the place of execution, the victims were offered their lives on condition of abjuration. One executioner took the fancy of saying to a father that if he did not yield he would cut the throats of his two sons upon his breast. They were two little lads, the eldest of whom might have been about fourteen and who, red with their own blood and with calcined flesh, listened coolly to this dialogue. The father answered, crouching on the ground, that he was ready, and the elder of the boys, claiming with some importance his right of seniority, demanded to be slaughtered the first. At last all was finished; night fell upon a mass of mangled flesh; heads were hung in baskets to the scaffold of justice and the dogs of the suburbs met in troops on that side of the city."

That happened in 1852. The sect of Mazdak under Chosroes Nouschirvan, was suffocated in a similar bath of blood. Absolute devotion is, for simple natures, the most exquisite of joys and a species of necessity. In the affair of the Bab, people who were hardly members of the sect, came forward to denounce themselves, so that they might be joined with the sufferers. It is so sweet for man to suffer for something, that in many cases the thirst for martydom causes men to believe. A disciple who was companion of Bab at his execution, hanged by his side on the ramparts of Tabriz and momentarily expecting death, had only one word in his mouth:--"Are you satisfied with me, master?"

The persons who consider as miraculous or chimerical all that in history surpasses the calculations of ordinary good sense, find such things inexplicable. The fundamental condition of criticism is to know how to understand the varying conditions of the human mind. Absolute faith is for us wholly out of the question. Outside of the positive sciences, of a certainty in some degree material, every opinion is in our eyes only approximate, implying partial truth and partial error. The proportion of error may be as small as you will; it is never reduced to zero when morals implying a question of art, of language, of literary form, or of persons are concerned. Such is not the manner of seeing things which narrow and obstinate spirits adopt--Orientals for example. The eye of those people is not like ours; it is the glassy eye of men in mosaics--dull and fixed. They can see only only a single thing at a time; that thing besets them, takes possession of them; they are not then masters of their beliefs or their unbeliefs; there is no room for a reflective after-thought. For an opinion thus embraced a man will allow himself to be killed. The martyrs in religion are what the party man is in politics. Not many very intelligent men have been made martyrs. The confessors of the time of Diocletian would have been, after the peace of the Church, wearisome and imperious personages. Men are never very tolerant when they believe that they are altogether right and the rest of the world altogether wrong.

The great conflagrations of religion, being the results of a too definite manner of seeing things, thus became enigmas for an age like ours, when the rigour of conviction is weakened. With us the sincere man constantly modifies his opinions; in the first place, because the world changes, in the second, because the observer changes also. We believe more things at the same time. We love justice and truth; for them we would risk our lives; but we do not admit that justice and truth belong to a sect or a party. We are good French-men, but we admit that the Germans and the English are superior to us in many ways. It is not thus at the periods and in the countries where everyone belongs with his whole nature to his communion, race, or political school; and this is why all great religious creations have taken place in societies, the general spirit of which was more or less analogous to that of the East. Until now, in short, absolute faith only has succeeded in imposing itself upon others. A good serving maid of Lyons, named Blandina, who caused herself to be killed for her faith at seventeen years of age, caused a brutal brigand chief, Clovis, who found her to his taste fourteen centuries ago, to embrace Catholicism, makes laws for us to this day.

Who is there who has not, while passing through our ancient towns which have become modern, stopped at the feet of gigantic monuments of the faith of olden times? All is externally renewed; there is not a vestige of ancient habits; the cathedral remains, a little lowered in height may be by the hand of man, but profoundly rooted in the soil. Mole sua stat! Its massiveness is its law. It has resisted the deluge, which swept away everything else around it; not one of the men of old times returning to visit the places where he lived would find his home again; the crow alone, who has fixed his nest in the heights of the sacred edifice, has not seen the hammer threatening his dwelling. Strange prescription! These honest martyrs, these rude converts, these pirate church builders, rule us still. We are Christians because it pleased them to be so. As in politics it is the barbarous foundations only that live, so in religion there are only spontaneous, and, if I may dare to say so, fanatical affirmations that can be contagious. This is because religions are wholly popular works. Their success does not depend upon the more or less convincing proofs of their divinity which they bring forward; their success is in proportion to what they say to the heart of the people.

Does it follow from thence that religion is destined to diminish little by little, and to disappear like popular errors concerning magic, sorcery, spirits? Certainly not. Religion is not a popular error; it is a great instinctive truth, imperfectly seen by the people, expressed by the people. All the symbols which serve to give a form to the religious sentiment are incomplete, and it is their fate to be rejected one after another. But nothing is more false than the dream of certain persons, who, seeking to conceive a perfect humanity, conceive it without religion. It is the very reverse which ought to be said. China is a very inferior species of humanity, and China has almost no religion. On the other hand, let us suppose a planet inhabited by a humanity whose intellectual, moral and physical power are double those of terrestrial humanity, that humanity would be, at least, twice as religious as ours. I say, at least, for it is probable that the augmentation of the religious faculties would take place in a more rapid progression than the augmentation of the intellectual capacity, and would not be done in a simple direct proportion. Let us so suppose a humanity ten times as strong as ours, that humanity would be infinitely more religious. It is even probable, that in that degree of sublimity, disengaged from all material cares and from all egotism, gifted with perfect tact, and a divinely delicate taste, seeing the baseness and the nothingness of all that is not true, good, or beautiful, man would be exclusively religious, plunged in a perpetual adoration, rolling from ecstasies to ecstasies, being born, living and dying, in a torrent of bliss. Egotism, in short, which gives a measure of the inferiority of being, diminishes in proportion, as the animal is got rid of. A perfect being would be no longer an egotist; he would be altogether religious. Progress then will have for its effect the increase of religion and neither its destruction nor its diminution.

But it is time to return to our three missionaries, Paul, Barnabas and John--Mark, whom we left at the moment when they went out of Antioch by the gate, which led to Seleucia. In my third volume I will endeavour to trace these messages of good news by land and by sea, through calm and tempest, through good and evils days. I am in haste to retell that unequalled epic, to describe those infinite routes of Asia and of Europe by the side of which the seed of the gospel was sown, those seas which they traversed so many times under circumstances so diverse. The great Christian Odyssey is about to commence. Already the apostolic barque has spread its sails; the wind sighs and aspires only to carry upon its wings the words of Jesus.

THE END